Political Contingency

Political Contingency

*Studying the Unexpected, the Accidental,
and the Unforeseen*

EDITED BY

Ian Shapiro and Sonu Bedi

New York University Press

NEW YORK AND LONDON

NEW YORK UNIVERSITY PRESS
New York and London
www.nyupress.org

© 2007 by New York University

Library of Congress Cataloging-in-Publication Data
Political contingency : studying the unexpected, the accidental, and the
unforeseen / edited by Ian Shapiro and Sonu Bedi.
p. cm.
Includes bibliographical references and index.
ISBN-13: 978-0-8147-4044-6 (cloth : alk. paper)
ISBN-10: 0-8147-4044-8 (cloth : alk. paper)
1. Political science—Methodology. 2. Causation—Political aspects.
3. World politics—1989– 4. Imaginary histories. I. Shapiro, Ian.
II. Bedi, Sonu.
JA71.P6123 2007
320.01—dc22 2007020644

New York University Press books are printed on acid-free paper,
and their binding materials are chosen for strength and durability.

Manufactured in the United States of America
10 9 8 7 6 5 4 3 2 1

For Bob Dahl
Whose idea it was

Contents

Introduction

Contingency's Challenge to Political Science

Ian Shapiro and Sonu Bedi

At its starkest, contingency challenges the very possibility of science. By calling something contingent, at a minimum we are saying that it did not have to be as it is. Things could have been otherwise, and they would have been otherwise if something had happened differently. Science is usually seen as geared to uncovering laws that account for what *must* be the case. If the universe is law-governed, how can there be genuinely contingent events? Perhaps they seem contingent to us, but for the committed scientist this perception must mark our incomplete understanding. Either things are necessary and science is possible, or they are contingent and it is not. Contingency's challenge is thus about the nature of reality, not just about the limits to our grasp of that reality. In the lingo: it is about ontology, not just epistemology.

Suppose that Israeli Prime Minister Yitzhak Rabin had not been assassinated by Yigal Amir in November of 1995, or that South African President F. W. De Klerk had been killed by a disgruntled white right-winger in January of 1992. Because no other National Party leader was willing to face down the Afrikaner hard right, as De Klerk did in March of that year by calling an unprecedented referendum on whether to conclude an agreement with the African National Congress, his death would almost certainly have derailed the negotiations between his National Party government and the ANC. This would have greatly strengthened NP reactionaries and ANC radicals, quite likely sending the country spiraling into chaos if not civil war.[1] By contrast, had Rabin escaped Amir's bullet in 1995, he might well have concluded the agreement to which he was then close with Yassir Arafat and the Palestine Liberation Organization and which his successor, Shimon Peres, did not pursue. The subsequent collapse of the Oslo accords and second intifada might have been avoided, ushering in agreements on Jerusalem, the status of refugees, and Jewish settlements that can scarcely be imagined today. We might have been looking today at a Middle East "miracle" while the ongoing the South Africa basket-case would have surprised no one.[2]

A bullet kills one leader, not another. Democratic settlements and civil wars occur in different countries as a result. Small contingencies with vast effects. History is replete with such instances of what might, or might not, have been. Had the just-appointed Prime Minister Winston Churchill—widely seen as a hothead at the time—not prevailed in his uphill battle with Foreign Secretary Lord Halifax in May of 1940, Britain would probably have capitulated to Hitler along with Belgium and France.[3] How much twentieth-century history would then have been different?

Yet many social outcomes do not depend radically on contingencies in this way. My decision to vote or not to vote is unlikely to affect an election's outcome. Any of the thousands of New Englanders who headed west in the nineteenth century could have stayed home without affecting America's westward expansion. In these cases had a great many people acted differently—which they might have done—the results would have been different, but the actions of any given individual were inconsequential.

Choice is often the hallmark of contingency, but not always. Had an infected monkey not bitten someone in Africa in the 1980s, the AIDS pandemic might never have erupted.[4] True, there is *a* connection with a human choice here—the person might have chosen to stay home on the day she or he was bitten. But contingency's connection to human choice might itself be contingent. The monkey might have been eaten by a lion the day before it bit the person who became the initial human carrier. Then again, the lion might have been shot by a hunter the day before it would otherwise have eaten the monkey. And the hunter might have missed his flight to Africa the day before he would otherwise have shot the lion . . .

There are countless contingencies, massively consequential for human existence, that have nothing at all to do with human action—let alone human choice. Had a meteorite not struck what is now the Yucatán peninsula some 65 million years ago, the dinosaurs and thousands of other species of plants and animals might not have become extinct.[5] How different would our world be in that case? And, of course, we might be rendered extinct by a future meteorite. We might be wiped out by a deadly microbe that is sitting under a rock somewhere and happens not to have been disturbed for thousands of years—but could be knocked over at any time. In short, important contingencies for human affairs may be, but need not be, related to human choice, and many particular human choices, while contingent in that the person might have done otherwise, may not be especially consequential for larger social and political outcomes.

This means that when we consider the challenge of contingency to the possibility of *political* science, or even to the social sciences generally, the questions we have to ask, while a subset of contingency's general challenge to science, are not easily quarantined. The social sciences might differ from the natural sciences in being concerned with human contrivances and the vicissitudes of voluntary action, but this is unlikely to map neatly onto the problem of contingency. Social and political arrangements can affect, and be affected by, the nonhuman world as well as the human world, and the degree, if any, to which these effects are law governed may not vary in any systematic way with the discipline of study. Indeed, as David Wootton's discussion of the origins of contemporary debates about contingency in chapter 1 makes clear, early modern thinkers who wrestled with the idea of contingency did not work with the disciplinary terrain that most of us take for granted today.

Political science, conceived as that branch of the social sciences focused on the nature and dynamics of political regimes, may at times be in the inescapable vice of contingencies, yet immune to them at others. How much contingency has been thought to matter to the scientific study of politics has varied with theoretical fashion. Proponents of such architectonic theories as Marxism, elite theory, and modern rational-choice theory have been concerned to divine laws of politics, cousins of the laws of physics, that would render the apparent effects of contingency epiphenomenal or illusory, or relegate them to the error terms in powerful explanatory equations—to be minimized if not done away with entirely. Skeptics of these views range from those who see everything as contingent—partisans of the quip that history is just one damn thing after another—to those who recognize that much is contingent yet nonetheless aspire to develop a science of politics. Their strategies range from limiting attention to the noncontingent features of political life, to studying what is contingent in one context as necessary in another, to dealing with contingency through the lens of probability, to minimizing contingency—as Machiavelli urged—by understanding it and controlling it. The advantages and limitations of these various strategies for coping with contingency's challenge to political science are the central focus of this volume.

I: Roots of Contingency

It is tempting to see contingency's challenge as an artifact of the Enlightenment—and in particular its erosion of religious understandings of natural law. As Wootton's chapter makes clear, however, although contingency's challenge was thrown into sharp relief by the eclipse of providential views of the universe, the core conundrum is traceable to older conflicts within the natural law tradition itself. These centered on two paradoxical tensions. One, arising from seeing God as all-powerful and natural law as universal, was captured in the question: Is God bound by natural law? If an affirmative answer seemed to threaten the idea of God's omnipotence, then conceding that natural law might be altered by God's will—or in formulations like John Locke's that it simply *is* God's will—undermined natural law's universality. Put differently, if nothing in the universe is contingent on God's will, in what meaningful sense can He be omnipotent? But if He *is* omnipotent, then how can there be laws that are truly universal? It seems that natural law must be, yet cannot be, binding on God.[6]

Closely related to this dilemma was the tension between the idea of an omniscient God and the intertwined doctrines of the fall and the possibility of redemption. If God created human beings with the capacity to choose between courses that lead to salvation or damnation, what they will in fact choose must in some sense be an open question. Yet this seems at odds with the idea of an all-knowing God who exists outside time and space and who knows, therefore, how everything turns out. How can the choices confronting humans really be choices at all if the outcome is not in doubt? We see the paradox at its starkest when we ask: Can an omniscient God create a world in which there are contingent outcomes? It seems that God must be able to do what it is impossible for him to do. Wootton's chapter chronicles and illuminates the ways in which early modern thinkers grappled with these tensions.

The idea that all knowledge is corrigible, and that science advances not by making knowledge more certain, but rather by producing more knowledge, is a creature of the mature—post-Humean—Enlightenment.[7] Philosophers of the early Enlightenment were wedded to the idea that only knowledge that is certain can be genuine. Sometimes this position was rooted in theology, sometimes in secular arguments like the Cartesian *cogito*. Whatever the source, indubitability was the gold standard for knowledge as distinct from opinion or speculation. Due to their identification of knowledge with certainty, it would have been anathema to thinkers of the early Enlightenment to couple knowledge with contingency. Just as it seemed paradoxical to affirm that an omniscient God could exist in a contingent universe, so it seemed equally problematic to say that there could be knowledge of contingencies. Contingencies were conceived of as random, illogical, arbitrary, and impenetrable—by definition beyond the realm of knowledge. At the same time, however, they were not beyond the realm of experience. Under the circumstances, perhaps there could be an enterprise geared to reducing the influence of contingency in human affairs. This was one early modern approach championed by Machiavelli, who defended republics as superior to monarchies on the grounds that they are more flexible and therefore better able to adapt to unforeseen developments. Likewise, he contended that powerful polities, like Sparta and Venice, are comparatively likely to endure because they would be costly to attack. They were models of the kind of regime best suited to a world beset by contingencies.

Implicit in Machiavelli's reasoning was the attempt to deal with contingency through the lens of probability: he was thinking about how to increase a regime's chances of survival. As contingency displaced providence as the source of the unfathomable in human affairs, probability seemed to a number of early modern thinkers the best means to try to get a grip on it. Wootton notes thinkers like Pascal and Bayle who invented the notion of possible worlds, radically expanding contingency's reach. Their attempts to bring order to unpredictability via the notion of probability were partly successful, but hampered by their almost congenital inability to entertain the idea that any proposition that was less than certain could rise to the level of knowledge. Hume, in particular, grappled mightily with this problem without resolving it.

In the course of trying to reconcile the realities of a contingent world with an epistemology that made certainty the hallmark of genuine knowledge, a number of eighteenth-century thinkers considered that there might be feedback mechanisms among the apparently disparate and chaotic events and—perhaps opaque—underlying forces that would render them coherent. This was the start of modern thinking about social processes by reference to such concepts as invisible hands and equilibrium processes for which Adam Smith is perhaps best known. But Wootton shows how several of Smith's predecessors and contemporaries began thinking about politics in ways analogous to Smith's *homo economicus*—the self-interested inhabitants of Mandeville's *Grumbling Hive*. Not only did they reason that apparently contingent events might be understood—and perhaps even predicted—by reference to underlying equilibrating mechanisms, they also carried this thought into the realm of institutional design. For it was but a small step from this thought to the Madisonian agenda that the selfish and aggrandizing actions of politicians could serve to offset and balance one another—that "[a]mbition must be made to counteract ambition"[8]—so long as their contingent actions were channeled through the right institutional structure.

Wootton's history reveals that many contemporary debates about contingency were prefigured by early modern theorists. They were perplexed by contingency's challenge to any ordered conception of the universe that the scientific outlook seems to require. Indeed, their distinctive epistemological assumptions, linking authentic knowledge to indubitable certainty, threw this tension into sharp relief. Their attempts to grapple with this tension involved taking a number of tacks, all of which would subsequently be explored more systematically. Mastering contingency so as to reduce its influence, using the ideas of probability and equilibrium to square the circle, and designing institutions to take advantage of contingency are all strategies taken in the contemporary literature that are explored in this volume. As a prelude to these considerations, we begin, in chapters 2 and 3, respectively, with analytical treatments of the meaning of contingency by Andreas Schedler and Philip Pettit.

What does it really mean to call something contingent, asks Schedler? His answer draws on a wide-ranging exploration of the term's uses in both scientific and ordinary language. He finds that the meaning of *contingency* is partly, but only partly context-dependent. To call something contingent is to invoke a semantic architecture that rests on three pillars: indeterminacy, conditionality, and uncertainty. By *indeterminacy* Schedler means that when we call an event or phenomenon contingent, we invoke the idea of possible worlds alongside the actual world—what Max Weber once described as "objective possibility." The world that exists might not have existed, and other worlds might have existed in its stead. "Things could be different," as Schedler puts it. "They could be otherwise in the present. They could have been different in the past. They could be different in the future."

But calling something contingent also invokes the notion of conditionality or causal dependence. Contingencies may often be what social scientists think of as dependent variables—they vary with the independent variables on which they depend. If there is no movement in the independent variable, then there is none in the dependent variable. The distinction between dependent and independent variables is artificial inasmuch as an independent variable in one context may be a dependent one in another. Fertility rates might be contingent on women's education and labor force participation rates, and these, in turn, might be contingent on social policies on education and child support subsidies. Conversely, changes in fertility rates might have an impact on public attitudes toward immigration. Whether everything—the existence of the universe and perhaps, even, the laws of physics—is in some ultimate sense contingent is a profound epistemic question, as we have seen.[9] So is the matter of how well we can theorize about contingencies.

Often contingencies are unanticipated—think of the earthquakes and hurricanes once denoted "acts of God" in the contingency or *force majeure* clauses of insurance contracts. This is not to say that unexpected contingencies are uncaused; only that no theory is likely to anticipate them. They might be explained after the fact, but not predicted.

Or at least not predicted with certainty. At best we will be able to make probabilistic claims about future contingencies—such as that a major earthquake will very likely occur in California at some point in the next fifty years. Even when more focused predictions are made, as with the claim that when per capita incomes in democracies fall below $1,000 their chances of surviving for one year falls substantially, there is always an error term. It encapsulates contingencies—perhaps specifiable, perhaps not—that might forestall the predicted result in a given instance. Political scientists have yet to reach consensus about why India has survived as a democracy for decades against these odds. Contingencies produce outliers.

What do we mean when we call a contingent event more or less likely? Phillip Pettit illuminates this question in chapter 3 via the notion of *resilience.* Recognizing that contingent phenomena are conventionally understood as those things that are simply not necessary (that is, they may have occurred in the actual world but "do not figure in every possible world"), he finds such a definition lacks specificity. The traditional definition is a "catch-all category" that includes too many phenomena to be helpful. Pettit suggests, instead, that we focus on possible worlds. The larger the proportion of possible worlds in which a phenomenon would exist, the more resilient it is in Pettit's sense. In other words, whereas necessary phenomena are those that occur in all possible worlds, their resilient (contingent) counterparts arise in many but not all such worlds. He goes on to argue that rational-choice and functionalist explanations ought to be understood as explaining the resilience of a particular behavior or pattern rather than its emergence or historical continuance. That is, proponents of both these kinds of explanation end up proffering reasons why the behavior or pattern "continues across a certain range of contingencies." The explanations in question tell us why particular phenomena withstand and persevere in the face of possible (but not yet actualized) disturbances, drifts, pressures, or crises. Institutions that are flexible in Machiavelli's sense are resilient in Pettit's.

II: Contingency's Challenge

If Schedler and Pettit give us useful conceptual tools for thinking about contingency's meaning, they do not tell us how serious a challenge contingency poses to the systematic study of politics. If contingent political outcomes can be predicted with high degrees of probability, if many political outcomes are strongly robust in Pettit's sense, then the fact of contingency may pose no particular threat to the systematic empirical study of politics. In chapter 4, by David Mayhew, and chapter 5, by Jennifer Hochschild and Traci Burch, we find disquieting reasons for supposing that in politics contingencies do a lot more than lurk in *de minimus* error terms.

Mayhew makes a powerful case for the central importance of contingencies in accounting for many developments political scientists try to explain in other ways. The gravamen of his claim is that political scientists have been insufficiently attentive to causes that are "proximate, contingent, or short-term" rather than "basic, underlying, or long-term." Whereas institutions, social forces, and enduring incentives predominate as explanatory factors in the study of American politics, Mayhew demonstrates the critical significance of such "chance events" as depressions, riots, assassinations, and wars, which often create "openings" that alter political outcomes decisively. There is a good chance that much New Deal legislation would not have been enacted but for the Great Depression. Ronald Reagan's soaring popularity after the failed attempt on his life in March 1981 rescued his huge program of tax and spending cuts that had been headed for the rocks. The Great Society legislation was helped immeasurably by John F. Kennedy's assassination. His legislative record had been so-so, but his death both sanctified and supplied impetus to his legislative program under Lyndon Johnson, as well as helping make 1964 "possibly the most productive legislative year since the 1930s."

Nor are these isolated instances of "events as causes." Mayhew cites a stunning array of major changes in taxes, tariffs, suffrage expansion, race relations, and veterans' benefits that have been ushered in by wars. Indeed, the Second Bank of the United States and the Bureau of Internal Revenue (the ancestor of the Internal Revenue Service) were "durable institutions" brought about by the War of 1812 and the Civil War, respectively. At a minimum, Mayhew concludes that political scientists should pay more attention to the interactions among "underlying" causes and the types of events he identifies. Beyond this, they should focus less on elections and electoral competition in trying to explain political outcomes and more on what goes on between elections and how that interacts with electoral politics. They should also attend more to executive politics—which often drives and responds disproportionately to events—and less to legislative politics. Moreover, Mayhew suggests that students of American politics should invest less than scholars of Congress have recently done in devices like the Poole-Rosenthal left/right ideological scale for explaining congressional outcomes. Events can widen or narrow ideological differences in ways that are not captured by such ordinal scales. They can even shift entire ideological spectrums in unanticipated ways. Indeed, events can shape and re-shape what the "right" and "left" wing positions are understood to be. Events can also swamp ideological differences—as with the near unanimous declaration of war on Japan following Pearl Harbor, the creation of NASA after the Soviet launch of Sputnik, or the Use of Force Resolution in the wake of the September 11, 2001, attacks.

In chapter 5, Jennifer Hochschild and Traci Burch reveal that political actors, no less than political scientists, can be victims of contingencies that they do not understand. Whereas Mayhew's analysis calls into question much of the conventional scholarship in the study of American politics, Hochschild and Burch's argument exposes the contingent nature of American law-making itself, an activity that presumably, by its very nature, should be subject to a certain amount of predictability. However, they show how in drafting even well-considered legislation, legislators can suffer from surprise. Here the surprise turns out to be the de-stabilization of America's inherited racial categories. Specifically, they argue that the unintended and, indeed, unforeseeable effects of the Hart-Celler Immigration Act of 1965 (which overturned much of the 1924 rules on immigration) and the ability to "mark one or more" racial categories on the 2000 Census are leading to the disintegration of racial categories.

Given the context of the Cold War and the civil rights movement, legislators and policymakers sought to remove the old system's country specific quotas that had favored immigration from the British Isles, Ireland, and Germany. The goal was to ensure that the United States was seen as a "fair and meritocratic society." Their primary goal in enacting the Hart-Celler Act of 1965 was not to increase immigration but rather to make it more fair—removing the bias in favor of immigrants from Northern Europe. If anything, these lawmakers thought that the act would only increase immigration from southern and Eastern Europe. As Hochschild and Burch argue, however, they were simply wrong—victims of contingency. The legislation was followed not only by an unexpected increase in immigrants from Asia, Mexico, the Caribbean, and South America, but also by an unanticipated decrease in immigrants from Europe. From 1970 to 2000, whites went from 83% of the American population to 69%, Asians and Pacific Islanders from 1% to 4%, and Latinos from 4% to 13%. These numbers stand in stark contrast to testimony given at that time by Attorney General Robert Kennedy (with the State Department and other experts concurring) that ending country specific quotas (passing the Hart-Celler Act) would not change the ethnic composition of America. The legislators could anticipate neither the complex incentives created by these actions nor the changes outside the United States about which they could not know.

More recently, in drafting legislation to permit one to mark multiple racial categories on the 2000 Census, lawmakers failed to see the combined effect of this decision with exogenous changes in immigration patterns. The debates in the 1990s to change the census reporting options involved little attention to immigrants or immigration law. They focused instead on multicultural issues of identity and choice, the artificiality of racial and ethnic categories, and the extension of anti-discrimination law to new realms. Even those who opposed the changes neglected the role of immigration, worrying instead about the possible impact on civil rights legislation. In fact, the two groups that stood at the center of the debate, whites and African-Americans, did not see it as related to immigration.

But as contingency would have it, most of those who turned out to define themselves by reference to more than one ethnic or racial category were immigrants, and the children of immigrants, from groups whose members had not been part of the public debate on multiracial categories. Moreover, since, as Hochschild and Burch argue, Anglo/Hispanics constitute the largest number of those who self-identify as mixed on the census, an increase in Hispanic population will probably result in more people eschewing traditional categories of race. Here contingency took as its victim an entire group of political actors (lawmakers, analysts, lobbyists) who simply could not comprehend the effects of these two legislative changes, or how they would interact with other changes in patterns of immigration.

Whereas chapters 4 and 5 explore contingency's challenge across time —events as causes of American development, the unintended interactive effects of legislation, and various developments that are sometimes call path-dependent—the next chapter focuses on the contingencies of space. Just as certain temporal contingencies can have great political consequences, so can spatial contingencies shape politics as well. On this point, Susan Stokes demonstrates in chapter 7 that regions or locations can have significant effects on democratization.

Defining a region "as a contiguous and compact space constituted by a set of countries in the world or by an area within a country," Stokes argues that spatial factors can affect the transition to and, more importantly, the consolidation of democracy. She distinguishes between those regional effects that are "spurious" from those that are genuine and "proper." In the former case, rather than the role of region, it is some other underlying independent variable (such as income, age, education, housing quality) doing the actual explanatory work. True regional dynamics arise when a certain quality particular to the region in question best explains the relevant behavior. Moreover, these dynamics can occur within a political jurisdiction or between and among regions that are in close proximity to one another. Thus, a wave of democratization in nearby trading partners can exert more powerful effects than such a wave that is far away.

Stokes buttresses her case through an exploration of the regional unevenness in the consolidation of democracy in various parts of Argentina. Treating "regional quality of democracy" as an independent variable, she finds that out of four different regions within Argentina, one (the area of Mar del Plata) exhibited a more robust democracy (with, *inter alia*, less clientelism and a greater tilt toward programmatic politics) than the others. Rejecting factors such as income, education, gender, age, and party preference, Stokes contends that "distinctive regional characteristics" of Mar del Plata better account for this variation in democratic consolidation. These characteristics include more widely held beliefs in responsive government. But why do such regional differences arise? Here Stokes looks to the results of decades of distinctive types of regional leadership. In this way, contingency is important in accounting for political outcomes in intersecting ways: regional differences have contingent effects on political outcomes, yet these regional differences are themselves the result of contingent factors.

III: What Is to Be Done?

The chapters in Part II establish the inescapable importance of contingency in accounting for political outcomes. Repudiating any notion that contingency is a minor error term to be quietly ignored, Mayhew, Hochschild and Burch, and Stokes establish that politics is influenced by the contingencies of time and space that scholars ignore at their peril. The study of politics is fraught with the vicissitudes of nagging counterfactuals, non-generalizable conclusions, and unexpected events. Acknowledging the omnipresence of contingency, how should political scientists proceed? The final chapters take up the challenge of contingency with an eye to providing some useful guidance. In a way, we end where we began. The early modern debates that Wootton explored in chapter 1 return in a contemporary idiom.

In chapters 7 and 8, Gregory Huber and Elisabeth Wood handle contingency by changing the terms by which the authors of previous chapters approached it. In their view it is misguided for political scientists to focus on the causes and consequences of particular events. They should not ask questions like: What would have happened had Rabin not been assassinated or if De Klerk had been? How much of the Great Society would have been enacted had J.F.K. not been shot in 1963? Would it have mattered if a particular individual had found himself living in a different region of Argentina? Instead, Huber and Wood think the focus should be on how strategic actors are likely to behave and what makes institutions endure, given the contingent political world.

Huber suggests that rather than attend to how "realized contingencies" influence political outcomes, political scientists would do better to study the strategic behavior of political actors "in the face of uncertainty." Instead of approaching contingency as a backward looking enterprise—where the question is: Could this event have happened differently?—political scientists should address the forward-looking question: How are strategic actors likely to behave given the unavoidable existence of contingency? From this perspective, concern with truly exogenous events (earth-quakes, assassinations, etc.) does not further our knowledge of politics. After all, if something is not at all foreseeable, it will have little effect on the way people act. Simply put, Huber turns the tables on the apparent threat of contingency by charging political science to focus on political actors, not events or causes. Game theory, he contends, can aid in this endeavor.

Huber takes as his case study the effects of judicial elections on the be-havior of judges. That is, how does the practice of selecting judges bear on the various kinds of sentences that judicial officers impose? Again, the wrong (and largely fruitless) question is to ask why did a certain newly elected judge impose a particular penalty on a criminal. The answer to this kind of question would depend on a host of contingent factors—the pres-ence of one judge instead of another, the features of the case, securing an election win for the next race, to name but a few. But political scientists should leave such questions to others. Instead, the question should be: How should judges be expected to behave, knowing that they will be up for reelection? Here a probabilistic calculus becomes an important tool. As judges contemplate how harsh a sentence to impose, the chance the crimi-nal may recidivate is always present. By using models of strategic action, we can hypothesize that, given the desire to be reelected, judges in certain situations will be more likely to impose higher than warranted penalties. For example, when faced with a high probability that the public will get wind of a sentence, a judge will probably dole out a harsher penalty, refus-ing to take a chance on the possibility that the criminal may not recidivate. In this way contingency's effect on the strategic behavior of political actors becomes something we can study systematically.

Whereas Huber examines these effects of contingency on strategic ac-tors, Wood is more interested in Machiavelli's and Pettit's question. She analyzes contingency's impact on an institution's robustness and how this robustness shapes the effect of contingent events. While some political ar-rangements (institutions, peace agreements, alliances, settlements) appear robust when confronted by unanticipated, contingent events, others un-ravel. Some emerge and persist independently in a variety of settings; oth-ers are rare or short-lived.

Wood invites us to think of an institution as an equilibrium pattern of interaction. An example of such an institution is a convention. Driving on the left side of the road, for example, is a convention that is characterized by individuals driving on a particular side of the road. Contingent events —in this case a perceived need to attract business from neighboring countries in which they drive on the right—might disrupt such a stable pattern (or equilibrium), leading individuals to follow another convention, which might in turn produce a new institutional equilibrium. Wood uses stochastic game theory to model and analyze how contingencies cause such institutional shifts and give rise to new stable patterns. Her analysis seeks to ascertain why certain patterns endure or remain in the face of contingent challenges, which, she contends, can lead to insights about how to craft comparatively robust political arrangements.

Recognizing that not all contingencies are the same, she proposes three different models of for thinking about destabilizing and restabilizing equilibrium in institutional patterns: individuals randomly engaging in idiosyncratic behavior (a new stable pattern arises by simple error); exogenous shocks—Mayhew's events as causes (an assassination or earthquakes); and organized, collective challenges by a group of political actors (a labor movement or sit-in). In Pettit's terms, Wood offers three different ways of analyzing an institution's resilience—depending on the kind of contingency involved. In each of the three models, she finds that the "basin of attraction" has much to do with an institution's robustness or resilience. The larger the basin, the more likely it is that the institution will persist. By studying the resilience of institutions in the face of these different types of contingency, Wood renders tractable the seemingly intractable problem posed by theorizing about contingency *itself.*

In chapter 9 Courtney Jung brings comparable considerations to the study of democratic transition negotiations, but she refuses to punt so quickly on the challenge of accounting for contingency in politics. In comparing South Africa's successful transition to democracy to its stalled Middle Eastern and Northern Ireland counterparts during the 1980s and 1990s, she explores the generalizable, though nonetheless contingent, features of attempts at negotiated settlements. The settings share in common the fact that neither the regime nor the opposition is powerful enough to impose a settlement unilaterally; they are also similar in that the regimes, while subject to an electoral constraint, are manifestly flawed democracies. In such quasi-democratic contexts, she argues, contingencies arise in certain patterns. There are opportunities and constraints in the various phases of potential peace negotiations.

Different actors might be more and less willing or able to take advantage of them for various contingent reasons, but one can still theorize fruitfully about the types of circumstance that will lead windows of opportunity for settlements to open and to close, what is likely to happen if and when negotiators move through them—or fail to do so—at certain critical moments, and, indeed, what factors make it more and less likely that actors in these settings will be inclined to try to reach settlements. For instance, because politicians are critically reliant on popular support to legitimate their actions, one can tell a good deal about how likely they are to risk making agreements by studying their levels of popular support and the support for potential agreements. The very weak—low single digit—Palestinian support for a two state settlement as envisaged in the 1993 Oslo accords in the summer of 2000 made it vanishingly unlikely that Arafat would agree to such a settlement—no matter how strong the pressure from the Clinton administration and the Barak government in Israel. It would have finished him in Palestinian politics.

But the situation was very different in 1995. Had Rabin survived, or had his successor, Shimon Peres, called a snap election immediately following the assassination when there was strong Palestinian and Israeli support for the settlement, he would have won and been able to reach a deal. In this, he would have followed the model of De Klerk, who faced down his hard right flank by calling a snap referendum on the negotiations after he had lost a series of by-elections to the conservatives. That Peres lacked the appetite for risk, or perhaps the imagination, of De Klerk turned out to be a vital contingency that could not have been predicted. Nonetheless, the political science of transition negotiations advances when we gain a more accurate understanding, as we do here, of what the constraints and opportunities actually are, and what the costs and benefits of acting on them will be likely to be. We cannot predict when settlements will be reached, but Jung demonstrates that we can often get close to understanding conditions that are necessary for success. At a minimum, this will allow us to predict failure as with the Camp David attempt in 2000. But it also holds out the possibility of enhancing our understanding of what makes success achievable, and more and less likely.

In Chapter 10 Robert Shulman puts our deliberations about contingency's challenge to political science into a larger perspective by recognizing its presence in the natural sciences, notably biochemistry. As political scientists we squirm at the thought that if events could always be otherwise, the very enterprise of generating law-like conclusions seems in jeopardy, but Shulman offers comfort in exploring the role contingency plays in the laboratory of the scientist. It is often said, as we noted at the outset of this introduction, that science is impossible if things are contingent all the way down. Shulman rejects this formulation as wrongheaded, contending that contingency and science need not be mutually exclusive. If biochemists can successfully minimize contingency—which he argues that they can—then perhaps there is hope for political science as well.

Shulman highlights two ways in which scientists work to diminish the impact of contingency. First, in a spirit reminiscent of Huber, he illustrates by reference to the study of diabetes that it is the "well-defined medical question" that can overcome contingency. Scientists presently do not understand why some patients predisposed to diabetes fare better than others or why, despite the odds, some sedentary obese subjects remain healthy and some vigorous lean, subjects fall ill. Nonetheless, the focus on the question why for some the pancreas overproduces but glucose levels remain tolerable can turn such contingences into comprehensible outcomes. Knowing what to look for, then, is a simple, but vital task. Defining the parameters of the study—here the relationship between the functioning of the pancreas and the body's glucose level—can aid in managing contingency. In this his claim is comparable to that of Huber and Jung who suggest that knowledge of politics can advance if we look at the relatively enduring incentives and constraints in different political circumstances, rather than at how a given individual in a given situation will respond to them.

Second, Shulman maintains that multi-method approaches can help tackle contingency. He sees this possibility at work in the study of the Brain/Mind. Here, contingency is inherent in the very definition of the subject, he argues. While some scientists appeal exclusively to a computational theory of the mind—maintaining a "top-down," "fixed view" of the mind as a rational computer, others take a "bottom-up" approach, radically contextualizing mental concepts. Nevertheless, Shulman maintains that most of the time biological scientists actually reject both reductionism and holism. They move freely in both directions, looking for the interacting effects, and science is better for it. There might be lessons in this for the study of politics. Rather than run to deterministic theory (sweeping contingency under the "error term" rug along the way) or embrace contingency with the gusto of an event driven historian, perhaps political scientists should multitask more. In effect this is Mayhew's advice in arguing for greater attention to the interactions between underlying dynamics and events as causes. Taken together, the chapters in this volume suggest that this is most likely to be achieved with a mix of methods—quantitative, qualitative, and axiomatic. Taking our cue from Shulman, we should realize that we are more likely to domesticate contingency if we surround it rather than either run from it or chase it over the horizon.

NOTES

1. In an interview with Ian Shapiro on 8 December 2003, De Klerk confirmed that he consulted no one in the cabinet or National Party leadership on the decision to hold the referendum following a series of lost by-elections in conservative strongholds because he knew they would have opposed it. He described the choice as "the only unilateral act I took as President," and speculated that had he been assassinated before the referendum, it would have been unlikely that any of the probable successors would have wanted to call such a referendum and, even if one did, the need to establish and consolidate his position as leader would have made it impossible to do so.

2. See Jung et al., "Problems and Prospects," pp. 277–326.

3. See Lukacs, *Five Days.*

4. For an exhaustive assessment of the "monkey bite" and other theories, see Hooper, *The River.* See also Barnett and Whiteside, *AIDS,* chapter 2, pp. 34–38.

5. See Frankel, *The End of the Dinosaurs.*

6. See Tuck, *Natural Rights* and Riley, *Political Legitimacy,* pp. 87–110.

7. See Shapiro, *Moral Foundations,* chapters 1–2.

8. Madison, "Federalist #51."

9. One group of physicists has recently questioned whether the laws of physics might not be unchanging. See Webb et al., "Cosmological Evolution."

BIBLIOGRAPHY

Barnett, Tony, and Alan Whiteside. *AIDS in the Twenty-First Century: Disease and Globalization.* New York: Palgrave Macmillan, 2003

Frankel, Charles. *The End of the Dinosaurs: Chicxulub Crater and Mass Extinctions.* Cambridge: Cambridge Press, 1999.

Hooper, Edward. *The River: A Journey Back to the Source of HUV and AIDS.* London: Allen Lane, 1999.

Jung, Courtney, Ellen Lust-Okar, and Ian Shapiro. "Problems and Prospects for Democratic Settlements: South Africa as a Model for the Middle East and Northern Ireland?" *Politics and Society* 33, 2 (June 2005): 277–326.

Lukacs, John. *Five Days in London: May 1940.* New Haven: Yale University Press, 2001.

Madison, James. Federalist #51. *The Federalist* (ed. Jacob E. Cooke). Middletown, CT: Wesleyan University Press, 1961.

Riley, Patrick. *Will and Political Legitimacy.* Cambridge: Harvard Press, 1982.

Shapiro, Ian. *The Moral Foundations of Politics.* New Haven: Yale University Press, 2003.

Tuck, Richard. *Natural Rights Theories: Their Origin and Development.* Cambridge: Cambridge Press, 1979.

Webb, J. K., M. T. Murphy, V. V. Flambaum, V. A. Dzuba, J. D. Barrow, C. W. Churchill, J. X. Proschaska, and A. M. Wolfe. "Further Evidence for Cosmological Evolution of the Fine Structure Constant," *Physical Review Letters* 87 (August 2001): 091301–091601.

Part I

Roots of Contingency

Chapter 1

From Fortune to Feedback
Contingency and the Birth of Modern Political Science

David Wootton

Events, dear boy, events.
—Harold Macmillan when asked what might prevent
his government achieving its objectives

Hydraulic Engineering: Machiavelli and Naudé[1]

This chapter is about a curiously elusive subject: the idea of contingency in early modern thought. It is not that the subject does not exist, for the concept of contingency was clearly understood. But early modern thinkers, with a few striking exceptions, found it almost impossible to focus on contingency: for most authors it was at best something glimpsed at the periphery of their vision, a liminal concept that represented the point where knowledge inevitably shaded into ignorance. In 1623 Sir Edward Digby wrote, "The eyes of human knowledge cannot see beyond its [human knowledge's] horizon; it cannot ascertain future contingents."[2] In 1625 Francis Bacon wrote, "But it is not good to look too long upon these turning wheels of vicissitude, lest we become giddy." The world of contingency was thus also the world of the unpredictable and the disorderly. John Donne, in a sermon of 1616, spoke of being "Exposed to the disposition of the tyde, to the rage of the winde, to the wantonness of the eddy, and to innumerable contingencies"; over three centuries later Macmillan was to find himself similarly at the mercy of events.

The problem early modern thinkers had with the contingent was not just that they saw it as shapeless, formless, disorderly, to be compared to a wind or an eddy. For scholastic philosophers and for Cartesians all knowledge was knowledge of things which were *necessarily* true (in the case of the scholastics, capable of being expressed in the form of a syllogism). By definition, the contingent thus lay outside the territory of the truly knowable, in a world where one had to make do with prudence, at best, or else with opinion: for Abraham Fraunce, writing in 1588, there were necessary reasons, "whereof cometh science," and contingent reasons, "whence cometh opinion." To enter the world of the contingent was to enter the world of homespun wisdom, of the maxim and the adage: a stitch in time saves nine, forewarned is forearmed, buyer beware. It was also to enter the world of human agency: "As these impediments are contingent," wrote William Petty in *Political Arithmetick* (1687), "so also are they removeable."

This brings us to a third order of difficulty. For orthodox early modern Christians, God's omniscience meant that He had perfect foreknowledge of all future events. The future, seen from God's point of view, was never contingent but always necessary. As Robert Burton put it in the *Anatomy of Melancholy* (1621), "Columbus did not find out America by chance, but God directed him . . . it was contingent to him, but necessary to God." A particular problem within the general territory of foreknowledge was presented by the question of freedom of the will. Some thinkers defined the contingent as everything that was not determined in advance, as Thomas Hobbes did: "By contingents, I understand all things which may be done and may not be done, may happen or may not happen, by reason of the indetermination or accidental concurrence of the causes." But others defined the contingent as specifically that territory of uncertainty that was associated with freedom of choice and voluntary action. Thus for John Salkeld (1613) the contingent was synonymous with that which is "dependent of man's will." For these authors the whole territory of the unknowable was made up of the contingent together with the accidental, which consisted of unpredictable events, such as an ax head flying off its shaft and killing a passer-by.

Theologians divided into two groups. The Augustinians (Jansenists, Calvinists) denied that there was such a thing as free will. Jonathan Edwards, in 1754, described it as "This contingency, this efficient nothing, this effectual no-Cause." For them, contingency was either an illusion or, at best, a purely subjective experience, a sense of not being compelled by any external agent. The will was in fact determined and enslaved, and thus there was nothing inherently unpredictable about human action. Their opponents (Jesuits, Arminians, Socinians) argued that human beings had real freedom of choice. At the extreme, this might lead to the claim that even God could not know for certain what would happen, that he too could only know the future conjecturally. More conservatively, it led to the claim that where free choices were involved, one could not predict the future on the basis of the past, and so no human being could know in advance what would happen. God, however, being outside time, did not need to predict in order to see the future. The whole of this vast literature can be briefly summarised in a single sentence from David Hume: "To reconcile the indifference and contingency of human actions with prescience; or to defend absolute decrees, and yet free the Deity from being the author of sin, has been found hitherto to exceed the power of all philosophy."[3]

Moreover all orthodox Christians believed in divine providence: thus they held that God not only foreknew what would happen, but also ensured that what happened served his purposes. The doctrine of divine providence was generally held to be incompatible with the view that there might be random or chance outcomes, even, for example, when drawing lots. Rather, the underlying purpose behind events had been concealed from us. Columbus's discovery of America was thus doubly necessary: God knew it would happen, and it was part of God's plan that it should happen.

There were thus four good reasons for dismissing the contingent as unknowable: it was random; it was illogical; it was arbitrary; it was impenetrable. And yet, despite these apparently insuperable obstacles, there is an early modern discourse on contingency in the context of both politics and history.

To be sure, this discourse has not been widely acknowledged in recent literature on the subject. Thus, for example, in *The Science of Conjecture*, James Franklin represents Machiavelli as someone unable to formulate an account of decision-making under conditions of uncertainty. Franklin points to Machiavelli's discussion of trade-offs in *The Discourses* (bk. 1, ch. 6): all courses of action can have unfortunate unintended consequences, and so one must assess the costs as well as the benefits of a course of action before deciding whether to adopt it. Any consideration of costs needs to take into account the probability of different outcomes. "To consider only the payoff, and not the probability of occurrence, will not lead to a satisfactory decision theory," Franklin writes, accusing Machiavelli of doing just that.[4] But in fact in the course of the chapter Machiavelli does turn from payoffs to probabilities.

Sparta and Venice, Machiavelli argues, represent a type of republic well adapted to preserve itself over time, as both occupy a defensible site while presenting little threat to their neighbors. There is thus a high cost involved in attacking them, and only a limited motive to engage in such an attack. "But," he then adds, "since everything to do with human beings is always in movement, and cannot be held steady, things are always getting better or worse." A stable equilibrium is impossible to achieve, so one must construct a political system that is able to deal with unexpected eventualities. Only a state that is capable of conquering its neighbors has the capacity to respond to all possible eventualities. Thus Machiavelli identifies a course of action which appears to have high benefits and low costs, and rejects it precisely because what Franklin terms "the probability of occurrence" has been overestimated; instead he favors a course of action with higher costs (internal conflict and external hostility), higher benefits (imperial conquest), and a higher probability of occurrence (the capacity to deal with changing circumstances).

This is, I would argue, a paradigmatic example of Machiavelli's mode of analysis. At every point he recommends strategies that increase the capacity to control events, and reduce vulnerability to events outside one's control. A strong army is the central strategy. But a collective leadership is also a valuable resource. A leader whose style of decision- making ideally suits one situation—Fabius Cunctator resisting Hannibal, for example—may prove completely useless in a very different situation, such as when invading the territory of an enemy. Ideally leaders should adapt to changing circumstances, but this is normally beyond human capacity. In a monarchy leaders cannot easily be changed when new circumstances occur, but in a republic they can: republics are therefore inherently more resilient and adaptable than monarchies.[5]

In chapter 7 of *The Prince,* Machiavelli discusses what is for him a test case, the political strategy of Cesare Borgia. The paradox here is that Borgia failed, and yet Machiavelli recommends that anyone placed in his position should follow exactly the policies that he followed. On first seizing power, Borgia was dependent on support from his "uncle" the pope. He took every possible step to make his power independent of the papacy, so that when the papacy changed hands he would be able to survive; unfortunately it turned out that he only had five years before his uncle died, which was not quite enough time. Even so he would have been successful but for two things. First, although he had not acquired enough power to ensure the appointment of a pope of his choice, he did have the capacity to exercise an effective veto over who was selected, and he misused this veto. Second, none of his preparations allowed for the possibility that he might be severely ill at the key moment. This unforeseen event was fatal to his plans.

The key elements of Borgia's strategy were thus entirely sound; he was defeated by a minor misjudgment and by an unlucky occurrence. One of Machiavelli's central points here is that no policy can be guaranteed success. Borgia had a very high chance of succeeding; as it happens, he failed, but his failure is not in itself proof that his strategy was misconceived.

Franklin says "probabilistic discussions never occur with those of fortune," for fortune is seen as a form of fatality, incompatible with the calculation of odds.[6] If we turn to the famous penultimate chapter of *The Prince*, it is apparent that Franklin has once again misunderstood Machiavelli's argument. There Machiavelli argues against those who believe that events are governed by chance, by fortune, by God, even though he admits that events are highly unpredictable. Roughly speaking, he thinks, half of our actions have the intended outcomes. Fortune, he goes on, is like a river which breaks its banks, destroying crops and buildings as it floods. But if one builds banks, barrages, and flood channels before the rains come, then one can either prevent the flood or minimize its consequences. He compares the Italy of his day to a plain without banks or barrages, while other states have taken better precautions and are more resilient and robust. Thus Machiavelli's argument is that the extent to which one is at the mercy of events depends to a considerable degree upon the long-term strategies one has adopted. There are, he believes, strategies that give you the capacity to survive any deterioration in your circumstances—a deterioration that is bound to come one day, just as every river floods at some point—while others leave you defenseless. In short, the core of what Machiavelli tries to teach in his political theory is how to adopt strategies that prepare in advance for unpredictable events.

Machiavelli is also concerned with the more immediate tactics of contingency-control. The longest chapter in *The Discourses* is on conspiracies, more specifically assassinations. In it he seeks to establish the tactics that give one the maximum chance of killing a ruler before one's plot is discovered: involve as few people as possible in the conspiracy; put nothing in writing; act as rapidly as possible; and be prepared to change plans quickly in response to unforeseen eventualities. Thus, whether a ruler or a subject, one does not have to be swept away by the flood of events, but can stand firm against it. Machiavelli may not use the language of probabilities, but it is quite clear that he thinks flood defenses are a perfect example of intelligent decision-making under conditions of uncertainty; all one needs to do is to identify in politics the equivalent to flood defenses. It is worth remarking that Machiavelli had practical experience of hydraulic engineering: together with Leonardo da Vinci, he had been involved in a plan to divert the Arno so that it no longer flowed through Pisa, thus cutting off Florence's longstanding enemy from maritime trade.

Few later theorists followed Machiavelli's line of argument. There are some obvious reasons for this. One is that there was soon an effective ban on any discussion of fortune because the term was regarded as pagan and anti-Christian. Another is that in *The Prince* Machiavelli was explicitly concerned with new rulers who were building institutions from scratch: later reason-of-state theorists assumed they were advising established rulers with pre-existing institutions. In *The Discourses* he sought to show the superiority of republics over monarchies: later theorists assumed they were advising kings. Their focus therefore shifted from strategy to tactics. A third is that reason-of-state theorists primarily concerned themselves with rational actors. Their assumption was that if one's opponent acted irrationally, it would be easier to defeat him than if he acted rationally. Thus one need not consider the full range of possible human behavior; one need only consider and counter the likely actions of a rational agent. This enabled such theorists to treat political action as if it were highly predictable, even though they were aware that this was not in fact the case. Almost without exception, Machiavelli's successors cease to concern themselves with the contingent character of political events. For them, the key limit on what is predictable is the existence of secret information known to one side but not the other. If there was symmetrical access to information, they assume, politics would be just like chess. Conflicts might be complex and in their detail unpredictable; but more able players would consistently beat less able players.

Almost without exception, but not entirely. The key exception is Gabriel Naudé's *Considérations politiques sur les coups d'estat*, originally published (we are told) in a limited edition of twelve copies in Rome in 1639 and widely available only after it was reprinted by Elzevier in Amsterdam in 1667. The circumstances of the publication of this book are deeply puzzling, and I consider them in an appendix to this chapter. There I argue that the *Considérations* is not the book it appears to be: it was not published in Rome in 1639, and it is not the book on *coups d'estat* that Naudé wrote. Here I will assume that the argument of the appendix is sound and refer to the author of the *Considérations* as G.N.P., the initials (standing for Gabriel Naudé Parisien) that appear on the title-page of the first edition. G.N.P., I believe, is a fictitious character created by the unknown editor and reviser of Naudé's original manuscript.

Unlike conventional reason-of-state theorists, who all seek to bring the immoral actions of rulers within some moral framework, G.N.P. does not hesitate to endorse the most blatantly Machiavellian of actions, and he declares with pride that he is going to distinguish himself from his predecessors by not taking conventional morality seriously. By *coups d'estat* he means extralegal actions taken, not to overthrow the government, but to extend the government's power—the assassination of opponents, for example. In this context, he defends at length the Massacre of St. Bartholomew, which he thinks would have been an excellent stratagem if only no Protestants had survived.

In chapter IV he turns to the topic of the universality of change. Thanks to this, even the most ambitious of enterprises—the destruction or construction of a powerful state, for example—may prove not to be impossible. Moreover, just as Archimedes could move the heaviest weights with a lever, so a small change can have enormous consequences, a small spark can start a great conflagration. G.N.P. gives numerous examples, beginning with the Trojan War, of wars which had insignificant beginnings, and concludes, "So it is the duty of the good politician to consider all the smallest circumstances which one encounters in serious and difficult enterprises, in order to make use of them, in magnifying them, and so sometimes turning a fly into an elephant, and a little scratch into a large wound, and a spark into a conflagration; or alternatively in diminishing all these things, according as it may serve his purposes."[7]

Since the realm of contingency is the realm of the disorderly, it is not surprising that G.N.P. turns to a discussion of the populace, whose irrationality and unpredictability make them a disruptive force in politics: like contingency itself, they are compared to "a sea subject to all sorts of winds and tempests."[8] And this leads him on to the ways in which demagogues and religious impostors can provoke rebellions. Managing the populace, through tuning the pulpit and directing the presses, thus becomes the central task of politics as seen from the ruler's point of view. Out of this analysis comes a general account of how religion, cynically exploited, can further the goals of politicians (an account reminiscent of the chapter on politics in Naudé's *Apologie pour tous les grands personnages qui ont esté faussement soupçonnez de magie* of 1625). G.N.P. seems to believe that religion is always a matter of fraud and pretence; his paradigm cases are Cortez and Pizarro furthering their conquests by convincing the Aztecs and the Incas that they were gods, and Columbus using his knowledge of a forthcoming eclipse to convince the native peoples that he had superhuman powers. But it is striking that all G.N.P.'s examples of Christian religious fraud come from Catholics. Not a single example serves to discredit Protestantism. So too all his *coups d'estat* are committed by princes, none by republics. It was noticing this that first led me to doubt that G.N.P. could be straightforwardly identified with Gabriel Naudé.

G.N.P.'s long detour through religious hypocrisy leads him back in the end to the theme of contingency:

> Since, then, it is natural for most rulers to be charlatans when dealing with religion, and to use it as a drug to maintain the credit and reputation of their theatre, one should not, it seems to me, blame a politician if, in order to accomplish some important enterprise, he makes use of the same resource, even if it is more respectable to say the opposite, and even if, to speak sense on the subject, "One should not reveal or expose such things to the common people, given that so many human beings are wicked and criminal." All these maxims, nevertheless, would be without shine or sparkle if they were not polished up, and as it were brought to life by another, which teaches us to use them when events are moving in the right direction, and to choose well the time and the circumstances to put them into execution. "The things which one makes use of at the right time, succeed and turn out well, but there are many which are very harmful if they are not used at the right time." And indeed it is not sufficient to have acquired this ordinary degree of prudence of which many politicians are capable, if we do not go on to another more refined level, one of which only the most experienced and cunning ministers are capable, and take profit and advantage from our opponent's omissions, or even from developments which might place us at a disadvantage . . . as with the stratagem by which King Tullus cleverly explained away the retreat of Metius Suffetius, indeed turned it brilliantly to his advantage, spreading the word from battalion to battalion that he had sent him off to surprise the enemy and cut off their retreat. In this case I am absolutely astonished that T. Livy and Cornelius Tacitus, who report these events, contented themselves with drawing limited conclusions from them . . . when one ought immediately to have drawn this general rule that "one must turn to one's advantage all unpredictable events."[9]

It is not a coincidence that this text which fully embraces the notion of contingency, and which urges its readers—with an obvious reference back to Machiavelli's discussion of fortune—to seize their opportunities by the hair, is written by someone who appears to have an entirely cynical view of religion and expresses views which he himself recognizes should never be expressed in public. Only an avowedly un-Christian author could hope to escape the idea of divine providence. Naudé, whose manuscript was the source of the text we now have, may once have intended his readers to conclude that power was to be pursued for its own sake. But when G.N.P.'s text was published in Holland (and later translated and published elsewhere in Protestant Europe), it was surely intended to evoke a very different response. Is the proper response to a Machiavellian politics an even more cynical Machiavellism? Or is it, perhaps, a pious trust in providence? Neither response can have seemed adequate. In the 1650s (which I take to be the true date of the first edition of the *Considérations*) reading G.N.P. must have seemed to justify a Machiavellian republicanism of the sort which was shortly to be advocated by the brothers de la Court, and it is in their circle, I suspect, that we should seek Naudé's unknown editor.

Cleopatra's Nose: Pascal and Bayle

No author writing for the public press dared embrace contingency in history. Machiavelli's political works were published posthumously; Naudé dared not publish, and G.N.P. was not a real person but a fiction. The only other author to embrace contingency was almost equally fictitious. In 1682 an anonymous work arguing that comets do not foretell the future was published; a year later there appeared a revised version under a new title: *Pensées diverses écrites à un Docteur de Sorbonne, à l'occasion de la Comète qui parut au mois de Décembre 1680*. This was, as we now know, the work of a Huguenot, Pierre Bayle, who had only recently been driven into exile by the religious intolerance of Louis XIV. But Bayle was writing anonymously and pretending to be not only a Catholic, but a Catholic who believed in freedom of the will. It was therefore easy for his fictional self to conclude (as no Calvinist could have done, and as he himself could not do when writing the *Continuations aux pensées diverses* a few years later, after his identity had been exposed) that there was a fundamental and irreducible contingency in human affairs. To reach this conclusion was simply to expose what Calvinists took to be a fundamental weakness in Catholic theology. In this he was helped by the philosophy of Malebranche, who had argued that God confines himself to a simple and economical system of causation. The result of this system is a whole range of particular events that God did not actually want to bring about; they are simply the unintended consequences of the divine parsimony when it comes to intervening in nature. Malebranche thus seeks to establish an overarching providential order, while insisting that God has not actually willed every particular outcome.

Bayle's *Pensées diverses* are famous for the paradox that a society of atheists is to be preferred to a society of idolaters (and, since Bayle implicitly equates Catholicism and idolatry, to a society of Catholics). The fear of God is not in fact, as had generally been assumed, necessary to preserve the fabric of society, for the threads of this-worldly self-interest are sufficient to bind even unbelievers. Later commentators were to conclude that the *Pensées diverses* was nothing less than a defense of atheism, and, as we shall see, the way in which the theme of contingency is handled might be taken to support that interpretation. The *Pensées diverses* are certainly a critique of conventional ideas of providence.[10]

Bayle argues that far-distant comets cannot really be the cause of disastrous events (wars, plagues, earthquakes, etc.) here on earth. Nor is it plausible that the time-scale within which comets reappear happens to coincide with the time-scale according to which disastrous events occur: wars occur unpredictably, and changes in nature, the draining of swamps for example, must mean that plagues and other natural events do not occur according to a predetermined and unchanging pattern. This leaves only a third possibility: God is responsible for the supposed coincidence in timing between comets and disastrous events. Either God miraculously brings about disastrous events whenever comets appear, or God miraculously makes comets appear whenever disastrous events are about to happen. Either way, the appearance of comets would, in pagan societies, reinforce idolatrous beliefs, and God would have performed miracles to benefit idolatry. Since we can be sure God would not do this, we can be sure that any coincidence between comets and disastrous events is not miraculous. It begins, in fact, to look as though any connection between comets and disaster is purely coincidental, which amounts to saying that there is no connection at all.

Bayle's ostensibly Catholic argument thus opens the way to an entirely secular understanding of nature and of history, one in which providence is supplanted by contingency. A comet appeared in the first year of Alexander's reign, but this does not make Alexander's conquests foreordained. He might have died before he could set out to war; he might have been killed in battle; he might have encountered a more effective resistance. All that was needed to change the course of history was for his horse, Bucephalus, to rear up at the wrong moment, breaking his rider's neck. Bayle's conclusion is that human affairs are contingent and that "it depends on the least nicety, that greatest events happen not quite contrary."[11] Bayle later returns to the same topic to argue that the most insignificant motives often bring wars about: Admiral Bonnivet persuaded Francis I to invade Italy because he wanted to revisit his mistress in Milan. Wars require an interlocking series of events, none of which is determined by the passage of a comet; and exactly the same sorts of events occur in the absence of comets, sometimes resulting in wars and sometimes not. So too the devil is an unnecessary hypothesis: even without him humans would be perfectly eager to do ill in the world.[12] Human nature on its own provides an adequate explanation for the evils human beings do to each other.

It is worth pausing for a moment to unpick the notion of contingency being employed by Bayle, or rather by his fictional self. He is not suggesting that were Bucephalus to rear up, the event would be a random occurrence or without a cause: he might rear because he had been bitten by a horse-fly. But, from the point of view of a military commander, of Alexander himself, the horse-fly which bites Bucephalus lies outside his frame of reference. His attention is concentrated on the size and disposition of his army and the training and equipment of his troops; from his point of view the horse-fly is entirely insignificant and Buchephalus's action entirely unpredictable. The notion of chance here is thus not an objective one, as it would be if the outcome of the battle were determined by the rolling of dice, but a subjective one: this appears to be a random event to someone whose mind is (quite naturally) on other things. One can see the Scottish philosopher Kames struggling with this distinction a hundred years after Bayle:

> When we say a thing has happened by *chance*, we do not mean that *chance* was the *cause*; for no person ever thought that *chance* was a thing that can act, and by acting produce events: we only mean that we are ignorant of the cause, and that, for ought we see, it might have happened or not happened, or have happened differently. Aiming at a bird, I shoot *by chance* a favourite spaniel: the meaning is not that chance killed the dog, but that as to me the dog's death was accidental. With respect to contingency, future events that

are variable, and the cause unknown, are said to be contingent; changes of the weather, for example, whether it will be frost or thaw tomorrow, whether fair or foul. In a word, chance and contingency applied to events, mean not that such events happen without any cause, but only that we are ignorant of the cause.[13]

Note that Kames's account is somewhat misleading. In the case of the spaniel, I am in no doubt as to the cause of his death after the event. I shot him. A bystander might even have seen that the spaniel was in danger before I pulled the trigger. But I, with my attention fixed on the bird and oblivious to everything else, was in no position to foresee his death before the event. It was the bird I was trying to kill, not the spaniel. *As to me,* as Kames puts it, the dog's death is accidental. Bayle tries to capture this subjective element by stressing the idea of *nicety:* the horse-fly is too small for the general to consider. But there is no need for the event that throws out our calculations to be small or insignificant: the outcome of a battle might be altered by an earthquake. What is essential is simply that the event should be one that I am not in a position to foresee.

Like Machiavelli and G.N.P., the imaginary author of the *Pensées diverses* (let us call him fictional-Bayle) is able to embrace contingency because he does not feel himself to be under an obligation to preserve our belief in providence. But, again like them, as soon as he has shown the power of contingency, he turns around to insist that events have a logic that makes them predictable. Cicero, for example, predicted the overthrow of the Roman Republic fourteen years before it happened. Political wisdom thus enables one to foretell the future; it is a species of secular divination. Often people claim to make predictions on the basis of fortuitous events such as the appearance of a comet or the failure to properly observe a religious ceremony, when underlying their prediction is a realistic analysis of the political conflicts of the day. In 1618 it was easy to predict that Europe stood on the brink of a vast war; the appearance of a comet was entirely irrelevant to the prediction.

Fictional-Bayle has a further purpose beyond those of displacing providence and of duly balancing the contingency and predictability of human actions. His aim is to write an attack on the foreign policy of Louis XIV under the guise of criticizing the policies of the house of Austria in the first decades of the seventeenth century. It is foolish, for example, for someone who wants to conquer others to declare that he intends to persecute their religion, for "people whom one wants to give in will resist like lions when they know that you intend to force them to adopt forms of worship that they believe are wrong."[14] When he then turns to contemporary events, he pretends to be praising Louis XIV when he is in fact criticising him. It is foolish, for example, to imagine that monarchies are capable of defeating republics: history shows that republics get the better of monarchies. Louis may be tempted to believe those who prophesy his success, but prophets are no more reliable prognosticators than comets. Louis may be confident that his opponents will be unable to coordinate their resistance, but leagues can often be effective. If Louis is wise he will not risk all he has gained so far on the unpredictable outcome of another war.

Fictional-Bayle himself described the *Pensées diverses* as a confused mess; his intention was to advance a number of paradoxes that would unsettle the orthodoxies of the day.[15] It would thus be a mistake to expect him to offer a coherent account of contingency. He is happy to maintain both that the future is unpredictable and that it is predictable, so long as the prediction stops short of prophecy. He is happy to invoke Machiavelli's discussion of fortune, but his fictional role as a faithful subject of a Catholic king prevents him from discussing the relative merits of different political institutions.[16] His game of self-misrepresentation gives him tremendous freedom, but at the same time it prevents him from pursuing his arguments to their conclusions. In the case of all three of our analysts of contingency, however, readers in the second half of the seventeenth century would have held that their texts would encourage, not only irreligion, but also republicanism. It is in monarchies, where the fate of an individual determines the fate of nations, that contingency rules supreme. Alexander's empire would never have come into existence had he fallen off his horse; under the Roman Republic, no one horse carried the fate of Rome's empire on its back.

Already implicitly present in the *Pensées diverses* is an argument that was to be amongst Leibniz's most original and important contributions to philosophy. In article "Xenophanes" of the *Historical and Critical Dictionary* Bayle argued that there was more evil than good in the world, thereby inventing the modern problem of theodicy. Leibniz replied that there was no more evil than was necessary, and that this was the best of all possible worlds. For the compilers of the OED, the article on Leibniz added to some later editions of the *Dictionary* is the first recorded usage of *possible* in this new sense, meaning that which is logically conceivable.[17]

There we read of Leibniz's view that "this world, which actually exists, being contingent, and an infinite number of other worlds being equally possible; the cause of the world [i.e. God] must have considered all these possible worlds to pitch upon one," and of his view that "there is an infinity of possible worlds." Leibniz argued that this was the best of all possible worlds, not simply, as Malebranche had argued, the best world, given God's commitment to a principle of parsimony in making exceptions to his own laws of nature. Leibniz's whole point was that there are no contingent events: everything is necessary.

The idea of alternative possible worlds, first clearly formulated (if only in order to reject it) by Leibniz, is, it should now be apparent, a ghostly presence in the argument of the *Pensées diverses*. In our world Bucephalus carries Alexander safely through the battle; in another he shies, and Alexander falls to his death. And then the whole face of history is transformed, for without Alexander's conquests Lysimachus, Ptolemy, Antigonus, Demeter, Seleucus, Cassander never become rulers; instead (fictional-Bayle tells us) they stay at home in Macedonia collecting their rents and managing their estates. The world we live in thus becomes one of many possible worlds; at key moments the passage from one world to another is controlled by entirely contingent events.

Neither chance nor necessity rules; the construction of a world such as ours requires a complex interweaving of the two. Bayle could not have known Pascal's *pensée* which says "Cleopatra's nose: if it had been shorter the whole face of the earth would have been different," for although a version of Pascal's *Pensées* had been published in 1670, this particular thought was not included in it.[18] But he had arrived at the same idea by his own means.

Pascal and Bayle were quite exceptional in allowing contingency such power. Science fiction has made the idea of possible worlds seem obvious and familiar to us, but Pascal and Bayle were the first to see themselves as living in one among many possible worlds. The ancient Epicureans had thought the world had come into existence because an atom had swerved; now it seemed that at any moment the swerve of an atom or the shy of a horse might bring a new world into existence, one quite different from that which would otherwise have appertained. Pascal found such thoughts alarming but salutary reminders of the sinfulness of human nature; Bayle seized on them as an excuse to secularize our understanding of man and of nature.

Rolling the Dice: The Logic of Port Royal and Hume

In 1662, the year of Pascal's death, Arnauld and Nicole published *La Logique ou l'art de penser,* often known as The Logic of Port-Royal, the first work of philosophy to give a central role to probability theory. Part 4, chapter 16 is entitled *Du jugement que l'on doit faire des accidents futurs.* Here they declare that probability theory enables one to judge if an event is likely to occur: "This is how doctors judge whether the outcome of an illness is going to be favorable or unfavorable, generals predict what will happen in a war, and this is how one judges in the world about most contingent events." They proceed to give examples from the purchase of lottery tickets and the risk of being struck by lightning, and end with a version of Pascal's wager.

Arnauld and Nicole were the first to argue that decision-making under conditions of uncertainty involves the same mathematical principles as gambling. At the heart of their argument was the notion of iteration: what mattered was not just what one might win or lose on any one occasion, but also the relationship between the size and frequency of wins as against the size and frequency of losses. Few things could be worse than to be struck by lightning; yet (by their estimate) only one person in two million dies this way; and so a rational person should regard the risk as being negligible. There was enormous resistance to this new way of thinking. Mathematicians, for example, showed how life expectancies could be calculated, and how this could be used to calculate the true cost of pensions and of life insurance policies; and yet governments continued to sell pensions and life insurance policies at the same price to people of all ages, and people continued to buy them without calculating the odds.

A particularly striking example of this inability to think straight about probabilities is to be found in the work of one of the greatest of all philosophers, David Hume. Hume was certainly acquainted with the work of Arnauld and Nicole, and yet his notion of science is that it consists always of establishing constant conjunctures. "How could *politics* be a science," he asks, "if laws and forms of government had not a uniform influence upon society?"[19] We identify chance, he argues, only where we are unable to recognize causation, so that "chance is nothing real in itself, and, properly speaking, is merely the negation of a cause."[20] From this he draws the conclusion that since chance is about ignorance, all chances are really equal chances ("perfect and total indifference is essential to chance"); where there are favorable odds on something happening this must be redescribed in terms of a superior number of equal chances. "This truth," he tells us, "is not peculiar to my system, but is acknowledg'd by every one, that forms calculations concerning chances." But "everyone" here certainly does not include Arnauld and Nicole, and I am mystified as to whom it did include.[21] It would seem, in fact, that Hume had somehow confused a fair chance when gambling, where the odds are the same for all the players, with an equal chance, where the odds are 50%. Hume is in fact upholding, within a superficially modern account of probabilities, the ancient belief that "chance and causation be directly contrary," so that if knowledge is knowledge of causation, there can be no knowledge of chance.[22] What appear to be chance events never "proceed from any contingency in the cause," but are always the result of "the secret operation of contrary causes."[23]

In both the *Treatise* (1739–40) and the *Enquiry* (1748) Hume illustrates his thinking on probability with the example of a die which has two-thirds of its sides marked with one figure, and one third with another figure. (The word "figure" is significantly ambiguous: at one point Hume suggests he has in mind spots representing a number, but his argument is designed to cover also a symbol such as hearts or clubs.) What interests him is the degree of certainty with which we expect the first figure to turn up if the die (again, it is significant there is only one) is thrown once. He does not consider the possibility of the die being thrown several times, or of several dice being thrown; and he does not assign numerical values to the figures inscribed on its sides. He thus prevents us from considering the possibility of an average or mean outcome, or from identifying a best case scenario or a worst case scenario. He never considers the possibility that anything might depend on the fall of the die, other than the falsification or verification of an expectation. He isolates his die from all those features that would make it possible to use it to illustrate a problem in decision-making theory, and reduces it to a machine for illustrating degrees of confidence. Thus he assimilates the probabilities involved in throwing a die to another set of probabilities, the probabilities involved in assessing the reliability of testimony for past events. "Of Miracles," originally written for inclusion in the *Treatise,* and eventually published in the *Enquiry,* is a case study in this backward-looking form of probability theory, which also was originated by Arnauld and Nicole.[24]

Reading Hume on the throwing of a die, it is as if Arnauld and Nicole had never written, even though the problems Hume is addressing clearly

derive from those they discuss. Where they take judgments about the outcomes of medical treatment to be probabilistic judgments about contingencies, Hume insists they are (perhaps imperfect) judgments about necessary and uniform connections, and this despite the fact that these supposed necessary and uniform connections are directly contrary to our
actual experience:

> Thus, for instance, in the human body, when the usual symptoms of health
> or sickness disappoint our expectation; when medicines operate not with
> their wonted effect; when irregular events follow from any particular cause;
> the philosopher and physician are not surprised at the matter, nor are ever
> tempted to deny, in general, the necessity and uniformity of those principles
> by which the animal economy is conducted. They know that a human body
> is a mighty and complicated machine: That many secret powers lurk in it,
> which are altogether beyond our comprehension: That to us it must often
> appear very uncertain in its operations; And that therefore the irregular
> events, which outwardly discover themselves, can be no proof that the laws
> of nature are not observed with the greatest regularity in its internal opera-
> tions and government.[25]

Hume presents his choice as a simple one. He can either see the human
body as a machine capable of generating random outcomes as the result,
say, of the throw of an internal, invisible die (as we do when we say there is
a 40% chance of a cancer recurring); or he can see it as producing necessary outcomes as the result of constant conjunctions. It never occurs to
him that the first choice might be a real one: that certain events in nature
might be objectively random. But what he is also doing, without acknowledging the fact, is systematically excluding any subjective definition of
contingency. He acknowledges that *to us* the operations of the body are
unpredictable, but he is reluctant to draw the conclusion that consequently they might as well be random. After an autopsy, I might be able to
establish why the patient died, and even be able to say that her death was
inevitable; but before the operation all I can do is state her prospects in
terms of probabilities.

One would expect this insistence that the future is in principle knowable to break down as soon as Hume turns from what he terms "the probability of chances" to what he terms "the probability of causes," cases
where an outcome is uncertain although the causes at work are perfectly
well understood: whether a ship, for example, will return safely from a

voyage. But here Hume argues that although we know there is, say, a 5% chance that the ship will sink, yet we *believe* it will return. Instead of imagining nineteen ships returning safely and one sinking, Hume insists that we imagine only one ship, and consequently imagine that ship returning safely: for "the belief, attending any reasoning, consists in one conclusion, not in a multitude of similar ones."[26] Where we have a number of conflicting experiences, we expect the future to correspond to our most frequent (what Hume calls our "superior") experience in the past: "as the contrary views are incompatible with each other, and 'tis impossible the object can at once exist conformable to both of them, their influence becomes mutually destructive, and the mind is determin'd to the superior only with that force, which remains after subtracting the inferior."[27] Hume does not dismiss this as a species of false reasoning (what he calls "unphilosophical probability"). Instead where Hume first dismissed subjective uncertainty in order to emphasize objective predictability, here he dismisses objective unpredictability in order to emphasize subjective confidence. In both cases, however, the effect is the same: to downplay the radical unpredictability of future events.

If Hume struggles in this way to exclude unpredictability from the picture, it can only be because he finds the idea of genuine, irreducible uncertainty profoundly troubling. For what *might* happen affects the passions, even if it never comes to pass. Perceived possible worlds, in which someone does me harm, or does me a favor, invade the present by stirring up emotions, even if they never become actual worlds. We cannot help but inhabit them in our imagination, and as a consequence we must always to some degree be caught up in an unending struggle between hope and fear.

In the *Treatise* (although not in the *Enquiry*) Hume explains very clearly why people find the idea of uncertainty troubling, and this explanation needs to be applied to his own discussion of probability. There he gives an account of hope and fear as being fluctuating conditions of the mind that are paradigmatically produced by uncertainty regarding the prospect of experiencing grief or joy.[28] Thus hope and fear are characteristically produced by the possibility or probability of a future state of affairs. (Although it is also true that other circumstances may produce passions indistinguishable from hope and fear. For example, if I am sentenced to be tortured, I will feel a sensation indistinguishable from fear even if there is absolute certainty that I will be tortured, for a fluctuation will occur in my mind's capacity to think about this awful event, and thus what I will feel is equivalent to the uncertainty of fear.) In this way possible future events cast what Hume elsewhere calls a "shadow" or "image" in the present.[29] (It should be noted that the argument here is scarcely compatible with the earlier account of the mind settling upon the most likely event; now it is seen to fluctuate between a number of possible outcomes.)

Hume is, to the best of my knowledge, the first to think about the psychological effects of living in a world that is only one of many possible worlds. One might think that overall the effect would be neutral—there would be much to hope for and much to fear, and the two would balance each other out. But Hume insists that this is not the case. For a contingent world is a world full of surprises, and "everything that is unexpected affrights us."[30] Hume puzzles over the reason for this, and concludes that it is not because human beings are inherently timorous; it is because surprise causes commotion, commotion causes uneasiness, and uneasiness is experienced as being so like fear, as being such an exact "image of fear," that it "naturally converts in to the thing itself . . . Thus all kinds of uncertainty have a strong connection with fear." Hume thus believes that when we leave the worlds of deductive certainty or providential order to inhabit a world of contingent uncertainty, we pay a very high psychological price, for we increase our experience of "terror, consternation, astonishment, anxiety, and other passions of that kind," which "are nothing but different species and degrees of fear."[31] In Hume's view part of the purpose of philosophy is to show you how to live well in the world, and it is part of philosophy's task, then, to curtail as strictly as possible the sensation of living in a world of uncertainty. So his account of chance and probability needs to be read in conjunction with his account of hope and fear, an account which stresses the way in which possible futures project images and shadows in the real world, images and shadows which give rise to anxiety and fear.

We can now see why Hume seeks as far as possible to eliminate contingency from his philosophy. A simple indication of this is the care with which he avoids the word itself, which appears only three times in the *Treatise* and twice in the *Enquiry* (I have already quoted both the occurrences in the *Enquiry*). The word "accident" is likewise avoided in his philosophical writing, and, as we have seen, chance is invoked only to be defined out of existence. "Liberty" too turns out to be almost a non-concept (there is no liberty of indifference, or freedom of choice, although there is a liberty of spontaneity, which one experiences when one senses that one is doing what one wants to do, as opposed to being forced to do something against one's will).[32] The words "probable" and "possible" occur, but only within a larger theory designed to ensure the triumph of "necessity." It is as if providence, driven out of Hume's philosophy by the front door, had returned by the back, redescribed as "science."

Hume was to become a great historian, and when he comes to consider the course of actual events, he has to recognize the power of accident. Of William I's conquest of England he writes that "he was indebted to fortune for procuring him some assistance, and also for removing many obstacles, which it was natural for him to expect in an undertaking, in which all his neighbours were so deeply interested."[33] When writing about the Spanish Armada he invokes "a strange concurrence of accidents," and describes how the English admiral expected the outcome to be determined by "winds, currents, or various accidents." If the Armada was, as contemporaries believed, "the critical event" that decided "for ever" the fate of Protestantism, then there was nothing predictable about the outcome of that event. Had the Marquis of Santa Croce, the intended commander of the Spanish fleet, not died of a fever, Protestantism might have been wiped out across Europe.[34]

In exactly the same way Edward Gibbon recognizes that there are moments when the tiniest of events could have the most enormous of consequences. When Mahomet was forced to flee Mecca in 622 A.D., he took shelter in a cave: "the providential deceit of a spider's web and a pigeon's nest" misled his pursuers. When eventually they caught up with him, he escaped. "In this eventful moment, the lance of an Arab might have changed the history of the world." So too in 732 A.D. the Battle of Poitiers, between Muslims and Christians, was "an encounter which would change the history of the world." Had the outcome been different, "perhaps the interpretation of the Koran would now be taught in the schools of Oxford, and her pulpits might demonstrate to a circumcised people the sanctity and truth of the revelation of Mahomet."[35]

Nevertheless Enlightenment historians, including Hume and Gibbon, were deeply loath to admit the possibility that outcomes are fortuitous, random, contingent, accidental, or the result of chance. They were obliged to do so when writing narratives, but when thinking about understanding history, their mantra was that the same causes always have the same effects. Given that real history seems to contain a good deal of contingent material, many of them, including Hume himself in his *Natural History of Religion*, turned with relief to a conjectural history in which one needed to explore only conceptual connections, without worrying about the messy complexities of real events. When they did have to acknowledge that this world was only one of many possible worlds, they were most willing to do so when it came to considering the possibility of alternative histories of religion, for here they were merely reiterating Montaigne's argument that we owe our religious beliefs not to the fact that they are true, but, like our mother tongue, to the fact that we happen to have been born in one place or another. Gibbon was happier to consider a Muslim England than an England without cities or universities.

Machiavelli, G.N.P., and fictional-Bayle were struggling, as we have seen, to clarify the relationship between contingency and predictability: they believed both that human behaviour was predictable, and that outcomes were contingent; they thought that outcomes were more predictable in some circumstances than others; and they thought that certain types of action increased or decreased the predictability of outcomes. They sought methods of reducing contingency and increasing predictability, but they were not prepared, as some theologians (Calvin, Jansenius) and some philosophers (Spinoza, Leibniz) were, to simply define contingency out of existence. In this ongoing debate Hume holds a peculiarly ambiguous place. Like Machiavelli, G.N.P., and fictional-Bayle, he saw no need to defend the idea of providence. He was the beneficiary of the intellectual revolution brought about by the Logic of Port-Royal. But he constantly sought to escape the tides and currents of accident and contingency and ground himself in a world of uniformity and necessity. He knew that a mere accident might determine the outcome of a surgical operation or of a battle, but one must face this uncomfortable fact as Elizabeth faced the Armada, with an "intrepid countenance"; one must not allow oneself to be "surprised," or even allow oneself to imagine being surprised, because surprise was indistinguishable from anxiety.[36] One must seek reassurance in the conviction that however "irregular" events may seem, yet the laws of nature are still observed "with the greatest regularity." Thus Hume constantly turns from contingency to predictability, from chance to certainty, from irregularity to regularity. So too Gibbon at one moment imagines Christianity being overwhelmed by Islam, and then reassures himself that even in a Muslim England, Oxford would still have developed into a university town, and the regular routine of lectures and sermons would have existed in that possible world just as it did in the actual world. At the very moment that the power of contingency is acknowledged, and an Arabian fleet is envisaged sailing up the Thames, its significance is undermined, and the world carries on largely unaffected. But what is it about the world which would enable it to be largely unaffected by seemingly significant events?

The quest for order and stability in a seemingly chaotic world was transformed in a very short period of time by the discovery of the feedback mechanism.

Windmills: De Lolme and the Federalist[37]

Feedback mechanisms such as thermostats have a long history, but in the second half of the eighteenth century they suddenly took on an added importance. New technologies depended on them: the fan-tail was invented to point windmills into the wind. (Strangely, the French failed to adopt this invention; with windmills as with markets they were *dirigistes*.) It was on the basis of contemporary windmill technology that in 1788 James Watt invented the centrifugal speed governor for steam engines. But intellectual systems (Adam Smith said that "a system is an imaginary machine") had also begun to rely on feedback mechanisms. The idea of a balance of power became commonplace after 1713. Hume's account of the balance of trade (1750) shows how international trade is self-stabilizing. Smith's account of markets (1776) shows how markets regulate themselves to eliminate sectors with unduly high or low profits and work to bring production into line with demand. Although the concept of a feedback mechanism had not been clearly articulated, such mechanisms lay at the heart both of the new social sciences and of the technologies of the industrial revolution.

In politics, there was a tradition going back to Polybius that argued that if power was divided, the quality of decision-making would be improved and conflicts of interest would be negotiated. By the late seventeenth century it was common to compare governments to machines far more complex than any envisaged by Polybius. And by the mid-eighteenth century feedback mechanisms began to be recognized not only in international but also in domestic politics. Thus in the preface to his translation of Polybius (1743), Edward Spelman offered a defense of party conflict, arguing that the opposition, even if it never won power, helped to improve the quality of government:

> whatever may be the success of the opposer, the public reaps great benefit
> from the opposition; since this keeps ministers upon their guard, and, often,
> prevents them from pursuing bold measures which an uncontrolled power
> might, otherwise, tempt them to engage in. They must act with caution, as

well as fidelity, when they consider the whole nation is attentive to every step they take, and that the errors they may commit will not only be exposed but aggravated.[38]

Here the opposition acts like a fan-tail on a windmill, constantly pushing the government to act in the interests of the nation as a whole, rather than in their own personal interests.

We find a similar argument in Jean Louis de Lolme's *Constitution of England* (1771):

> As the representatives of the people will naturally be selected from among those citizens who are most favored by fortune, and will consequently have much to preserve, they will, even in the midst of quiet times, keep a watchful eye on the motions of power. As the advantages they possess will naturally create a kind of rivalship between them and those who govern, the jealousy which they will conceive against the latter will give them an exquisite degree of sensibility on every increase of their authority. Like those delicate instruments which discover the operations of nature while they are yet imperceptible to our senses, they will warn the people of those things which of themselves they never see but when it is too late; and their greater proportional share, whether of real riches or of those which lie in the opinions of men, will make them, if I may so express myself, the barometers that will discover, in its first beginning, every tendency to a change in the constitution.[39]

The representatives thus serve as a thermostat, inflaming or damping down public opinion depending on the presence or absence of a threat to liberty and property. De Lolme had a similar account of the workings of a free press.

In Federalist 51 (1788), Madison presented what is now the most famous statement of this idea that political systems should be self-regulating or self-stabilising:

> To what expedient, then, shall we finally resort, for maintaining in practice the necessary partition of power among the several departments as laid down by the Constitution? The only answer that can be given is that as all these exterior provisions are found to be inadequate the defect must be supplied by so contriving the interior structure of the government as that its several constituent parts may, by their mutual relations, be the means of

keeping each other in their proper places. Without presuming to undertake a full development of this important idea I will hazard a few general observations . . . the great security against a gradual concentration of the several powers in the same department consists in giving to those who administer each department the necessary constitutional means and personal motives to resist encroachments of the others. The provision for defense must in this, as in all other cases, be made commensurate to the danger of attack. Ambition must be made to counteract ambition. The interest of the man must be connected with the constitutional rights of the place. It may be a reflection on human nature that such devices should be necessary to control the abuses of government. But what is government itself but the greatest of all reflections on human nature? If men were angels, no government would be necessary. If angels were to govern men, neither external nor internal controls on government would be necessary. In framing a government which is administered by men over men, the great difficulty lies in this: you must first enable the government to control the governed; and in the next place oblige it to control itself. A dependence on the people is, no doubt, the primary control on the government; but experience has taught mankind the necessity of auxiliary precautions.

Here the government works like a market: a large number of competing departments prevent the emergence of a monopoly; the self-interested behavior of individuals serves the broader interest of the public.

Conclusion

My chapter has fallen into four parts. In the first, I argued that Machiavelli and Naudé, or rather G.N.P., believed that the politician could understand, influence, and limit the power of contingency. In the second, I showed how Pascal and Bayle invented the notion of different possible worlds, thereby radically expanding the power of contingency in human affairs. In the third, I suggested that, despite the birth of probability theory, the Enlightenment was surprisingly resistant to the idea of contingency, which it still associated with the irregular and the inexplicable. In the fourth section I have shown how the idea of a feedback mechanism served to bring new order into the world of contingent actions. In international relations, in markets, in the conflicts between parties and political institutions, it became apparent that individuals pursuing their own interests did not behave in an unpredictable fashion. Despite the fact that their goal might be only profit or power, their behavior served to discourage war, to lower prices, and to prevent politicians being corrupted by power. The apparently contingent world of individual agents pursuing private objectives had been found to conform to general principles that made it possible to predict outcomes.

At the beginning we saw that the word "contingent" could sometimes be used to refer to the whole range of unpredictable events, and sometimes, in opposition to "accident," to those forms of unpredictable action which resulted from free will. From the Logic of Port-Royal onwards, probability provided a new account of the laws governing accidents. Death, disease, and lotteries turned out to be describable in terms of statistical regularities. The accidental became predictable. In the eighteenth century, laws began to be formulated to account for the free actions of individuals, and the idea of a social science was born. Now the contingent too became predictable.

This final development casts new light on my third section. David Hume played a key role in the development of the idea that human behavior could be understood and predicted. He not only formulated the theory of the balance of trade, but he also studied the ways in which the public "fluctuated" between supporting government and opposition, and he argued that "the skillful division of power" could help harness politics to the public interest.[40] In my third section I argued that Hume's reluctance to recognize the importance of contingency meant that he had no adequate account of decision-making under conditions of uncertainty. Yet this irrational quest for certainty also meant, we can now see, that he was ideally placed to be a pioneer in that taming of contingency in matters of social action which was the greatest achievement of the eighteenth-century philosophers.

By 1788, when Madison wrote Federalist 51, the vast ocean of contingency was beginning to be explored, but much still remained to be done. If we think back to Donne's tides, winds, and eddies, then the laws governing the tides had been identified by Newton; modern meteorology was to begin with the naming of the clouds in 1803; and in recent years there has been much progress in understanding the mathematics of eddies. But we still live in a world of uncertainties, of unrealized possibilities, of surprises and irregularities. In some measure we can prepare, as Machiavelli urged, for the unknown. We can, in the manner of Arnauld and Nicole, calculate our chances. We can seek reassurance, as Gibbon did, in the conviction that life will go on, that the Dark Ages will never return. We can put on an intrepid countenance. But still, as Hume reluctantly recognized, we must acknowledge that "the passions are not only affected by such events as are certain and infallible, but also in an inferior degree by such as are possible and contingent."[41] What is at stake in the idea of contingency is not only the limited nature of our knowledge, not only the giddiness that the contemplation of unpredictable change inevitably induces, but also the potentially unlimited scope both of our hopes and of our fears.

Appendix: The Authorship and Publication of the Considérations politiques sur les coups d'estat

There is no doubt that the first edition of the *Considérations* is the one that claims to have been published in Rome in 1639. Nor is there any doubt that Naudé was in Rome in 1639, and that he did write a book on *coups d'estat*, so that at first sight there seems no reason to doubt the authenticity of the Rome 1639 edition. Yet on closer examination everything suggests that this edition is a fake. According to the preface it was written for Naudé's employer, the Cardinal de Bagni, who had been papal nuncio to France, and was printed only because de Bagni disliked reading manuscripts and preferred reading print. This is a puzzling story, for reading manuscript was an almost inescapable fact of life for seventeenth-century readers; and the most obvious way of escaping reading a manuscript would be to have it read aloud, not to have it printed. Moreover, the story is also at odds with Naudé's own statement, in a letter to Cardinal Mazarin written in 1642 but unpublished until 1870, that he had written the book for Cardinal de Bagni, who had had it read aloud (*s'en faire lire*) and had liked it. But de Bagni had been so astonished by the boldness of Naudé's argument, Naudé tells us, that Naudé had since not wanted to show the manuscript to anyone but the late Jean-Jacques Bouchard, whose written comments Naudé had kept with the manuscript, a manuscript he would one day, he promised, show to Mazarin.[42] Naudé's account implies that only four people had been acquainted with the text: Naudé himself, de Bagni, de Bagni's secretary or whoever had read aloud to him, and Bouchard. It is straightforwardly incompatible with the existence of any printed edition known to Naudé himself.

Second, the preface to the Rome 1639 edition claims that only twelve copies had been printed. There is something odd about the care with which the preface seeks to explain the publication and at the same time announces that there is no intention to make the book public—one would expect that if this was really intended to be a clandestine printing, each of the twelve copies would have been carefully numbered, but at the same time the author (identified on the title-page as G.N.P., standing for Gabriel Naudé Parisien) and his employer (identified as "son Eminence") would have been much more carefully concealed. Were only twelve copies printed? As early as 1706 the claim was circulating that in fact the print run had been of over a hundred. Six copies are known to survive, a proportion that seems exceptionally high for an original print run of twelve, but perfectly compatible with an original print run of one hundred.[43]

Third, the printer's device on the title-page, a twin compass with the motto *Labore et Constantia,* is not that of any Roman printer, but, as Peter S. Donaldson has noted, that of the Dutch printer Christopher Plantin and his heirs. Judging by this that the book was printed in Holland, Donaldson has argued that the forgery is Naudé's own: sometime after the death of de Bagni and Bouchard in 1641 but before the letter to Mazarin of 1642 (which Donaldson reads as a deliberate attempt to deny responsibility for a printed edition already in existence), Naudé had arranged for the *Considérations* to be printed with a false date and place of publication, and a false story that they were being published in an edition of only twelve copies at de Bagni's request. The letter to Mazarin is designed to displace responsibility for any such edition onto Bouchard.[44]

Donaldson's argument changes everything and nothing. An edition of twelve copies printed in Rome in 1639 is really, on his account, an edition of a hundred copies printed in Leyden in 1641; it is in any case an authentic edition of Naudé's text. But Donaldson's solution will not do. The "Rome 1639" edition of the *Considérations* is some 45,000 words long (the second edition, of 1667, is somewhat longer because in it a French translation is provided for all passages quoted by Naudé in Latin). In 1642 Naudé told Mazarin that his book on *coups d'estat* would, if printed, be much longer than Guy de Balzac's *Le Prince* or Jean de Silhon's *Le Ministre.* The first of these books is some 50,000, the second some 80,000 words long. Nor is this the only evidence for the original length of Naudé's book. In 1637, in *De studio militari,* Naudé described it as *disceptatione gravissima,* a very weighty disquisition. In 1633 Allacci, who clearly had some knowledge of the work in manuscript (on Naudé's own account it had been written the year before), described it as *discursum ingentem,* a huge discourse. There is a striking discrepancy between these three accounts, two of them Naudé's, and the text as we have it. Donaldson fails to notice this discrepancy because he has misread Naudé's *Bibliographia politica* of 1633 and thinks that Naudé has there used, in his description of his newly written book on *coups d'estat,* the non-existent word *contractatio,* which he takes to imply a short book, when in fact he describes it as *tractatio,* a treatise.[45]

This is not the only discrepancy between the book we have and the book Naudé appears to have written. In his letter to Mazarin, Naudé explains that he has written a text on *coups d'estat,* and then helpfully explains what he means by the term: "*comme par exemple celuy des vespres Siciliennes, de la Saint-Barthélemy, du changement de religion en Angleterre, de la mort de messieurs de Guise, de la conversion de Henry IV, et de l'exécution du Marquis d'Ancre.*" He then tells us that he worked for six months on this book. It is hard to read the list of *coups d'estat* he offers as anything other than a guide to the contents of the book he had written. Yet when we turn to the *Considérations,* only one of these topics, the St. Bartholomew's Day Massacre, is discussed. The others are not even mentioned.

There is, I think, only one way of making sense of all these puzzles. It is clear that in 1631–32 Naudé wrote a very large book on *coups d'estat* for the Cardinal de Bagni, probably in French, a language de Bagni spoke. In 1642 that book was still unpublished and very few people had read it. There is no good reason to think that it was published during Naudé's lifetime, and every reason to think that Naudé regarded it as unpublishable. By 1659 a version of that book, claiming to have been published in Rome in 1639, existed in print—the earliest reference to it known to me is in a list of Naudé's publications printed by Father Louis Jacob.[46] The *Considérations* is clearly a work close to Naudé's original text: it appears, for example, with a dedicatory poem by Bouchard, who, Naudé tells us, had read the original manuscript. But it is far too short to be the text that Naudé had written; it is therefore an edited or filleted version of Naudé's text.

Publishing Naudé in Holland at some point between Naudé's death in 1650 and 1659, Naudé's unknown editor presumably sold copies of the book as secondhand rarities which had somehow reached him from Naudé's own library: the claim that only twelve copies had been printed is a transparent device to ensure the highest possible price for each copy sold. In fact what had reached him was the unpublished manuscript itself, but this he had no interest in making public because it did not serve his own polemical purposes. This editor was almost certainly a Protestant, for he omitted topics that would make Protestant readers uncomfortable, topics such as Henry VIII's divorce and the conversion of Henri IV. And he may have added things, for Naudé tells us his book was written in 1632, but the published text, which passes itself off as printed in 1639, contains a passing reference to events which occurred in 1638.[47]

If this reconstruction is correct, and I think it must be, then it would be quite wrong to read the *Considérations* as a book of the 1630s written by a learned French Catholic absolutist who had lost his faith in religion—which is how it is normally read. In its edited and revised form, it is presumably in part a work of the 1650s, produced by a learned Dutch Protestant republican who wants to represent Catholics as cynical unbelievers. Indeed it is worth noting that it is precisely at the end of the 1650s that the Dutch seem to have first discovered republicanism.[48]

My argument has a number of striking consequences. First, we now have almost no reliable evidence as to Naudé's views on religion, for René Pintard, the great authority on Naudé in particular and the *libertins érudits* in general, himself stressed that without the *Considérations* it would not be obvious that Naudé was a *libertin,* an unbeliever.[49] Second, our evidence for Naudé's understanding of politics now appears to be hopelessly contaminated: our only reliable source is the letters to Mazarin. It is essential that henceforth we recognize that we are dealing not with one person but with two: Gabriel Naudé, the famous author of the advice on building a library, librarian to Mazarin, and "G.N.P.," the author whose initials appear on the title-page of the spurious edition "A Rome, MDCXXXIX." G.N.P. is a fiction, the result of someone cutting and reworking Naudé's original text to serve quite different purposes from those that motivated its original composition. And because the *Considérations* is in effect the result of a collaboration between two people with very different religious and political commitments, we cannot expect to find in it a coherent and consistent argument. Only if the text is seen as having been wrested away from its original author can we hope to understand its peculiarities.

NOTES

1. I am grateful to David Norton for correcting some errors in my discussion of Hume: he is not responsible for those that remain. I am also grateful to Peter Donaldson for corresponding with me about Gabriel Naudé, and to David Womersley for helping me with Gibbon.

2. All the quotations in the first few paragraphs come from the *Oxford English Dictionary* articles for "contingent" and "contingency," except for the quotation

from Bacon which comes from "Of Vicissitude of Things" in the *Essays:* the word "vicissitude" was new in English in 1590–96; in this essay Bacon uses "flux" in a new sense, as a synonym for "vicissitude."

3. Hume, *Enquiries,* p. 103.

4. Franklin, *Science of Conjecture,* pp. 191–92.

5. I used the word "resilient" before reading Philip Pettit's discussion of "resilience" in this volume, but I think my argument here could usefully be recast in the terms he employs: Machiavelli is looking for strategies that will work in the maximum number of possible future worlds.

6. Franklin, *Science of Conjecture,* pp. 336–37.

7. Naudé, *Considérations,* 1639 ed., p. 150; 1667 ed., p. 242.

8. Naudé, *Considérations,* 1639 ed., p. 154; 1667 ed., p. 248.

9. Naudé, *Considérations,* 1639 ed., pp. 179–82; 1667 ed., pp. 289–93.

10. For an account of Bayle's core views, see Wootton, "Pierre Bayle, Libertine?"

11. Bayle, *Pensées diverses* and *Miscellaneous Reflections,* §213–14.

12. Bayle, *Pensées diverses* and *Miscellaneous Reflections,* §238.

13. Home, *Sketches,* II, p. 308.

14. Bayle, *Pensées diverses,* II, p. 262.

15. Bayle, *Pensées diverses,* II, p. 311.

16. Bayle, *Pensées diverses,* II, p. 261.

17. Bayle, *Dictionary,* VI (1738), p. 674, column 1. For an earlier usage (presumably also derived from Leibniz) see King, *An Essay* (1731), II, p. 298.

18. Pascal, *Pensées,* no. 90. The nearest equivalent in the first edition is a thought on Cromwell, no. 203.

19. Hume, *Enquiries,* p. 90.

20. Hume, *Treatise,* p. 125.

21. Hume is defended on this and other issues by Gower, "Hume on Probability"; but Gower equivocates over the meaning of the word "equal." It is clear from Daston, *Classical Probability,* p. 32, that Montmort (1708), Bernoulli (1713), and De Moivre (1718) would not have agreed with Hume, and he cannot have been familiar with their work. Earlier theorists, such as Huygens, had argued that games of chance are fair if each player has an equal chance of winning (Daston, *Classical Probability,* pp. 28, 30), but this is very different from the claim (which I think would have puzzled Arnauld and Nicole, who discuss a case where each player has an equal chance, but the odds for any player of winning are 1:9—they see no need to redescribe these odds in terms of equal chances [Daston, *Classical Probability,* p. 18]) that all chances are equal chances. We later find a view similar to Hume's in Laplace (Daston, *Classical Probability,* p. 29), but I am not clear who had held Hume's view before Hume.

22. Hume, *Treatise,* p. 125.

23. Hume, *Enquiry,* p. 87; see also *Treatise,* p. 132.

24. Wootton, "Hume's 'Of Miracles.'"

25. Hume, *Enquiry*, p. 87.

26. Hume, *Treatise*, p. 138.

27. Hume, *Treatise*, p. 138.

28. Hume, *Treatise*, pp. 443–48.

29. Hume, *Treatise*, pp. 315, 408.

30. Hume, *Treatise*, p. 446.

31. Hume, *Treatise*, p. 447.

32. Hume, *Treatise*, p. 407.

33. Hume, *History of England*, I, p. 151 (spelling and punctuation modernized).

34. Hume, *History of England*, IV, pp. 258–71.

35. Gibbon, *Decline and Fall*, III, pp. 193–94, 336–37.

36. Hume, *History of England*, IV, p. 265; Hume, *Enquiry*, p. 87; Hume, *Treatise*, p. 446.

37. For a fuller discussion of this topic, see Wootton, "Liberty, Metaphor, and Mechanism."

38. Spelman, *A Fragment*, introduction.

39. De Lolme, *Constitution of England*, p. 259.

40. Hume, *Essays*, pp. 65, 43.

41. Hume, *Treatise*, p. 313.

42. Naudé, *Mémoire confidentiel adressé à Mazarin*, pp. 8–12. Discussed in Donaldson, *Machiavelli and Mystery of State*, p. 162, where *s'en faire lire* is mistranslated.

43. See the editor's discussion in the facsimile reprint of the "Rome" edition, Naudé, *Considérations politiques*, ed. F. Charles-Daubert, pp. xxxvii–viii.

44. Donaldson, *Machiavelli and Mystery of State*, pp. 160–5.

45. Naudé, *Syntagma*, p. 2; Allacci, *Apes urbanae*, p. 116; Naudé, *Bibliographia politica*, p. 47; Donaldson, *Machiavelli and Mystery of State*, p. 163. Judging by his note on p. 142, the only one of these sources Donaldson consulted directly is the letter to Mazarin; otherwise he relied on the account in Pintard, *Libertinage érudit*, p. 615.

46. The reference is quoted by Charles-Daubert on p. xviii; the work he is quoting is evidently Louis Jacob, *Gabrielis Naudei tumuli* (1659).

47. Pintard, *Libertinage*, p. 615.

48. For surveys of the concept of "republicanism," see my review of *Republicanism: A Shared European Heritage*, ed. Martin van Gelderen and Quentin Skinner, and Wootton, "The True Origins of Republicanism."

49. Pintard, *Libertinage*, p. 475. My argument here thus significantly strengthens the argument of Kristeller, "Between the Italian Renaissance and the French Enlightenment," which takes the position that the posthumous *Naudeana* cannot be trusted as a guide to Naudé's thought. I do not imagine Naudé was a conventional Catholic; but it is clear that much of the discussion of his attitude to religion has been based on unreliable evidence.

BIBLIOGRAPHY

Allacci, Leone, *Apes urbanae, sive de viris illustribus, qui ab anno MDCXXX per to-tum MDCXXXII Romae adfuerunt, ac typis aliquid evulgarunt.* Rome: L. Grignanus, 1633.

Arnauld, Antoine, *The Art of Thinking.* New York: Bobbs Merrill, 1964.

Bacon, Francis, *The Essayes or Counsel, Civill and Morall,* ed. Michael Kiernan. Oxford: Clarendon, 1985.

Bayle, Pierre, *A General Dictionary, Historical and Critical,* 10 vols. London: James Bettenham, 1734–41.

Bayle, Pierre, *Miscellaneous Reflections Occasion'd By The Comet,* 2 vols. London, J. Morphew, 1708.

Bayle, Pierre, *Pensées diverses sur la comète,* ed. A. Prat, 2nd. ed. Paris: Librairie Nizet, 1984.

Daston, Lorraine, *Classical Probability in the Enlightenment.* Princeton: Princeton University Press, 1988.

De Lolme, Jean Louis, *The Constitution of England,* rev. ed. London: Robinson and Murray, 1789.

Donaldson, Peter S., *Machiavelli and Mystery of State.* Cambridge: Cambridge University Press, 1988.

Franklin, James, *The Science of Conjecture: Evidence and Probability Before Pascal.* Baltimore: Johns Hopkins University Press, 2001.

Gibbon, Edward, *The History of the Decline and Fall of the Roman Empire,* ed. D. Womersley. 3 vols. London: Allen Lane, 1994.

Gower, Barry, "Hume on Probability," *British Journal for the Philosophy of Science* 42 (1991): 1–19.

Hamilton, Alexander, James Madison, and John Jay, *The Federalist,* ed. Jacob E. Cooke. Middletown, CT: Wesleyan University Press, 1961.

Home, Henry, Lord Kames, "Upon Chance and Contingency," in *Sketches of the History of Man,* 2 vols. Edinburgh: W. Creech, 1774.

Hume, David, *A Treatise of Human Nature,* ed. L. A. Selby-Bigge, 2nd. ed. Oxford: Clarendon Press, 1978.

Hume, David, *Enquiries Concerning Human Understanding,* ed. L. A. Selby-Bigge, 3rd. ed. Oxford: Clarendon Press, 1975.

Hume, David, *Essays, Moral, Political, and Literary,* ed. E. F. Miller, rev. ed. Indianapolis: Liberty Classics, 1987.

Hume, David, *The History of England,* 6 vols. Indianapolis: Liberty Fund, 1983.

King, William, *An Essay on the Origin of Evil,* 2 vols. London: W. Thurlborn, 1731–32.

Kristeller, Paul Oscar, "Between the Italian Renaissance and the French Enlightenment: Gabriel Naudé as an Editor," *Renaissance Quarterly* 32 (1979): 41–72.

Machiavelli, Niccolò, *Il Principe,* ed. L. Arthur Burd. Oxford: Clarendon, 1891.

Naudé, Gabriel, *Bibliographia politica.* Venice: Franciscum Baba, 1633.

Naudé, Gabriel, *Considérations politiques sur les coups d'Etat,* ed. F. Charles-Daubert, facsimile reprint of "Rome 1639" edition. Hildesheim: Georg Olms Verlag, 1993.

Naudé, Gabriel, *Considérations politiques sur les coups d'estat,* facsimile reprint of 1667 edition. Caen: Université de Caen, 1989.

Naudé, Gabriel, *Mémoire confidentiel adressé à Mazarin par Gabriel Naudé après la mort de Richelieu.,* ed. A. Franklin. Paris: L. Willem, 1870.

Naudé, Gabriel, *Syntagma de studio militari.* Rome: Giacomo Facciotto, 1637.

Oxford English Dictionary, 2nd edition, on compact disk. Oxford: Oxford University Press, 1992.

Pascal, Blaise, *Pensées sur la religion,* ed. Louis Lafuma, 2nd ed. Paris: Delmas, 1952.

Pintard, René, *Le libertinage erudit.* Paris: Boivin, 1943.

[Spelman, Edward], *A Fragment out of the Sixth Book of Polybius.* London: J. Bettenham, 1743.

Wootton, David, "Hume's 'Of Miracles': Probability and Irreligion," in *The Philosophy of the Scottish Enlightenment,* ed. M. A. Stewart. *Oxford Studies in the History of Philosophy,* vol. I. Oxford: Oxford University Press, 1990: 191–229.

Wootton, David, "Liberty, Metaphor, and Mechanism: The Origins of Modern Constitutionalism," in *Liberty and American Experience in the Eighteenth Century,* ed. David Womersley. Indianapolis: Liberty Fund, 2006: 209–74.

Wootton, David, "Pierre Bayle, Libertine?" in *Oxford Studies in the History of Philosophy,* vol. II, ed. M. A. Stewart. Oxford: Oxford University Press, 1997: 197–226.

Wootton, David, "The True Origins of Republicanism: The Disciples of Baron and the Counter-Example of Venturi," in *Il repubblicanesimo moderno. L'idea di repubblica nella riflessione storica di Franco Venturi,* ed. Manuela Albertone. Naples: Bibliopolis, 2006: 271–304.

Wootton, David, review of *Republicanism: A Shared European Heritage,* ed. Martin van Gelderen and Quentin Skinner, 2 vols. Cambridge: Cambridge University Press, 2002, *English Historical Review,* 120 (2005): 135–39.

Chapter 2

Mapping Contingency

Andreas Schedler

Political science, striving to uncover the *regularities* of political life, has paid scarce attention to its *contingencies*. As any discussion of contingency is contingent on the conception of contingency it embraces, we have to understand first of all the conceptual morphology of contingency, before we can proceed to examine the causal role it plays in politics. We have to understand what contingency is, what the notion is good for in the language and practice of politics. The present chapter takes up this task of clarifying the conceptual structure of contingency. After briefly discussing some scholarly intuitions, ordinary uses, and lexical definitions of contingency, it extends a worrisome initial diagnosis. Contingency, it claims, suffers from a double conceptual liability: It is indeterminate in its *empirical referents* and unclear in its *semantic structure*. On the one hand, contingency is a concept of high abstraction which is not anchored in concrete empirical spheres. Everything is, or may be, contingent, but if contingency is to be a useful concept for the study of politics, we have to anchor it in concrete realms of application. On the other hand, contingency inhabits a somewhat disorderly semantic field. It is an elusive abstraction commonly defined by other elusive abstractions, like chance, uncertainty, freedom, and unpredictability, whose boundaries and internal relations are rather opaque. To resolve the semantic problem of meaning, much of this chapter addresses the empirical problem of reference. It draws a roadmap through multiple locations of contingency: individual actors and actions, conceptual, normative, and practical commitments, objective and subjective facts, causal relations, catastrophic and ordinary events. Mapping the multiple referents and uses of contingency allows me in continuation to treat contingency as a three-dimensional concept that involves indeterminacy (possible worlds), conditionality (causal justifications), and uncertainty (open futures).

Conceptualizing Contingency

Broad and elusive, contingency is a bit of a conceptual pudding. Given appropriate childhood socialization, we know it when we see it, and may appreciate its taste and consistency. Still, the academic enterprise of nailing it to the wall of conceptual clarity presents a certain degree of difficulty. According to the well-known concept of concepts represented by the Ogden-Richards triangle, a concept consists of three basic elements. The peak of the triangle is formed by its name (term), its basis by its defining attributes (connotation or intension), on one side, and the empirical phenomena it applies to (denotation or extension), on the other. Contingency's problem is two-fold. Its definitional attributes are unclear, while its empirical referents are indeterminate. The notion of "contingency" forms the terminological peak of a conceptual triangle whose basis is shrouded in linguistic fog.[1]

Unclear Attributes

It is tempting to open a conceptual text on contingency by offering, first of all, a formal definition. Quite plausibly we might stipulate, for example, that "contingency is a name for accident and chance," that "contingent events are under-determinate and unpredictable," that "contingency is a label for things we cannot explain," that "contingencies are small causes with big consequences," or that "contingency means freedom from fate and necessity." Such and similar stipulations resonate in recognizable ways with intuitions that guide the language of contingency in philosophy and the social sciences. Overall, though, they pose more questions than they answer. Do they have anything in common? Which are their underlying dimensions? How do they relate to everyday uses of the word "contingency"?

On everyday uses of "contingency" in ordinary language there is, actually, not much to report. Contingency is a theoretical concept whose high level of abstraction seems to confine it to specialized spheres of debate like philosophy and the sociology of modern life. Philosophy, in particular, enjoys a well-entrenched popular reputation for "seeing difficulties nobody else sees"[2] as well as for seeing things, like contingency, no one else sees or cares about. Apparently, in our everyday lives, we have little use for the language of contingency. We do not regularly get up in the morning and worry about the "contingency" of our human condition, or the innumerable "contingencies" that may happen to us over the course of one day.

Contingency may be a central part of our personal hopes and anxieties, but not of our ordinary language.

To capture, with a wide fishing net, current non-academic uses of contingency, I searched the *LexisNexis* news content database. The results suggest that contingency is a phenomenon that afflicts lawyers and budget planners more than anyone else. Almost four-fifths of the first fifty hits are situated in the spheres of law and money.[3] They refer to contingency clauses in public finances ("contingency budgets" and "contingent liabilities"), the remuneration of legal services ("contingency fees" and "contingency work"), insurance business ("contingency commissions"), and real estate transactions ("financing contingency" and "inspection contingency"). In these contexts, "contingency" refers to forms of conditionality. Contingency budgets make provisions for unexpected expenditures, while contingency clauses in commercial transactions define certain events (like victory in a lawsuit) that must occur to trigger certain contractual obligations (like the payment for legal services).

The remaining hits of "contingency" in *LexisNexis* refer to strikes of catastrophe, be they natural or social. They refer to private or public agencies "planning for disasters large and small." The contingent list of "unplanned and unexpected emergency situations" to be taken care of, according to the *LexisNexis* print media search, includes military aggression by foreign powers, the transmission of BSE among European sheep, floods, landslides, and typhoons, the loss of vital satellites, the collapse of the Palestinian Authority, as well as, unsurprisingly, "the specter of terrorism."[4] The common thread underlying these references to contingency is readily discernible: Contingency carries the mark of chance, uncertainty, unpredictability. Uncontrolled disasters may strike us out of the blue. Although we may be able to anticipate them, we can neither predict nor control them.

Moving to less casual registers of usage and meaning, we find the theme of uncertainty reappearing in a prominent fashion in the entry on "contingency" the *Oxford English Dictionary* offers. As the dictionary states in overlapping formulations, in the kingdom of contingency, things are "liable to happen or not," "open to the play of chance, or of free will," "subject to chance and change," "without preordination," "free from predetermining necessity." They are a matter of "chance," "casualty," "accident," "fortuitousness," "uncertainty."[5]

Academic intuitions, ordinary language, and lexical stipulations open interesting windows to the hazy landscape called "contingency." They do not point towards a single definition of the word that could gain widespread consent. Taken together, though, they do point towards three central attributes that constitute, as I will argue towards the end of the chapter, the semantic columns the abstract edifice of contingency rests upon: indeterminacy (*y* could be different), uncertainty (*y* is unpredictable), and conditionality (*y* depends on *x*). At the end of the chapter, I will not pull a single conceptual rabbit out of the hat of multiple meanings. Rather, I will try to clarify how these three semantic dimensions hang together. Do they form necessary attributes of any intelligible use of the term "contingency"? Or do they represent optional building blocks within a more open architecture of "family resemblances"?[6] To answer these questions, I shall first examine actual uses of "contingency" in the field of politics.

Open Referents

Contingency is an abstract property (or bundle of properties) we can attach to almost any kind of empirical phenomenon. Rather than referring to a circumscribed class of cases, its empirical referents are radically open. Compare the breadth of contingency with the relative narrowness of concepts like passion and violence. The latter two are abstractions that are anchored in concrete spheres of reality. Passion is a property of human subjectivity; violence is a property of human action (even if we may stretch the concept and apply it to speech acts, social structures, and natural phenomena, too). Thus, if we talk about the role of passion in politics, or the role of violence, we know where to look. Contingency is different. It is a free-floating abstraction, a ship adrift without a home port. Rather than drawing our attention to particular spheres of experience, it disperses our attention by opening up a wide and shifting horizon.

In modern times (and perhaps even more so in postmodern times), almost everything appears to be contingent. As our religious empires of certainty and necessity have collapsed, our horizons of possibilities have expanded. Modern men and women, similar to psychiatric patients who lose their confidence in the solidity of everyday life, cannot be certain of anything. As the Austrian lottery advertises: Everything is possible. Marshall Berman claimed this to be the core "experience of modernity"—the both distressing and exhilarating sensation that "all that is solid melts into air."[7] So far into the twenty-first century, there are (almost) no non-contingent things anymore, nothing is built, nothing is meant, for eternity. At the very latest, with the collapse of the twin towers in New York on 11 September 2001, we have lost our sense of non-contingency.

The Double Task

Given the unclear connotation and open denotation of "contingency," the task of conceptual clarification at hand is two-fold: we have to clarify the meaning of the word as well as its empirical referents. Accomplishing the former presupposes the latter. As semantic questions are pragmatic questions (after the linguistic turn of modern philosophy), establishing "the meaning of contingency" demands understanding the things we do with the notion of contingency (in the academic study of politics). What do we do when we talk the language of contingency? What is it good for? What kinds of claims do we make, and what kinds of commitments do we accept, if we describe empirical phenomena as "contingent"? To ascertain the meaning of contingency in political life, we have to pull it down from the heaven of abstraction to the earth of concrete politics. We have to convert the free-floating abstraction into a notion anchored in specific empirical fields.

Anchoring Contingency

Even if (almost) everything looks contingent (or may be shaken into a consciousness of contingency), not everything looks contingent in the same manner and for the same reasons. If we wish to understand the role of contingency in politics (as well as in the study of politics), we must examine the specific meaning "contingency" acquires in specific contexts of usage. By specifying the empirical referents of political contingency (extension), we will be concretizing its meanings (intension). In the following, I discuss some major types of political contingency that rest upon diverging empirical referents and theoretical justifications. The map of political contingencies I trace is neither complete nor, of course, immune to contestation. Simple, yet fundamental, sociological categories provide its basic guideposts: actors and actions; their conceptual, normative, and practical commitments; subjective and objective facts; causal relations; and, last but not least, events—catastrophic as well as ordinary. Of course, we could choose different coordinates to draw our map. Even if we were to redraw them, our basic point would still hold: "Contingency" carries different meanings in different contexts of usage; the claims we make and the commitments we accept when we talk about it (in the study of politics or elsewhere) depend on the empirical phenomena we are talking about.

Contingent Actors

No issue provides more vivid testimony to the gulf that separates the academic world of political science from the so-called real world of politics than the contrasting assumptions they entertain about the nature of political actors. Striving to reach general insights on the workings of politics in different structural and institutional contexts, students of politics tend to operate upon the assumption of motivational homogeneity: all actors are expected behave in similar ways under similar conditions. Practitioners of politics, by contrast, tend to assume that few things matter more to political outcomes than the identity of individual decision-makers. To them, political actors are not fungible. Quite to the contrary, they are unique carriers of ideological profiles, intellectual capacities, communicative abilities, moral commitments, motivational strength, risk aversion, emotional intelligence, and a long et cetera. In either perspective, the rules and institutions that regulate access to political power (like democratic elections) are central to politics. Yet, political practitioners tend to conceive them primarily as selection devices, while political scientists tend to analyze them primarily as incentive systems.[8] In sum, while political actors assume the personal qualities of individual actors to be contingent, political science treats them as non-contingent. Political actors may look different on the surface, it assumes, but at a profound level of fundamental motivations they all look alike.

As a consequence, political science is fundamentally incapable of incorporating the contingent qualities of individual decision-makers into its theories, except through vague conceptual crutches like "charisma" and "leadership."[9] It is with great suspicion that scholars tend to receive the idea that particular historical processes would have taken different turns, depending on contingent qualities of political protagonists. Within the political science community, a counterfactual judgment like Fareed Zakaria's affirmation that the defeat of the August 1990 Communist coup in the late Soviet Union was contingent on the "extraordinary courage" and "gift for political theater" displayed by Boris Yeltsin[10] is likely to be considered typical of a journalist, but somehow unworthy of a political scientist. If the idea of heterogeneous actors constitutes an optical illusion, the attribution of political outcomes to contingent qualities of individual actors constitutes a causal illusion.

If political science treats actors as constants and their structural and institutional environments as variables, professional sports give us an idea of how the study of social reality may look like under the inverse assumption. Contemporary professional sports resemble quantitative political science in their deep enthusiasm for numerical descriptions. Side by side with the modern state, modern capitalism, and modern science, professional sports are among the largest producers of quantitative data in the contemporary world. Professional soccer, for example, is a living cemetery of descriptive statistics about everything: number of goals, timing of goals, shots on goal, active and passive ball possession, corners, penalties, off-sides, fouls, yellow and red cards . . . all that and more, computed per player, per team, per competition, per season, and all over the recorded history of soccer. Since soccer games are (temporally and socially) insulated episodes of athletic competition in which rules remain constant, while players vary, the statistics of soccer, unlike the statistics of political science, do not measure structural or institutional variables. Rather, they link outcome and process data (their dependent variables) with information about the identity of players and teams of players (their independent variables). Sport journalists, by locating empirical contingency within actors, while taking their structural environment as given, produce explanations of outcomes that focus on actors, too, rather than structural environments.

Contingent Actions

Under the premise of human freedom, all human actions are contingent. Except for psychiatric syndromes of compulsive behavior that involve a radical loss of individual sovereignty, we can always act differently. We can vote or abstain. We can condemn or excuse political violence. We can seek redemptive love or psychotherapeutic counseling. We can contemplate our navel or the future of the Middle East. We can shake off our chains or escape from freedom. Several contributions to this volume focus on the contingency of human actions: Inhabitants of poor countries may stay at home or migrate (Hochschild and Burch); within given facts and rules, judges may give harsh or light sentences (Huber); voters in conflict-ridden countries may support peacemakers or warmongers (Jung). However, even if (almost) everything we do is contingent, not everything we do is uncertain and unpredictable. Human decisions may have elements of randomness, but we do not usually conceive actors as decision lotteries. We try to explain their actions by understanding them.[11]

For the present purpose of distinguishing, in an illustrative way, possible grounds for human action that differ in their degree of contingency or unpredictability, we may draw on four broad sociological categories: passions, reasons, routines, and ideologies. *Passions* are intense individual preferences that tend to conflict with the demands of rationality. They are reasons reasonable people are not willing to accept as legitimate motives of action. *Reasons* are justifications reasonable people are willing to accept as valid currencies in the exchange and examination of arguments. *Routines* are self-reproductive regularities that do not require rational justification for their continuing sustenance. *Ideologies*, finally, are justifications for action that are immune to deliberation, that is, to change through argumentation.[12]

Passions are assumed to be sources of disorder, reasons and routines sources of order. Passions sit at the extreme pole of contingency as indeterminacy, routines and ideologies at the other extreme of non-contingency as predictability. Assuming that rational choice (however conceived) is not fully determinate either, the middle ground of rational motivation constitutes the privileged terrain of the social sciences (see also Huber, in this volume). In this perspective, the movement from passion to reasons augments predictability, while the movement from routines and ideologies to rationality decreases predictability. Depending on the point of departure, the "rationalization" of politics may thus represent a move towards lesser or greater contingency.

Margaret Levi's concept of "contingent consent," to cite a prominent example, builds upon the distinction between predictable ideologies and contingent rationality. While "ideological" attitudes towards military conscription do not waiver in the face of external circumstances, citizens' "contingent consent" to conscription depends on governmental trustworthiness and the fairness of conscription rules and practices.[13] In an analogous manner, secular changes in partisanship exemplify a slow transition from ideological non-contingency to rational contingency: In Western European democracies, traditional party loyalties have been weakening over the past decades. Captive voters have given way to floating voters who, cut loose from life-long social and political identities, have become "available" to rational appeals (as well as to irrational appeals). As a result, citizen support for political parties has turned "contingent."[14] By turning from stable ideologies to rational calculation, voters have injected new "contingencies" into the electoral market.

Contingent Commitments

Actors may harbor strong desires as well as clear preferences, but desires and preferences rank lowly in the hierarchy of authoritative reasons. Their normative authority is "derivative" from rational commitments— the queen of concepts occupying "the center of rational agency."[15] Different types of commitments relate in different ways to the idea of contingency. Here, I shall briefly discuss the contingency of conceptual, normative, and practical commitments.

CONCEPTUAL COMMITMENTS

In political science, it is not uncommon to hear colleagues conclude inconclusive conceptual debates by saying: "I do not mind how we call things. Labels are not important. As long as we know what we are talking about, the words we choose do not matter." Such combined expressions of frustration and indifference in the face of long-winded conceptual discussions are meant to say, I gather (drawing again on the triangular Odgen-Richards concept of concepts): The basic elements of concepts are their definitions (intension) and their referents (extension). The former delimitates the attributes we have in mind, the latter the cases we wish to cover. The specific names (terms) we attach to our conceptual containers are matters of arbitrary choice. Essentially irrelevant to our enterprise of uncovering empirical regularities in the objective world, terms are contingent.

The methodological conviction that language does not matter is an heir to a pre-Wittgensteinian conception of language in which words are just arbitrary etiquettes we attach to pre-existing things in the objective world. Language has no substantive relevance on its own; it is a neutral carrier, a mirror glass, an empty basket to collect discrete objects lying around "out there" in the objective world. Yet, if we switch from a "naïve" to a "pragmatic" perspective on language, concepts do not appear as contingent classification devices, but as carriers of non-contingent claims and commitments.[16]

In our academic definitions of concepts, we routinely distinguish the "necessary" attributes of concepts from their "contingent" features. The non-contingent core of a concept consists of those essential claims competent and responsible members of a language community commit themselves to when they use the concept (in certain contexts). Its contingent periphery consists of those variable claims reasonable language users may legitimately reject when using the concept (in certain contexts). Defining concepts then involves defining the commitments they make on us. Of course, the content of core and peripheral commitments may change over time. In their contribution to this volume, Jennifer Hochschild and Traci Burch reflect on the irritations that may arise from the insight that a conventional classification device like "race" (which some language communities embrace as commonsensical and natural, while others reject it as a pernicious social construct) is not given and immutable, but subject to change. The boundaries between central and secondary conceptual commitments may be open to dispute, too. The politics of language, the public struggle over the meaning of concepts, is a struggle over the claims we underwrite, or refuse to underwrite, by employing the concepts under dispute. This is precisely what the present chapter strives to accomplish: delineating the claims and commitments we accept when we take recourse to the language of contingency in the study of politics.

NORMATIVE COMMITMENTS

Normative commitments may display various layers of non-contingency or contingency. We may invoke transcendental sources of certainty and declare ultimate foundations to be non-contingent. We may accept the elusiveness of ultimate foundations in post-transcendental and post-traditional societies, but still embrace fundamental values (like human dignity and human equality) as non-contingent. We may take recorded narratives or written codifications of rules and principles as non-contingent (like the Bible, the U.S. Constitution, or the Universal Declaration of Human Rights). Finally, we may hold the interpretation and application of basic values and texts to be non-contingent.

Conceiving any of the steps between ultimate foundations and concrete norm applications as non-contingent serves the purpose of withdrawing them from doubt and controversy. It serves the purpose of closing public debate. The non-contingent is immune to normative change, the contingent open to normative contestation. The dividing line between "dogmatic" and "reasonable" forms of religiosity is often said to run between those who accept the contingency of norm application (the lowest level of normative regulation) and those who do not. The troubles modern political philosophy has been going through in constructing and deconstructing ultimate foundations suggests, however, that "in reality" all levels are contingent (although we may decide to ignore or deny their contingency, for good or bad reasons).

Budgetary contingencies, contingency payments, and other kinds of financial and legal "contingencies" that turned out prominently in our *LexisNexis* news search make the effectiveness of practical commitments *y* dependent on the uncertain realization of factual conditions *x*. Contingency funds provide funds in case of emergencies. Contingency payments foresee legal honoraria in case of victory in court. Given their rule-like nature, such contingent commitments are similar to moral and legal rules in at least three aspects. First, just like moral and legal rules, they intend to govern the future by establishing conditional relationships. If *x*, then *y*. Second, the nexus between empirical conditions and practical consequences is intentional, not causal. Third, conditions *x* may be contingent, but the conditional nexus itself is non-contingent.

In opposition to moral and legal rules, however, rules of contingency do not address sovereign actors. They do not inform them about the consequences (rewards or sanctions) of their future behavior. Rather, they formulate responses to uncertain events that lie outside the control of the actors involved. Rules that regulate social behavior stipulate: If you do *x*, then *y* happens to you. Rules that regulate contingent events stipulate: If *x* happens, then we do *y*. Social rules are instruments of discipline we formulate to prevent and punish deviant behavior. Rules of contingency are insurance schemes we formulate to protect us against future eventualities we do not control. By declaring our commitments to be contingent, we avoid binding our hands in absolute ways, regardless of future surprises.

Contingent Facts

The attributes of the objective world we call contingent are those we deem to be liable to change. Non-contingent facts are constant by necessity: All humans are mortal. Contingent facts are subject to variation: Human beings may die at any time. While our mortality is not contingent, the timing of our death is. To use Karl Popper's well-known metaphor, non-contingent facts are *clocks* that are "regular, orderly, and highly predictable in their behaviour," while contingent facts are *clouds* whose irregular "coming and going" is "hard to predict."[17]

In the face of doubt, we may defend claims of factual contingency by pointing either at descriptive patterns or causal connections. Since claims of factual non-contingency are *descriptive generalizations,* we may disprove them through the identification of empirical exceptions: Not all swans are white; not all teachers know more than their students; not all democracies ban religious issues from the political sphere.[18] Claims of factual contingency face the inverse challenge: Critics may deny the existence of empirical exceptions. Why do you think *y* could be different, if it is the same everywhere? Why do you think history should allow for an exception? The age-old indictment to reformers and revolutionaries: It has always been this way!

In addition to descriptive justifications, claims of contingency may call for *causal justifications*. While the former point at variations of factual phenomena, the latter point at variations of causal factors to back claims of contingency. From this point of view, the indeterminacy of causes *x* determines the indeterminacy of consequences *y*. We describe *y* as contingent because it is contingent on variable causes *x*. For example, our research results depend on our research practices which depend on our ontological assumptions: "What one finds is contingent upon what one looks for, and what one looks for is to some extent contingent upon what one expects to find."[19] Or to quote two examples from comparative politics: The survival of democracy in interwar Europe was contingent on the behavior of "border parties" located between anti-democratic extremes and the democratic center;[20] in divided societies, the outbreak of communal violence is contingent on pre-existing structures of communal relations.[21] As causal factors vary across cases, outcomes of interest vary across cases, too.

Contingent Causation

In the social sciences, our explanations differ widely in scope. Some are universal (capable of explaining all relevant cases), others are punctual (capable of explaining only one relevant case), most lie in between. Often, causal variables do not act in isolation, but interaction. Their explanatory role depends on the presence or absence of intervening variables that modify (decrease, increase, or invert) their causal impact. Whether democracies survive critical times depends on the dynamics of elite polarization.[22] Whether majoritarian electoral systems produce bipolar electoral competition depends on the preference structures of candidates and voters.[23] Whether ethnic heterogeneity turns into ethnic violence depends on strategic choices by nationalist entrepreneurs.[24] We may describe such conditional, non-universal explanations as "contingent generalizations."[25]

The notion of contingency here serves to specify causal connections. It explicates that causal effects are not invariant, but context-dependent (see also Stokes, in this volume).

Contingent Events

When we talk about contingencies (in the plural), we tend to talk about events—things that happen to happen—irritations, accidents, surprising changes of circumstances. Events are different from variables: Variables are factors open to change; events are episodes of actual change. According to a recent definition, an event represents "an instance of substantial and relatively quick change in an independent or dependent variable of theoretical interest."[26] Along with variables of theoretical interest, we may wish to include variables of practical interest, too. For instance, the personal identity of the foreign minister murdered by a lone killer may not be a variable of theoretical interest to political scientists, even as it may be one of profound practical interest to political actors. While variables are the factors that sustain institutional equilibria, events are the "punctuations" that may tip the equilibrium.[27] Not all events are equal, though. In the following, I wish to distinguish between catastrophic and ordinary events.

CATASTROPHIC EVENTS

Catastrophes are instances of contingency even laypersons outside law firms and philosophy departments recognize as such. Civil or military "contingency planners" who work in anticipation of earthquakes, hurricanes, contagious diseases, political violence, or foreign invasion do not need to explain the meaning of "contingency" to the general public. Even without being offered, or able to offer, any formal definition, ordinary language users are likely to understand the nature of catastrophic contingencies. Clearly set apart from the preceding categories of contingency, catastrophes involve four distinctive features.

Anticipation

Coping with contingent events means coping with the future. Contingent events are contingent (indeterminate and uncertain), as they may or may not happen in the future. The past is a source of certainties: We know what happened at given times and places. The future is the motherland of uncertainty: Y may happen or not. Even when we analyze contingencies that took place in the past, we analyze them as contingencies from the viewpoint of "past futures,"[28] the forward-looking calculations of actors inhabiting the historical past. Despite their relative infrequency, catastrophes are not necessarily unforeseeable, but may well occur with calculable probabilities. In some cases, we ignore the frequency distribution of possible catastrophes, which prevents us from attaching probability values to their occurrence. We may know in principle that such *chaotic* events can happen, but have no idea how often they do. For example: a branch falling from a tree, hitting your head, and killing you, while walking the Champs Elysées in Paris, just days after escaping from National Socialism (as happened to Austrian writer Ödön von Horváth in 1938). In other cases, though, we do know the frequency distribution of the events under consideration, which enables us to estimate the probability of their occurrence (across time, space, or groups). We know such *stochastic* events are bound to happen with calculable probabilities, although we can predict neither their actual occurrence nor their concrete timing and trajectory. For example: the formation of hurricanes per year in the Caribbean basis.

Damage

The objects of bureaucratic, political, and military "contingency planning" are not neutral events, and even less so, pleasing events. Planning for the day we win big in the lottery does not count as "contingency planning," but daydreaming. Contingencies are events that bear clear, often dramatic, negative consequences. They are the "disasters large and small" we wish to prevent from happening or, if we cannot, whose damaging consequences we wish to mitigate. In domestic security and foreign affairs, contingency planning typically relates to dramatic menaces like war and terrorism, including the "double contingency of external invasion and internal contention" the Federalist Papers warn against.[29]

External Causation

While conditional formulations (if x, then y) are essential to most other forms of contingency, catastrophic contingency largely dispenses with conditionality. Rather than describing contingent effects depending on contingent causes, or contingent acts depending on contingent reasons, it describes the irruption of exogenous forces that disrupt the orderly interplay of independent and dependent variables. We may understand the causal chains that lead to natural catastrophes, but we cannot control them. We cannot intervene and prevent the catastrophe from forming. Catastrophic contingencies are external shocks. Their indeterminacy is not epistemic (unknown causes), but practical (exogenous causes).

Infrequency

Catastrophes are uncertain: They may or may not happen. And they are unpredictable: We do not know whom they will hit, nor when and where (social, temporal, and spatial indeterminacy). What distinguishes them from other contingencies, however, is neither their uncertainty nor their randomness, but their infrequency. Contingent events are rare events. In the continuous flow of normality, they stand out as abnormal occurrences, as "unusual" and "unexpected."[30] They do not hit us very often (though when they do, they may knock us out). Contingency is the exception to the rule, the accident that interrupts the flow of routine, the thing that happens against our expectations, against our best guesses. Contingency is what ruins our day, our investment schemes, our wedding plans, our carefree contemplation of this weekend's soccer broadcast. Lola, the heroine in the movie Run Lola Run (Tom Tykwer, 1999)—she is the Queen of Contingency. Always punctual, she comes late once, and sets off a vertiginous chain of calamities.

In his contribution to this volume, David R. Mayhew discusses the "underinvestigated" causal impact of political events, placing considerable emphasis on catastrophic events like floods, earthquakes, war, assassinations, and economic collapse. As he argues persuasively, unexpected events may have influenced in decisive ways a long series of significant political outcomes over the past one hundred years of U.S. history.

ORDINARY EVENTS

Even if they sometimes appear as paradigmatic embodiments of contingency, catastrophes form a very specific subset of contingent events. The broader family of contingent events includes an infinite number of much smaller, less dramatic, and more benign "variable changes" that accompany us, with consequences deep or shallow, in our ordinary life. Over a normal day, we often manage an innumerable number of contingencies: My alarm clock fails to ring; my head aches from excessive milk consumption the night before; I put on the wrong trousers; my breakfast toast burns to ashes; I consider the alternative between cathartic yodeling and nervous breakdown. Such petty contingencies mold the rhythm of our lives, they are the stuff of our evening conversations, they punctuate our routines without unsettling them. They may be profoundly unnerving (at the moment), at the same time that they are fundamentally irrelevant (in the long run). We refer to them as "the contingencies of everyday life" or, in our sphere of study, "the contingencies of politics."

In political science, we usually overlook these contingencies as we survey political life from the heights of scientific abstraction. The higher we climb the ladder of abstraction, the more orderly the world will appear to us; the closer we look at it, the more contingent it appears. Streams of "contingent" phenomena looked at from a distance, if they are visible at all, often appear as trivial, non-consequential, not worth remembering. Consider, again, the sphere of sports. The whole excitement of sports games derives from their contingency. We know the rules, we know the players, but the game itself is open. Neither its concrete development nor, of course, its outcome are predetermined. Citing again from the film *Run Lola Run* that opens its breakneck concatenation of fateful contingencies with a metaphorical reference to soccer: "The ball is round. The game lasts 90 minutes. This is for sure. Everything else is pure theory." Meaning: Here are the rules, the rest escapes theory. The development of the game itself transcends our predictive capacities. It is a matter of strategic intelligence, individual virtuosity, precise coordination, physical endurance, mental calmness, and collective passion—plus a measure of chance and coincidence, of luck good and bad.

Yet if we climb a helicopter and look at the stadium from a bird's perspective, the contingencies of the game withdraw from our field of vision. The stadium itself looks pretty non-contingent, and so does the empirical regularity that soccer games take place every Sunday within the stadium, in the presence of larger or smaller crowds, cheering or booing. We, the students of politics, tend to adopt such an aerial perspective. Indifferent to the "contingencies of politics," we strive to decipher its structural logic. We are not interested in political games—but in their origins, their outcomes, their evolution over time, their institutional structure, their mechanisms of dispute resolution, their material and cultural bases, their consequences. Our passion pertains, if anywhere, to game statistics. The game itself we store away in a methodological black box.

In every black box, though, sits a white box striving to get out.[31] Political scientists often do try to throw light into the black box of politics by watching political games in similar ways that we watch the games of sport. Delivering narratives of dramatic quality, they reconstruct decisive sequences of action, zoom in on exciting moments, record times of inactivity, celebrate success and defeat. They report on strategic plans and tactical moves, on the virtuosities and failures of teams and players, on justice and chance, on opportunities exploited and given away. Journalists look at politics that way. They recount politics from the perspective of politics, from a short distance and a short time horizon. Country studies in comparative politics sometimes adopt such a close perspective on political life, too, which makes them vulnerable to the charge of falling captive to the contingencies of politics and loosing their distinctiveness vis-à-vis journalism. In general, the discipline tries to avoid becoming absorbed by the excitement of political contingencies. It keeps the black box sealed, detaches itself from the game of politics, and shifts its attention from processes to structures, and from proximate to distant causes.[32]

Unpacking Contingency

The preceding inventory of things contingent is not complete. It has been silent, for example, on the contingencies of collective actors and collective action. Yet, even if it contains blank spaces, our roadmap conveys a rough idea of the multiple sites inhabited by contingency; and it puts us in a position to respond, with a certain degree of confidence, to our initial question about the semantic core of contingency: Is it only a vague "family resemblance" the different usages of the word "contingency" share, or can we plausibly identify a structure of meaning common to all uses of "contingency" across different contexts? The answer is positive, I believe, but somewhat more complicated and less parsimonious than one would hope for. As I wish to argue, the semantic architecture of "contingency" is built around three abstract pillars: indeterminacy, conditionality, and uncertainty. The three of them appeared in my initial exploration of the *Oxford English Dictionary* and *LexisNexis* news sources and have been accompanying us in the subsequent discussion of empirical referents of contingency. They form a chain of inference I hold to be constitutive for all usages of the word, even if any of them may remain implicit or recede to the background in some contexts of usage (see Table 2.1).

Indeterminacy

The negative notion of indeterminacy (the negation of determinacy) points to the existence of possible worlds alongside the so-called real world.

TABLE 2.1
The Three Dimensions of Contingency

Referents/ Dimensions	Indeterminacy "It could be different."	Conditionality "It depends."	Uncertainty "We cannot know."
Individual actors	**Non-contingent traits are universal (actor homogeneity). Contingent traits may, or may not, be present (actor heterogeneity).**	The degree as well as the content of human individuation depend on social and personal circumstances.	Personality traits are not the mechanical (predictable) outcome of social circumstances and biological programming.
Individual action	**Contingent acts: Actors may, or may not, do *y*. Non-contingent acts: Actors always do *y*.**	Acts depend on motives (passions, reasons, ideologies, routines).	Decisions are uncertain, if the parameters of decision-making are uncertain.
Conceptual commitments	**Necessary attributes: claims we cannot reject when employing a concept. Peripheral attributes: claims we may reject when using a concept (contingent commitments).**	The logic of linguistic communication: Conceptual choices entail claims and commitments we cannot change by decree.	The border-line between contingent and non-contingent commitments is contingent itself. Language users may reject inherited conceptual tools and meanings.
Normative commitments	**Contingent claims are open to change and contestation. Non-contingent claims are universal, inviolable, beyond dispute.**	The logic of normative argumentation: Normative conclusions depend on normative premises.	Normative premises are not fixed and given, but a matter of social and individual choice.
Practical commitments	Contingent commitments are conditional on future parameter changes. Firm commitments are unconditional.	**Contingent commitments *y* depend on the occurrence of future events *x*.**	Contingency *x* occurs in the future. We do not know whether it will happen, or not.
Objective facts	**Contingent facts may, or may not, be the case. Non-contingent facts always hold.**	Contingent facts *y* vary, for they depend on variable causes *x*. Constant facts depend on constant causes.	We may not know whether *x* will occur.
Causal relations	**Contingent effects *x* → *y* may, or may not, hold. Non-contingent effects are universal.**	Causal relations vary, because they depend on intervening contextual variables *z*.	We may not know whether *z* is the case.
Catastrophic events	Catastrophes are always possible, even if their probabilities of occurrence are low.	Catastrophes are external shocks. We may understand, but do not control, their causes.	**We do not know when, where, whom, and how catastrophes hit.**

NOTE: Cells in **boldface** indicate the primary meaning of contingency in the respective row.

71

One simple phrase describes the indeterminate essence of contingency: Things could be different. They could be otherwise in the present. They could have been different in the past. They could change in the future. When we talk about contingency, we issue statements of indeterminacy: what is, could not be; and what not is, could. Claims of contingency involve the "exclusion of necessity and impossibility."[33] They stipulate the "objective possibility"[34] that reality may look different. They mobilize the notion that "a different world is possible" (as the motto of the World Social Forum runs). In the centrality it accords to indeterminacy, contingency is a profoundly modern idea. It postulates a world cut free from the grip of transcendental forces. Reality is not a gift of God, but the combined creation of woman, nature, and chance.

Conditionality

To say something is contingent is to imply: It depends. Our claims of contingency rest at least implicitly upon claims of conditionality: The empirical phenomenon y is variable/indeterminate/contingent because *it depends* on variable/indeterminate/contingent causal factors x. In this sense, contingency equals covariation (between conditions and consequences) . . . and thus reveals itself to occupy the very center of social scientific methodology. In the methodological mainstream of contemporary social science, this notion of covariation provides the (orthodox and thus non-contingent) foundation of causal explanation.[35] Inescapably, the scientific observation of covariational evidence rests upon this double assertion of factual contingency—the related contingency of independent and dependent variables. Consequences y are variables, because causes x are variables. The former dependent, the latter independent. Neither one is constant, both are (necessarily) contingent. Contingency thus is not a variable. Rather, it is the magic wand that transforms any kind of phenomenon into a variable (indeterminate, conditional, uncertain).

Uncertainty

Indeterminacy may come along with highly variable degrees of uncertainty. Uncertainty may be radical, as in contingent events that are beyond our control and perhaps even beyond our comprehension: an act of terrorism, a heart attack at twenty, the lone assassin running amok in a supermarket. But uncertainty may also be quite limited, as in contingent events whose occurrence is conditional on specific, calculable conditions, such as the residence permit of a foreign citizen being "contingent" on her ability to secure formal employment. Catastrophic events, which ordinary language identifies as vivid instances of contingency, often go hand in hand with radical unpredictability. Other types of contingency, by contrast, contain elements of uncertainty only to the extent that we leave their origins (such as the motives for accepting contingent normative commitments) outside our analytical horizon.

The Semantic Architecture

In an intriguing semantic division of labor between grammatical forms, the noun "contingency" in the singular tends to stress the indeterminate nature of y, and the adjective "contingent" tends to express the conditional nature of y, while "contingencies" in the plural tend to highlight the unpredictable side of y. "Contingency" (the singular) is a regular participant in philosophical debate on the indeterminate foundations of human existence, as in Richard Rorty's "contingency of the liberal community."[36] In contradistinction, "contingencies" (the plural) describe catastrophic events like hurricanes and terrorist attacks, while the adjective "contingent" often refers to rather unexciting and predictable consequences of rather unexciting and predictable causal factors.

The three constitutive dimensions of contingency are not isolated attributes that would not speak to each other. Rather, they form a coherent structure of meaning. Together, they constitute an inferential chain that argues, in essence, that phenomenon y is contingent since it is contingent on contingent conditions x. Let us dissipate the air of tautology by briefly going through the three steps. All uses of "contingency" involve the notion of indeterminacy, the negation of necessity and impossibility. If we declare something to be contingent, we claim it could be different; we conceive it as only one realization among many possible worlds. Indeterminacy, however, is not the whole story, but only the concluding step of a larger argument about the conditions of indeterminacy. At least in an implicit manner, statements of contingency point towards the sources of indeterminacy. They mobilize claims of conditionality: Y could be different because it depends on causal conditions x. Finally, although they may remain relegated to the semantic backstage, statements of contingency regularly carry connotations of unpredictability or uncertainty. These elements of uncertainty, too, can be traced back to the underlying conditions of indeterminacy: Y is unpredictable to the extent that its causal conditions x are unpredictable. The three steps that form the inferential chain of contingency may be resumed the following way:

(1) y = indeterminate, since
(2) y = f (x), with
(3) x = indeterminate

The first line expresses indeterminacy, the second conditionality, and the third uncertainty. Table 2.1 cross-tabulates the referents of contingency I reviewed with these three dimensions I postulate. It conveys two basic messages. Firstly, there are no empty cells. All usages of "contingency" involve all three semantic dimensions of indeterminacy, conditionality, and uncertainty. Secondly, the three dimensions do not carry equal weight across different contexts of usage. Some of them may not be obvious in certain contexts, although we can still recognize them, make them explicit, and pull them to the semantic surface. Besides, in each context of usage, one of the three dimensions stands out, overshadowing the remaining two (see the boldface cells in Table 2.1). As the table suggests, indeterminacy dominates most contexts of usage, but conditionality takes the lead with respect to the contingency of practical commitments, and uncertainty with respect to the contingency of catastrophic events.

Conclusion

As the variegated map of contingencies I have been drawing suggests, contingency appears in manifold costumes and in many places of political life. If politics is the art of the possible, its practice involves the creation, management, and containment of multiple contingencies. At first sight, the very idea of contingency seems to be alien to the positive study of politics. Our official object of study, after all, are political realities, not political possibilities. Nevertheless, since given realities always unfold within a moving horizon of possibilities, with the so-called "real world" coexisting with and competing against other "possible worlds," the study of politics, too, has come to grips with the multifaceted plurality of contingencies that inhabit the public sphere. What seems clear from my review of uses and meanings of "contingency" is that contingency "as such," contingency in the abstract, may be of little use to found or frame an agenda for political reflection and research. If we wish to incorporate contingency into the study of politics, we have to make explicit where precisely we are locating it on the complex map of semantic structures and empirical referents.

As a matter of course, we should not expect the study of contingency to be a smooth consensual affair. In our private lives, tracing the distinction between contingent and non-contingent phenomena is a matter of personal judgment, as famously expressed (and religiously framed) in Reinhold Niebuhr's "contingency prayer": "God, grant me the serenity to accept the things I cannot change, the courage to change the things I can, and the wisdom to know the difference." In the realm of politics, drawing the boundaries between the contingent and the non-contingent is a matter of public contestation. The claims of political contingency we put forward may always be challenged by counterclaims of determinacy. If we declare things to be contingent, others may respond by asserting their "inevitability, 'naturalness,' or functionality."[37] In the sphere of academic inquiry, controversies over the boundaries of contingency may lose the dramatic quality they tend to carry in political life. Still, the invitation to incorporate the "contingencies of politics" into the study of politics may be read as an invitation for controversy. The outcomes of such controversy, of course, are contingent.

NOTES

1. On the Odgen-Richards Triangle (definition, referents, term), see Sartori, "Guidelines," and Gerring, *Social Science Methodology*, Chapter 3.

2. Rorty, *Contingency*, p. 12.

3. *LexisNexis Academic*. Search term: contingency. Date of search: 18 October 2004. Search period: previous six months. Searching the database by the adjective "contingent" yields similar results, although with additional references to "contingents" of soldiers and peacekeepers all over the world.

4. The literal quotations are from Joseph Goedert, "Disaster Contingency Plans: What Docs Need to Do," *Newsline* 12/6 (June 2004): 16; "Obasanjo Wants N2.5Bn Contingent Vote Restored," *Africa News* (21 May 2004); and Michael J. Martínez, "With managers leaving town, Wall Street has contingencies in place," *Business News* (27 August 2004).

5. "Contingency" (2nd edition 1989), *Oxford English Dictionary Online* (Oxford: Oxford University Press, 2004). www.oed.com.

6. Wittgenstein, "Philosophische Untersuchungen," pp. 277–286.

7. Berman, *All That Is Solid.*

8. See also Brennan, "Selection."

9. Political philosophy has fewer troubles in acknowledging the radical "contingency of self-hood" (Rorty, *Contingency*).

10. Zakaria, *The Future of Freedom*, p. 89.

11. The reference is, of course, to Max Weber: We explain social action by understanding it (see Weber, *Wirtschaft und Gesellschaft*, p. 1).

12. For richer treatments of reasons and passions, see Hirschman, *The Passions and the Interests*, and Holmes, *Passions and Constraint*. For a more complex conceptual analysis of ideology, see Gerring, *Social Science Methodology*, pp. 72–86.

13. Levi, *Consent.*

14. Webb, "Party Responses," p. 28.

15. Brandom, *Articulating Reasons*, p. 31.

16. Brandom, ibid.

17. Popper, *Objective Knowledge*, pp. 207–208.

18. Stepan, "Religion."

19. Gerring, "What Is a Case Study?" p. 351.

20. Capoccia, *Defending Democracy.*

21. Varshney, *Ethnic Conflict.*

22. Bermeo, *Ordinary People.*

23. Cox, *Making Votes Count.*

24. Snyder, *From Voting to Violence.*

25. Tetlock and Belkin, "Counterfactual Thought Experiments," p. 30.

26. Gerring, "What Is a Case Study?" p. 351.

27. Krasner, "Approaches."

28. Koselleck, *Vergangene Zukunft.*

29. Madison, Hamilton, and Jay, *The Federalist Papers*, No. 7.

30. Gerring, *Social Science Methodology*, p. 145.

31. I am paraphrasing Ranulph Glanville, "Inside Every White Box," with apologies for the inversion of the numbers and roles of escapist boxes.

32. Kitschelt, "Accounting."

33. Luhmann, *Soziale Systeme*, p. 152.

34. Weber, "Objektive Möglichkeit."

35. "All empirical evidence of causal relationships is covariational in nature" (Gerring, "What Is a Case Study?" p. 342). On the external observation of covariational evidence versus the internal critique of rational claims (with regard to judicial decision-making), see Schedler, "Arguing and Observing."

36. Rorty, *Contingency.*

37. Pierson, *Politics in Time*, p. 20.

BIBLIOGRAPHY

Berman, Marshall, *All That Is Solid Melts into Air: The Experience of Modernity.* New York: Penguin, 1982.

Bermeo, Nancy, *Ordinary People in Extraordinary Times: The Citizenry and the Breakdown of Democracy.* Princeton and Oxford: Princeton University Press, 2003.

Brandom, Robert B., *Articulating Reasons: An Introduction to Inferentialism.* Cambridge, Mass., and London: Harvard University Press, 2000.

Brennan, Geoffrey, "Selection and the Currency of Reward," *The Theory of Institutional Design,* ed. Robert E. Goodin. Cambridge, UK: Cambridge University Press, 1996, pp. 256–75.

Capoccia, Giovanni, *Defending Democracy: Reactions to Extremism in Interwar Europe.* Baltimore and London: Johns Hopkins University Press, 2005.

Cox, Gary, *Making Votes Count: Strategic Coordination in the World's Electoral Systems.* Cambridge, UK: Cambridge University Press, 1997.

Gerring, John, "What Is a Case Study and What Is It Good For? *American Political Science Review* 98/2 (May 2004): 341–54.

———, *Social Science Methodology: A Criterial Framework.* Cambridge, UK: Cambridge University Press, 2001.

Glanville, Ranulph, "Inside Every White Box There Are Two Black Boxes Trying to Get Out," *Behavioral Science* 27 (1982): 1–11.

Hardin, Russell, "Determinacy and Rational Choice," *Rational Interaction: Essays in Honor of John C. Harsanyi,* ed. Reinhard Selten. Berlin: Springer, 1992, pp. 191–200.

Hirschman, Albert O., *The Passions and the Interests: Political Arguments for Capitalism before Its Triumph.* Princeton, NJ: Princeton University Press, 1977.

Holmes, Stephen, *Passions and Constraint: On the Theory of Liberal Democracy.* Chicago and London: University of Chicago Press, 1995.

Kitschelt, Herbert, "Accounting for Postcommunist Regime Diversity: What Counts as a Good Cause?" Durham, NC: Duke University, 2002, unpublished typescript.

Koselleck, Reinhart, *Vergangene Zukunft: Zur Semantik geschichtlicher Zeiten.* Frankfurt am Main: Suhrkamp, 1989.

Krasner, Stephen, "Approaches to the State: Alternative Conceptions and Historical Dynamics," *Comparative Politics* 16/2 (1984): 223–46.

Levi, Margaret, *Consent, Dissent, and Patriotism.* Cambridge, UK: Cambridge University Press, 1997.

Luhmann, Niklas, *Soziale Systeme: Grundriß einer allgemeinen Theorie.* Frankfurt am Main: Suhrkamp, 1987.

Madison, James, Alexander Hamilton, and John Jay, *The Federalist Papers.* London: Penguin, 1987, orig. 1788.

Pierson, Paul, *Politics in Time: History, Institutions, and Social Analysis.* Princeton and Oxford: Princeton University Press, 2004.

Popper, Karl R., *Objective Knowledge: An Evolutionary Approach.* Oxford: Clarendon Press, 1979.

Rorty, Richard, *Contingency, Irony, and Solidarity.* Cambridge: Cambridge University Press, 1989.

Sartori, Giovanni, "Guidelines for Concept Analysis," *Social Science Concepts: A Systematic Analysis,* ed. Giovanni Sartori. Beverly Hills: Sage Publications, 1984, pp. 15–85.

Schedler, Andreas, "Arguing and Observing: Internal and External Critiques of Judicial Impartiality," *Journal of Political Philosophy* 12/3 (September 2004): 245–65.

Snyder, Jack, *From Voting to Violence: Democratization and Nationalist Conflict.* New York and London: W. W. Norton, 2000.

Stepan, Alfred, "Religion, Democracy, and the 'Twin Tolerations,' " *Journal of Democracy* 11/4 (October 2000): 37–57.

Tetlock, Philip E., and Aaron Belkin, "Counterfactual Thought Experiments in World Politics: Logical, Methodological, and Psychological Perspectives," *Counterfactual Thought Experiments in World Politics: Logical, Methodological, and Psychological Perspectives,* eds. Philip E. Tetlock and Aaron Belkin. Princeton, NJ: Princeton University Press, 1996, pp. 1–38.

Varshney, Ashutosh, *Ethnic Conflict and Civil Life: Hindus and Muslims in India.* New Haven and London: Yale University Press, 2002.

Webb, Paul, "Party Responses to the Changing Electoral Market in Britain," *Political Parties and Electoral Change,* eds. Peter Mair, Wolfgang C. Müller, and Fritz Plasser. London: Sage, 2004, pp. 20–48.

Weber, Max, *Wirtschaft und Gesellschaft: Grundriss der verstehenden Soziologie.* Tübingen: J. C. B. Mohr, 1985, 5th edition.

———, "Objektive Möglichkeit und adäquate Verursachung in der historischen Kausalbetrachtung," *Gesammelte Aufsätze zur Wissenschaftslehre,* ed. Johannes Winckelmann. Tübingen: J. C. B. Mohr, 1988, 8th edition, orig. 1906, pp. 266–90.

Wittgenstein, Ludwig, "Philosophische Untersuchungen," *Ludwig Wittgenstein, Werkausgabe Band 1.* Frankfurt am Main: Suhrkamp, 1984, orig. 1945–49, pp. 225–580.

Zakaria, Fareed, *The Future of Freedom: Illiberal Democracy at Home and Abroad.* New York: W. W. Norton, 2003.

Chapter 3

Resilience as the Explanandum of Social Theory

Philip Pettit

The notion of the resilience is of the first importance, I believe, for an understanding of some of the major styles of social explanation. This is because the resilience of various social phenomena is the best candidate for the *explanandum* of much social science. Here, drawing on earlier work that I have done in the area, I attempt to underline that message. The chapter is in three sections. In the opening discussion I introduce the notion of resilience, relating it to the more general notion of contingency. In the second section I argue for the importance of resilience as an *explanandum* of rational choice and in the third for its equal importance as an *explanandum* of functionalist theory. The aims of these enterprises, and the relationship between them, make excellent sense—and perhaps only make such sense—once they are seen as seeking to explain why one or another phenomenon is resilient.

Contingency and Resilience

Think about the actual world as one among an indefinite number of possible worlds, where each possible world represents a way that things could have been, and where two possible worlds need only differ in miniscule respects. Contingent phenomena, by standard accounts, are those that materialize in the actual world but that do not figure in every possible world: they are not necessary. Contingent phenomena do actually obtain but they do not have to obtain. While they figure in the actual world, there are ways the actual world might have been—possible worlds, that is—where they do not appear.

This received way of thinking about contingency has one obvious drawback. It makes the class of contingent phenomena into a large, catch-all category that includes every actual way things are that just might not have been so, however unlikely it is that they should not have been so. It lumps together the law of gravitation with the fact that I got up late this morning with the fact that ours is a social species, casting each of these truths as equally contingent; in each case, after all, there are some possible worlds where one or the other, or more, of these truths do not hold.

This drawback suggests that we should revise our approach and think about contingency, not as a property that something has or fails to have, period—not, in particular, as actuality-combined-with-non-necessity— but as a property that events and facts and the like can have in a lower or a higher degree. And the metaphor of possible worlds—we need only treat it as a metaphor[1]—can also help us to represent what contingency in this graduated sense involves.

A way things are in the actual world will be contingent in the graduated sense to the extent to which they are not found elsewhere, non-contingent to the extent to which they are found at other locations: found, that is, in other possible worlds. The less frequent their location in non-actual worlds, the more contingent they are; the more frequent, the less contingent. The limit of contingency will be realization in the actual world but nowhere else; the limit of non-contingency will be realization in every possible world—i.e., necessity. And there will be any number of in-between grades.

The word I use for the property of figuring in the actual world and being relatively common across other possible worlds is "resilience." Phenomena are high in resilience and low in (graduated) contingency to the extent to which they are realized, not just in the actual world, but under a relatively large number of variations on the actual world: across a relatively high number of other possible worlds. Take the actual world and ask of some phenomenon within it how far it is resilient, how far contingent. The answer will be fixed by how far it will continue to be realized under different variations on the actual world: experimentally and historically vindicated variations but also variations about which we can only theorize.

The discussion so far shows how resilience comes in degrees, with the more resilient phenomenon occurring in a greater number of possible worlds, the less resilient occurring in a smaller number. But resilience may vary in quality as well as degree, and this turns out to be an important observation from the point of view of political theory and social science. We will see why in later sections.

Suppose that two phenomena are equally resilient. Suppose that they occur in the same number of possible worlds and so have the same raw resilience score. It should be clear that they may still differ in an important aspect. The non-actual worlds in which one of them figures may be much more interesting for us as a class than the worlds in which the other figures. Let the one phenomenon be resilient across X-worlds, the other resilient across Y-worlds. It may be that X-resilience connects more deeply with our interests—say, our theoretical or practical interests—than Y-resilience, and so we will naturally attach more importance to it. X-resilience will be resilience of a different quality from Y-resilience, even when the degree of resilience is the same in each case.

How are we likely to assess possible worlds in determining the importance of resilience across those worlds? One obvious way would be by reference to the probability of the worlds: their chance of being actualized. The fact that a phenomenon is resilient across two worlds, where one is relatively more likely than another, is going to make resilience in the first world more interesting from many points of view. The greater probability of that world is going to mean, for example, that the information about the phenomenon's resilience in that world is of much greater predictive interest.

If we knew all the worlds where something was resilient, and had information on the exact probability of each of those worlds—the exact chance of its occurring—then we would know the absolute probability of that phenomenon. While it might be heuristically interesting and even indispensable, then, to approach the topic via a consideration of resilience, we could state our findings in simple probabilistic terms. But of course that information about probability will often not be available. We will have firm intuitions about the groups of possible scenarios where the phenomenon will occur—or that have such and such a probability of occurring—but no complete probability ordering of those worlds in relation to worlds where the phenomenon does not occur or is unlikely to occur. Thus we may grade the resilience of a phenomenon by reference to the probability of the worlds where it is resilient, while remaining unable to discharge the concept of resilience in favor of that of probability.

Is there any other sensible way in which we might want to grade the resilience of a phenomenon? Surprisingly, I think there is. Suppose the phenomenon involves our continuing to enjoy some good. We might take great consolation in the fact that the good will continue to be available in worlds where we behave well, even while admitting that it is more probable we will revert to type and behave badly; after all, this will mean that whether or not we enjoy the good is up to us: it is within our own control. Or we might be delighted to find that it will continue to be available regardless of how badly certain others behave, even while admitting that they are entirely benign and very unlikely to behave badly; this will mean that whether or not we enjoy the good is not up to them: it is not within their control.

If we prioritize probability or chance in grading resilience, that will be because we are concerned with whether the worlds where the phenomenon continues to be realized are probable or not; let a world be relatively unlikely to come about, and we will have less interest in whether the phenomenon remains in place there. If we take the other route, prioritizing our own control or that of others, that will be because we are concerned with whether the worlds where the phenomenon endures are ones that are within our own power of realization or the power of realization of others. We may also mix concerns, of course, being focused, among equally probable worlds, on those that are more easily controllable by us or less easily controllable by others; or being focused, among worlds where control is equal, on those that have a higher chance of realization. But for ease of presentation I shall not discuss that possible mixing further.

In the next section I will argue for the importance of chance-graded resilience for rational-choice theory and in the third section for its importance in functionalist theorizing. Control-graded resilience is important for political philosophy, in particular for explicating ideals like that of freedom, as I have argued elsewhere.[2] But I shall concentrate in this essay on social theory.

Resilience and Rational-Choice Explanation

The Explanatory Interest of Resilience

There are three different types of *explananda* that are of particular importance in social science, as I have tried to argue elsewhere.[3] We may be interested in explaining the emergence or appearance of a phenomenon: say, the emergence of a certain regularity, or norm, or organization, or whatever. We may be interested in explaining the survival or reproduction of the phenomenon over a certain time, perhaps through a series of crises. Or, I would say, we may be interested in explaining its resilience: explaining why it is that for a variety of possible scenarios, possible ways the world may go, it remains a fixture.

There are two deep reasons why resilience is a natural focus of social investigation. One is that we will often be unable to access the information that would tell us, or tell us with any degree of assurance, how something emerged or how it survived through this or that period or crisis. Thus the natural question will be how far we can tell resilient apart from non-resilient phenomena, how far we can distinguish fixtures on the social landscape from mere ephemera. Already in the eighteenth century, the Baron de Montesquieu[4] had made such an argument. He saw how difficult it would be to tell detailed stories about how things come about, identifying their "particular causes"—and how relatively uninteresting such very detailed stories might be. He recommended instead that we look for "general causes": that is, causes that make various phenomena more or less inevitable, establishing conditions such that the phenomena are likely to remain in place under all or most of the different scenarios that those conditions allow.

The second, perhaps deeper reason for the interest of resilience to social scientists—it surely had an influence on Montesquieu, too—is that the investigation of resilience is vital for choosing policies and designing institutions; a great deal of social science is pursed with these ends in view. Let our concern be whether we should go for this sort of institution or that other variety, this way of trying to achieve a certain result or that alternative means, and one of the main issues will be: which of those institutions is likely to prove more durable—likely to prove more durable in face of shifting fashions and uncertain levels of human commitment. The knaves principle,[5] dubious though it may be as a unique principle of institutional design,[6] was devised with precisely this sort of concern in mind. Bernard Mandeville[7] gave early expression to it when he hailed the constitution that "remains unshaken though most men should prove knaves." The principle remains in place among economists and others when they seek out ways of arranging things in the market or the polity that are "incentive-compatible": compatible with the ordinary run of human motivations, i.e., capable of surviving in the presence of such motivations.

Two major styles of explanation in social science over the past century have been rational choice, sought by economists and economically minded social scientists, and functionalist, associated with sociology, anthropology, and related disciplines. Rational-choice explanation seeks to make sense of various phenomena by reference, roughly, to the rational self-interest of individual agents. Functionalist explanation tries to achieve this end by displaying the phenomena as serving to promote one or another alleged social benefit.

I have argued elsewhere that each of these explanatory styles has tended, at least in the main, to be applied with a view to elucidating the resilience or the presumed resilience of various phenomena, rather than their emergence or survival. I now proceed to explain that claim, though I can do so only in a very sketchy way.[8] While I will not focus particularly on the issue, it should be obvious that resilience will be more interesting in each case to the extent that it is resilience across worlds that have a greater chance of being realized. Thus the suggestion is that chance-graded resilience is the focus of much social science.

Rational-Choice Explanation and Resilience

Economists and rational-choice theorists present human agents as relatively self-regarding creatures who act with a view to doing as well as possible by their predominantly self-regarding desires.[9] These desires are usually assumed to be desires for what is loosely described as economic advantage or gain: that is, roughly, for advantage or gain in the sorts of things that can be traded. But self-regarding desires, of course, may extend to other goods, too, and there is nothing inimical to economics in explaining patterns of behaviour by reference, say, to those non-tradable goods that consist in being well loved or well regarded.[10] The economic approach is tied to an assumption of relative self-regard but not to any particular view of the dimensions in which self-regard may operate.

But does the egocentric picture fit? Are human beings rational centres of predominantly self-regarding concern? It would seem not. Were human agents centres of this kind, then we would expect them to find their reasons for doing things predominantly in considerations that bear on their own advantage. But this isn't our common experience, or so at least I shall argue.

Consider the sorts of considerations that weigh with us, or seem to weigh with us, in a range of common, or garden, situations. We are apparently moved in our dealings with others by considerations that bear on their merits and their attractions, that highlight what is expected of us and what fair play or friendship requires, that direct attention to the good we can achieve together or the past that we share in common, and so on through a complex variety of deliberative themes. And not only are we apparently moved in this non-egocentric way. We clearly believe of one another—and take it, indeed, to be a matter of common belief—that we are generally and reliably responsive to claims that transcend and occasionally confound the calls of self-regard. That is why we feel free to ask each other for favours, to ground our projects in the expectation that others will be faithful to their past commitments, and to seek counsel from others in confidence that they will present us with a more or less impartial rendering of how things stand.

The claim that we ordinary folk are oriented towards a non-egocentric language of self-explanation and self-justification does not establish definitively, of course, that we are actually not self-regarding. We all recognise the possibilities of rationalisation and deception that such a language leaves open. Still, it would surely be miraculous that that language succeeds as well as it does in defining a stable and smooth framework of expectation, if as a matter of fact our sensibilities do not conform to its contours: if, as a matter of fact, we fall systematically short—systematically and not just occasionally short—of what it suggests may be taken for granted about us.

We are left, then, with a problem for rational-choice theory. The mind postulated in rational-choice theory is that of a relatively self-regarding creature. But the mind that people display towards one another in most social settings, the mind that is articulated in common conceptions of how ordinary folk are moved, is saturated with concerns that dramatically transcend the boundaries of the self. So how can we invoke the workings of the economic mind to explain behaviour, when the black box at the origin of behaviour does not apparently contain an economic mind? What I suggest is that in the most unlikely social settings self-regard may still have an important presence: it may be virtually if not actually there; it may be waiting in the wings, even if it is not actually on stage.

Suppose, first, that people are generally content in non-market contexts —we can restrict our attention to these—to let their actions be dictated by the cultural framing of the situation in which they find themselves: by the habits or perhaps the whims underpinned by that framing. Suppose, in the second place, that despite the hegemony of cultural framing in people's everyday deliberations and decisions, there are certain alarm bells that make them take their own interests into consideration. People may proceed under a more or less automatic cultural pilot in most cases, but at any point where a decision is liable to cost them dearly in self-regarding terms, the alarm bells will tend to ring and prompt them to consider personal advantage. And suppose, third, that attending to considerations of personal advantage will lead people, generally if not invariably, to act so as to secure that advantage: they become disposed to do the relatively more self-regarding thing.

Under these suppositions, self-regard will normally have no actual presence in dictating what people do; it will not be present in deliberation and will make no impact on decision. But it will always be virtually present in deliberation, for there are alarms which are ready to ring at any point where the agent's interests get to be possibly compromised, and those alarms will call up self-regard and give it a more or less controlling deliberative presence. The agent will run under cultural pilot, provided that that pilot does not carry him or her into terrain that is too dangerous from a self-interested point of view. Let such terrain come into view, and in most cases the agent will quickly return to manual; he or she will quickly begin to count the more personal losses and benefits that are at stake in the decision on hand. This reflection may not invariably lead to self-regarding action—there is such a thing as self-sacrifice, after all—but the assumption is that it will do so fairly reliably.

What will rational-choice theory explain under this hypothesis about virtual self-regard? My answer is: the relative resilience of the phenomenon or procedure or institution that is said to be in people's virtual self-interest.

Imagine a little set-up in which a ball rolls along a straight line—this, say, under Newton's laws of motion—but where there are little posts on either side that are designed to protect it from the influence of various possible but non-actualised forces that might cause it to change course; they are able to damp incoming forces, and if such forces still have an effect—or if the ball is subject to random drift—they are capable of restoring the ball to its original path. The posts on either side are virtual or standby causes of the ball's rolling on the straight line, not factors that have an actual effect. So can they serve any explanatory purpose? Well, they cannot explain the emergence or the continuation of the straight course of the rolling ball. But they can explain the fact—and, of course, it is a fact—that not only does the ball roll on a straight line in the actual set-up, it also sticks more or less to that straight line under the various possible contingencies where disturbance or drift appears. They explain the fact, in other words, that the straight rolling is not something fragile, not something vulnerable to every turn of the wind, but rather a resilient pattern: a pattern that is robust under various contingencies and that can be relied upon to persist.

The resilience explained in this toy example may be a matter of independent experience, as when I discover by induction—and without understanding why—that the ball does keep to the straight line. But equally the resilience may only become salient on recognising the explanatory power of the posts: this, in the way in which the laws that a theory explains, may only become salient in the light of the explanatory theory itself. It does not matter which scenario obtains. In either case the simple fact is that despite their merely standby status, the posts serve to resolve an important matter of explanation. They explain, not why the pattern emerged at a certain time, nor why it continues across a certain range of times, but why it continues across a certain range of contingencies: why it is modally as distinct from temporally persistent.

As a reference to the virtually efficacious posts explains the resilience with which the ball rolls on a straight line, so I suggest that a reference to a merely virtual form of self-regard may explain the resilience with which people maintain certain patterns of behaviour. Imagine a given pattern of human behaviour whose continuation is actually explained by the cultural framing under which people view the relevant situations and by their habit of responding to that framing. Suppose that that pattern of behaviour has the modal property of being extremely robust under various contingencies: say, under the contingency that some individuals peel away and offer an example of an alternative pattern. The factors that explain its actually continuing may not explain this robustness or resilience; there may be no reason, so far as they go, why the example of mutant individuals should not display a new way of viewing the situation, for example, or should not undermine the effects of inertia. So how to explain the resilience of the pattern? Well, one possible explanation would be that were the contingencies envisaged to produce a different pattern of behaviour, the alarm bells of self-interest would ring and self-regarding deliberation would lead most of the mutants and would-be mutants back towards the original pattern.

I said earlier that in all likelihood the thresholds at which people's alarm bells ring, and they begin to think in self-regarding terms, may vary from individual to individual. This means in turn both that a pattern of behaviour may be very resilient in some individuals and less resilient in others and that the individual-level explanations of resilience may not have the same force; they may support different predictions for different individuals. But this variation, of course, need not affect aggregate-level explanation. While allowing for individual differences in self-regard thresholds, for example, we may be confident that across the population as a whole a certain general pattern of behaviour enjoys resilience in relation to a certain degree of drift or disturbance in the producing causes; people's thresholds may generally be low enough to ensure that self-regard will kick in and stablise the pattern.

The analogy with the rolling ball serves to show how in principle the model of virtual self-regard may leave room for the economic explanation, at the level of individual or aggregate, of behaviour that is not actively generated by considerations of self-regard. But it may be useful to illustrate the lesson more concretely.

David Lewis's[11] work on convention is often taken as a first-rate example of how economic explanation can do well in making sense of a phenomenon outside the traditional economic domain of the market. He invokes the fact that conventions often serve to resolve certain problems of coordination; thus the convention of driving on the right (or the left) serves to resolve the coordination problem faced by drivers as they approach one another. But what is supposed to be explained by Lewis's narrative? He is clearly not offering a historical story about the emergence of conventions. And, equally clearly, he is not telling a story about the factors that actually keep the conventions in place; he freely admits that people may not be aware of the coordination problem solved by conventional behaviour and may stick to that behaviour for any of a variety of reasons: reasons of inertia, perhaps, or reasons of principle or ideology that may have grown up around the convention in question.

The best clue to Lewis's explanatory intentions comes in a remark from a later article when he considers the significance of the fact that actually conventional behaviour is mostly produced by blind habit. "An action may be rational, *and may be explained by the agent's beliefs and desires,* even though that action was done by habit, and the agent gave no thought to the beliefs or desires which were his reasons for action. If that habit ever ceased to serve the agent's desire's according to his beliefs, it would at once be overridden and corrected by conscious reasoning."[12] This remark gives support to the view that what Lewis is explaining about convention, by his own lights, is not emergence or continuance but resilience. He implies that the servicing of the agent's—as it happens, self-regarding—desires is not the actual cause of the conventional behaviour but a standby cause: a cause that would take the place of a habit that failed to produce the required behaviour in circumstances where that behaviour continued to be what self-interest required. And if the servicing of self-regard is a standby cause of this kind, then what it is best designed to explain is the resilience, where there is resilience, of the conventional behaviour.

But it is not only the Lewis explanation of conventional behaviour that lends itself to this gloss. Can we explain American slave-holding by reference to economic interests,[13] when slave-holders articulated their duties, and conducted their business, in terms of a more or less religious ideology? Yes, to the extent that we can explain why slave-holding was a very resilient institution up to the time of the Civil War; we can explain why the various mutants and emancipationists never did more than cause a temporary crisis. Can we explain the failure of people to oppose most oppressive states as a product of free-rider reasoning,[14] when it is granted that they generally used other considerations to justify their acquiescence? Yes, so far as the free-riding variety of self-regarding reasoning would have been there to support non-action, to make non-action resilient, in any situation where the other, actual reasons failed to do so and alarms bells rang. Can we invoke considerations of social acceptance to explain people's abiding by certain norms, when I freely grant that it is considerations of a much less prudential kind that keep most people faithful to such norms?[15] Yes, we certainly can. Self-regarding considerations of social acceptance can ensure that normative fidelity is robust or resilient if they come into play whenever someone begins to deviate, or contemplate deviation, and if they serve in such cases to restore or reinforce compliance.

The upshot will be clear. We can make good sense of the economic explanation of culturally framed, uncalculated behaviour in terms of the model of virtual self-regard. That model shows that the assumptions which economists make about the human mind, in particular about human motivation, can be rendered consistent with the assumptions of commonplace, everyday thinking. And it shows that so interpreted, the assumptions motivate a promising and indeed developing program for economic explanation: and explanation, not just in the traditional areas of market behaviour, but across the social world more generally.

I have concentrated on the sort of explanation available in non-market contexts where there is a particular problem about ascribing explicit, rational-choice calculation. But even in areas more closely related to the market, rational-choice theory often opts for explaining resilience rather than emergence or continuance as such. Equilibrium explanation serves to promote the explanation of resilience quite explicitly, for a stable equilibrium is precisely a point or area of resilient convergence; a region such that when individuals drift into behaving in a way that takes them away from it, then, other things being equal, they will be led to correct for this and to return to their original pattern. Not only is resilience the natural *explanandum* for rational-choice theory outside the market context, then; it also has a more general claim on that status.

Resilience and Functionalist Explanation

The problem that I used to motivate my argument about rational-choice theory was that if that theory is taken to explain the emergence or continuance of certain forms of behavior, at least outside the market context, then it faces the problem of an empty black box; the rational choice calculation that would presumably be required to explain the genesis of the behavior is not available to do the required work. It turns out that a similar problem besets the project of functionalist explanation in social choice, as is commonly alleged, and that the best way of construing the project so as to avoid that problem is also to take it to be focused on the explanation of resilience, not emergence or survival.

The biological model of functional explanation suggests that the aim of the functional approach in social science is to explain why certain social traits are to be found in this or that society or institution or whatever, as the biological analogue explains why certain traits are there to be found in this or that species or population. And the availability of a natural selection mechanism to make sense of functional explanation in biology raises the question as to what sort of mechanism underlies functional explanation in social science. The empty black box problem is that for most functional explanations in social science there is no obvious mechanism to cite and that the explanations, therefore, are apparently baseless.[16]

Why do we find religious rituals in various societies? Because they have the function of promoting social solidarity.[17] Why do we find common ideas of time and space, cause and number?[18] Because they serve to make mental contact and social life possible. Why do we find certain peacemaking ceremonies in this or that culture? Because they serve to change the feelings of the hostile parties towards one another.[19]

The problem with all of these bread-and-butter examples of functional explanation is that it is not clear why the fact that the trait in question has the functional effect cited explains why the trait is found there: explains why we find the relevant religious rituals or peacemaking ceremonies or structures of social stratification. It is not clear what mechanism is supposed to operate in the black box that links the functionality of the trait with its existence or persistence. No one supposes that intentional design plays the linking role. The only mechanism that could do so appears to be a mechanism of selection akin to that which is invoked in biology; there may be other mechanisms possible in the abstract but they would not seem to fit these standard sorts of cases.[20] And in most cases there is no evidence of a mechanism of selection having been at work.

There are some examples, it is true, where functional explanation in social science can be backed up by a selectional story. Some economists say that the presence of certain decision-making procedures in various firms can be explained by their being functional in promoting profits, and they back up that explanation with a scenario under which the firms with such procedures, being the firms which do best in profits, are the ones that survive and prosper: they are selected for the presence and effects of those procedures in a competitive market.[21] But it is very implausible to think that such selectional mechanisms are available for social-functional explanation in general.[22] The black box which functionalist thinkers apparently have to postulate is in most cases empty.

But if we can have recourse in the rational-choice case to the notion of a virtual mechanism of self-regard—a mechanism that may not operate under actual circumstances but that would operate under relevant counterfactual conditions—then we can equally well help ourselves in the functionalist case to the notion of a virtual mechanism of selection. The idea would be this. Maybe there has not been any historical selection of a given type of institution for the fact that its instances have a certain beneficial effect. But still it might be worth noting that were the type of institution in question to be in danger of disappearing—say, under disturbance or drift—then a selectional mechanism would be activated that would preserve it against that danger. The institution is not the product of actual selection, so it may be assumed—again, this is the worst-case assumption from our point of view—but it is subject to virtual selection: it would come to be selected in any of a variety of crises that put it under pressure.

The idea here is familiar from biology and extends readily to social science. Suppose we say that a certain trait is adaptive or that the gene responsible for the trait increases the inclusive fitness of the bearer in a certain environment: roughly, it increases the propensity of the bearer to replicate its genes. Just saying that a trait is adaptive does not amount to saying that it has actually been selected for in a historical process. After all, a trait might be adaptive or a trait might come to be adaptive due to a change in the environment, without ever having played a role in causing its bearers to be selected. What has to be true if a trait is adaptive is that were it to be put under pressure—as it will be, of course, under ordinary evolutionary conditions—then it would cause its bearers to be selected: they would stand a better chance of replicating their genes than relevant competitors. Adaptiveness goes with being virtually, if not actually, favoured by selectional processes.[23]

It is easy to imagine virtual selection at work in the social as well as the natural world. Imagine that golf clubs—that is, the institutions—have emerged purely as a matter of contingency and chance: imagine that their popularity and spread has been due entirely to the brute fact that people enjoy swinging strangely designed implements at a solid little ball and seeing how far and how accurately they can hit it. This is to suppose that golf clubs have not actually been selected for in anything like a history of competition with other institutions. Consistently with the absence of any such historical selection, however, what might well be the case is that golf clubs have certain effects—certain functional effects—such that were they to come under any of a variety of pressures, then the fact of having those effects would ensure that they survived the pressure. And if that were the case, then it would be natural to say that though not the beneficiaries of actual selection, golf clubs do enjoy the favour of a virtual process of selection.

The story is not outlandish. For golf clubs do have certain effects that are functional from the point of view of members. They are expensive to run and so generally exclusive of all but the well-to-do. They are accessible from a city base. And they enable the well-to-do in any city or town to make useful business and professional contacts. What better way to establish a business or professional relationship than in the course of a relaxed round of golf? It is plausible, then, that were golf clubs to come under various pressures—were the cost of maintaining them and the cost of membership to rise, for example—still they might be expected to survive; we might not find people leaving the clubs in the numbers that such pressures would normally predict. The members of the clubs would be forced to reconsider their membership in the event of this sort of pressure but that very act of reconsideration would make the functionality of the club visible to them and would reinforce their loyalty, not undermine it. And were some members to leave then it would become clear to them, and to others, that they lost out in doing so.

As it is reasonable to suppose that people display a virtual, if not always an actual, self-regard, so this sort of example shows that it is quite plausible to think that social life is often characterised by virtual processes of selection. Among the institutions of the society, there are many that have functional effects. And while those effects may not give us ground for thinking that the institutions were actually selected for the effects, they may well give us ground for believing that the institutions would be selected under various counterfactual conditions. The institutions are not the beneficiaries of actual selection but they do benefit from virtual selection.

In the example given, the virtual selection depends in part on virtual self-regard, and some may wonder if the two forces are really distinct; they may suggest that virtual selection is one particular pattern to which virtual self-regard gives rise. I don't think this is right, though I have no objection in principle. The causal processes underlying virtual selection may just not be the forces recognised in rational choice theory.

I have elsewhere suggested a functional explanation for the persistence of counter-productively high rates of criminal punishment, for example, that invokes decidedly non-rational forces.[24] The idea is that if legislators reduce rates of punishment, then no matter how beneficial this proves overall, it will lead sooner or later to a crime that would not have been committed without the reduction; that this will cause a hue and cry in the media, public outrage, and a demand on politicians to make some response; and that the only response that will be available to them in the sound-bite or the headline will be to call for a restoration of stiffer penalties. This pattern of interaction involves non-rational as well as rational motives—outrage is scarcely a rational force—and if it obtains, then high sentencing will be assured of virtual selection; it will be fit to survive many challenges that might have been expected to change it.

So what will functionalist theory explain under the hypothesis of virtual selection? Again, I say: resilience. The presence of a process of virtual selection enables us to explain the resilience of various behaviours and institutions by the fact that they have certain functional effects. Maybe we can't explain the historical emergence, or even the historical persistence, of golf clubs by reference to their functional effects for members; maybe there hasn't actually been any systematic selection of golf clubs for the fact of having such effects. But even in that surely unlikely case, we can explain the resilience of golf clubs—as we may come to recognize that resilience in the first place—through identifying those functional effects. We can see that because of serving business and professional members in the way they do, golf clubs are fit to survive any of a variety of challenges; at least for the foreseeable future, they are here to stay.

What is true of golf clubs, if this analysis is right, is likely to be true also of the counter-productively high levels of criminal sentencing that prevail, arguably, in many contemporary societies. Let decisions about criminal sentencing be left in the hands of elected politicians who have an incentive to respond in kind to emotional demands among their constituents; this incentive will be particularly strong, when politicians are not bound by the discipline of the Westminster system to toe a party line. There will then be firm ground for expecting criminal sentences to be lifted to levels at which they can satisfy the public outrage that crime often occasions. When they are lifted to that level, then there will be little chance of reducing the sentences or softening them in any way—even if criminological evidence suggests that such penalties serve no purpose and may even worsen the overall prospect of reducing crime.

The sort of role that I am holding out for functionalist theory is no mere invention of my own. It fits well with the tradition of functionalism in social science. Under the salvation offered to functionalists, the explanation they seek is the sort that would identify and put aside the features that may be expected to come and go in social life and that would catalogue the more or less necessary features that the society or culture displays: those that are resilient and may be expected to survive a variety of contingencies and crises. The tradition of thinking associated with the likes of Durkheim in the last century and Parsons in this is shot through with the desire to separate out in this way the necessary from the contingent, the reliable from the ephemeral. The idea in every case is to look for the core features of a society and to distinguish them from the marginal and peripheral. Functionalist method is cast throughout the tradition as a means of providing "a basis—albeit an assumptive basis—for sorting out 'important' from unimportant social processes."[25]

Conclusion

We have seen that both rational-choice theory and functionalist theory make good sense if they are each presented as focused on the explanation of the resilience of certain social phenomena, rather than the explanation of their emergence or even survival. The upshot is a way of viewing each enterprise that makes it inherently attractive, and attractive even to those who are adherents of the other, or adherents of neither. We could hardly have asked for more.

NOTES

1. Pace Lewis, *Plurality of Worlds.*
2. Pettit, *Republicanism.*
3. Pettit, *Common Mind.*
4. Montesquieu, *Considerations.*
5. Brennan and Buchanan, "Normative Purpose."
6. Pettit, *Republicanism,* ch.7.
7. Mandeville, *Free Thoughts,* p. 332
8. For more see Pettit, *Common Mind,* Part 3; *Rules,* Part 2.
9. Pettit, *Rules,* Part 2
10. Brennan and Pettit, *Economy of Esteem.*
11. Lewis, *Convention.*
12. Lewis, *Philosophical Papers,* p. 181, my emphasis.
13. Fogel and Engermann, *Time on the Cross,* p. 4.
14. North, *Structure and Change,* pp. 31–32.
15. Brennan and Pettit, *Economy of Esteem,* Part 3.
16. Elster, *Ulysses.*
17. Durkheim, *Elementary Forms.*
18. Durkheim, *Elementary Forms*; Lukes, *Durkheim,* p. 442.
19. Radcliffe-Brown, *Andaman Islanders,* pp. 238–39.
20. Van Parijs, *Evolutionary Explanation.*
21. Alchian "Uncertainty"; Nelson and Winter, *Evolutionary Theory.*
22. Pettit, *Common Mind,* pp. 155–63.
23. Cf. Bigelow and Pargetter, "Functions."
24. Pettit, "Criminal Justice."
25. Turner and Maryanski, *Functionalism,* p. 135

BIBLIOGRAPHY

Alchian, A. A. "Uncertainty, Evolution and Economic Theory." *Journal of Political Economy* 58 (1950): 211–21.
Bigelow, J., and R. Pargetter. "Functions." *Journal of Philosophy* 34 (1987): 181–96.
Brennan, G., and J. Buchanan. "The Normative Purpose of Economic 'Science':

Rediscovery of an Eighteenth-Century Method." *International Review of Law and Economics* 1 (1981): 155–66.

Brennan, G., and P. Pettit. *The Economy of Esteem: An Essay on Civil and Political Society.* Oxford, Oxford University Press, 2004.

Durkheim, E. *The Elementary Forms of the Religious Life.* New York, Free Press, 1948.

Elster, J. *Ulysses and The Sirens.* Cambridge, Cambridge University Press, 1979.

Fogel, R. W., and L. S. Engermann. *Time on the Cross: The Economics of American Negro Slavery.* Boston, Little, Brown and Company (Inc.), 1974.

Lewis, D. *Convention.* Cambridge, Mass., Harvard University Press, 1969.

Lewis, D. K. *On the Plurality of Worlds.* Oxford, Blackwell, 1986.

Lewis, D. *Philosophical Papers,* Vol 1. Oxford, Oxford University Press, 1983.

Lukes, S. *Émile Durkheim: His Life and Work: A Historical and Critical Study.* Harmondsworth, Middlesex, Penguin Books Ltd., 1973.

Mandeville, B. *Free Thoughts on Religion, the Church and National Happiness.* London, 1731.

Montesquieu, B. d. *Considerations sur les causes de la grandeur des Romains et de leur decadence.* Gonzague Truc, ed. Paris, 1967.

Nelson, R., and S. Winter. *An Evolutionary Theory of Economic Change.* Cambridge, Mass., Harvard University Press, 1982.

North, D. *Structure and Change in Economic History.* New York, Norton, 1981.

Pettit, P. *The Common Mind: An Essay on Psychology, Society and Politics,* paperback edition 1996. New York, Oxford University Press, 1993.

Pettit, P. "Is Criminal Justice Politically Feasible?" *Buffalo Criminal Law Review,* Special Issue ed. by Pablo de Greiff 5(2) (2002): 427–50.

Pettit, P. *Republicanism: A Theory of Freedom and Government.* Oxford, Oxford University Press, 1997.

Pettit, P. *Rules, Reasons, and Norms: Selected Essays.* Oxford, Oxford University Press, 2002.

Radcliffe-Brown, A. R. *The Andaman Islanders.* Glencoe, Ill., Free Press, 1948.

Turner, J. H., and A. Maryanski. *Functionalism.* Menlo Park, California, The Benjamin/Cummings Publishing Co., 1979.

Van Parijs, P. *Evolutionary Explanation in the Social Sciences.* London, Tavistock, 1981.

Part II

Contingency's Challenge

Chapter 4

Events as Causes
The Case of American Politics

David R. Mayhew

In explaining American politics, political scientists tend to follow a path that is normal for social scientists:[1] We reach for causes that are seen to be basic, underlying, or long-term rather than ones that are proximate, contingent, or short-term. Institutions, social forces, and enduring incentives tend to win attention as factors. Thus a good deal of scholarship assigns causal status to such phenomena as economic self-interest,[2] the interests of social classes,[3] party identification,[4] electoral realignment coalitions,[5] the American liberal tradition,[6] long-lasting party ideologies,[7] social capital,[8] political decisions that are said to attain a kind of constitutional standing,[9] congressional folkways,[10] fixed institutions such as congressional rules,[11] long-lived cleavage patterns in congressional roll call voting,[12] the American separation-of-powers system,[13] political movements that take a long time gaining momentum,[14] political party platforms that carry through many years,[15] and political "moods" that exhibit considerable durability.[16]

The Significance of Events

It would be a foolish political science that did not pursue causal factors like these. Yet as a collective explanatory enterprise, the profession may be under-investing in factors that are proximate, short-term, or contingent. I will make a case here for *events* as such explanatory factors. It may be answered that coverage of this sort of thing should be left to historians (of whom some, although not all, have emphasized short-term or contingent factors; imagine a dimension with A. J. P. Taylor at the short-term or contingent pole, Lewis Namier at the long-term or underlying pole, and Fernand Braudel making an appearance at both poles). Yet arguably the first aim of all us should be to provide satisfying causal accounts, regardless of our disciplinary locations or their boundaries.

Let me offer an example of a blinkered explanation brought on by a focus on underlying or long-term factors. In 1940, Paul F. Lazarsfeld and his associates undertook voter research that employed a pioneering panel study that ran from May through November of that year and emanated in *The People's Choice.*[17] To be probed were such matters as "cross pressures," an "index of political predisposition," a "reinforcement effect," "socio-economic status" (or "SES"), and "intentions at variance with their [the voters'] social environments"—that is, a variety of embellishments on an underlying theme of social determinism.[18] Then in May of that year the Nazis invaded France, in June they defeated France, and in September they came close to defeating Britain. Here was a chance for the Columbia University researchers to tear up their interview schedule. They could have accommodated head-on one of the richest environments of politically relevant events imaginable. Americans, so far as one can tell from casual evidence (consider the lore about Edward R. Murrow's radio reports) and single-shot commercial surveys, were riveted by the European disasters and their implications for this country. How do events of this nature and magnitude play into an election campaign?

Undeterred, the Columbia researchers carried on to their social-deterministic conclusion for which *The People's Choice* is well known. So far as one can tell, they did not ask any direct questions about voter reactions to these ominous events, the government's handling of them, or the candidates' capacity to handle them.[19] These were of course first-rate, serious scholars. They do present an event timeline for the 1940 campaign season, and they offer in passing some fascinating if scanty material: Voters apparently surged to President Roosevelt that year *during June when France was falling*—"mainly on the ground that the European crisis necessitated the continuance of an experienced administration in Washington."[20] But this result is presented as an aside rather than a fundamental finding, and it would probably be hard to find anyone who remembers it. Events are again off-message in the Columbia team's work on the 1948 election, *Voting,*[21] where the authors do not take seriously, for example, the Berlin airlift. That gripping exercise of American triumphalism, which I can recall myself from newsreels showing the big planes taking off and landing, extended through the last months of the 1948 campaign when Truman was apparently gaining his edge. Did it make a difference? In political science, the question is understudied. Rare is the account of the 1948 election that does it justice.[22]

Possibly events have been making a better showing in more recent scholarship than they once did. Wars, for example, have come to figure as dummy variables in time-series analyses of voting behavior.[23] Events during election campaigns and as determinants of public opinion have received attention.[24] Droughts and even shark attacks are said to move voters.[25] Crises and disasters have been broached as motors of policy change.[26] Even so, the case that events are under-investigated still seems valid.

A conceptual discussion is in order. What is an "event"? To use a very commonsensical formulation, an event is something that happens. Most events are irrelevant to the discussion here. In principle, the relevant events are ones that can change a political context by generating a new sense among publics or policymakers about what is important in public affairs, what problems need to be solved, what relevant causal stories are credible, or simply what should be valued or done. I do not see any clear criterion for deciding how elongated an "event" should be allowed to be. Here, I would like to accommodate, at least in principle, both quick happenings such as assassinations or earthquakes and lengthier ones such as wars or depressions that are perhaps better thought of as sets of events.

In tune with the theme of contingency, I will dwell here on "chance events"[27]—that is, ones that are contingent in the sense of being unpredicted or unpredictable. Not all events are chance events. The sun comes up every morning. American national elections, which are events, have been held regularly every two years since 1788. Elections are the obvious exhibit for the case that political scientists *do* study events—over and over again. Although American elections, at least in the sense they that do in fact regularly occur, are not chance events, they bear an interesting relation to chance events. They can take on an aspect of chance events in the sense that their results are often unexpected, even sometimes dramatically unexpected, and this can be interesting and important. For one thing, voters may correct later for an electoral "surprise."[28] For another, it is a good bet that an astonishing result like the Republican takeover of the Senate in 1980 can give a new incumbent party more temporary policy leeway that it might otherwise enjoy based on the bare congressional membership numbers. But even when an election result is more or less foreseen (thus taking the election out of the realm of chance events), voters are of course free to use the occasion of an election to channel their reactions to *earlier* chance events, as did voters, to cite a classic instance, who were weary of the course of the Great Depression in 1932.

Chance, contingency, and unexpectedness are not unproblematic ideas. Unexpected by whom? The catastrophic earthquakes that roiled the politics of Nicaragua in 1972 and Mexico in 1985 were a surprise to everybody. The attack on Pearl Harbor in 1941 was unexpected by Americans, but not by the Japanese government. Audience needs to be considered. For the most part, I will deal here with happenings that came along and surprised the U.S. government, this country's political elite, and most of American society. That is ordinarily the profile of, for example, strikes, domestic violence, and economic depressions. They are unexpected. The attacks on Pearl Harbor in 1941 and the Trade Center in 2001 were, from the American vantage point, unexpected. But "events" in the broad definition used here are of course themselves caused, like everything else, and the U.S. government can in principle itself be a cause as it was in the invasions of Mexico in 1846 and Iraq in 2003. I want to include American wars as events (or sets of events). In what sense are wars "chance events?" For one thing, all of them probably come as something of a jolt to American society even if the government initiates them. More important, wars have their own dynamics: As they go on, regardless of how they started, they are capable of generating unexpected new problems (as in the uncontrolled looting in Iraq in 2003), new causal stories (as in the idea that George W. Bush and Tony Blair lied their way into the Iraq war), and new preferences (as in the new American antipathy toward the French and vice versa). It is true that other kinds of government action might in principle qualify as "events" as defined here. The passage of the Kansas-Nebraska Act of 1854, for example, was a surprise development (given the expectations of, say, a year earlier) that roiled American society through engendering a new mix of perceived problems, causal stories, and preferences: It smelled of a southern slave-power conspiracy.[29] It rivaled Nicaragua's and Mexico's earthquakes in its political consequences. But in the body of this chapter I will steer clear of government-induced "events" with the complex and partial exception of wars.

What is a "cause"? In political affairs, a search for conditions that are anything like both necessary and sufficient, as in water boiling at 212 degrees, is probably fruitless. Here, I use the explanatory customs of historians as my chief guide to causation. In principle, the sense of "cause" I try to employ is: An X (that, is a politically relevant event) was a cause of a Y (any of a range of specified states of affairs) if it was a major contributory cause, and at least a necessary cause, of Y happening at least during the time frame it did and possibly at all. These requirements are perhaps modest in the sense that they allow ample room for additional causes. Even if an event was an important cause of a Y, a range of other things, ordinarily some of them "underlying," may have figured importantly or even necessarily in the explanatory mix too. But these requirements are not trivial: "Necessary" means exactly that,[30] and "major contributory" follows the conventional historians' practice of assigning relative importance to causes.[31]

In a statistical sense, no difficulty seems to arise, at least in principle, in juxtaposing events as causes to "underlying" factors as causes. The economic historian Robert W. Fogel, for example, has presented an interesting model mixing the two kinds of factors.[32] In a philosophical sense, these are of course deep waters. But in a practical sense, it is hard to see how the blend can be avoided. Causal factors that are obviously promising can range from the deeply underlying to the starkly proximate. Take the Spanish election of the spring of 2004 won by the Socialists. No doubt party identifications tracing back generations and regional antipathies tracing back centuries need to be adduced to explain this electoral pattern and outcome, as do many other considerations, but one factor has to be the election-eve demolition of the Madrid trains by Islamic fundamentalists. For another example, deep-seated party and ideological loyalties were probably fierce in the American North in the mid-1860s, but, so far as one can tell, absent General Sherman's victory in Atlanta in September 1864, the presidential election of the November of that year would have gone to the Democrat George B. McClellan and possibly been followed by an immediate armistice that preserved southern slavery. "The impact of this event [the capture of Atlanta] cannot be exaggerated."[33]

Below I offer some evidence on these matters that is suggestive and I hope thought-provoking even if it is selective and short of clinchingly systematic. It is drawn from American history back through 1789. For the most part, it centers on complex and extended events rather than simple and brief ones—the chief exhibits being entire wars (rather than, say, individual battles) and sometimes prolonged economic recessions or depressions. This is not to deny the importance of jolts like the battle of Atlanta. But a jolt-centered treatment covering two centuries might end up unduly anecdotal, at least on current readily available evidence. With larger events it is possible to aim for at least an ingredient of systematicness. Also, in the realm of *effects* I emphasize long-lasting rather than short-term ones (although not to the complete exclusion of the latter). This is on grounds of importance but also, in the case of wars, non-obviousness: It is a dog-bites-man story, for example, that wars cause the raising of troops and the short-term expenditure of immense money. Particular attention will be given here to *long-term electoral effects* (that is, not just the outcomes of single elections) and *long-term policy effects* (that is, ones that have lasted for decades or generations).

TABLE 4.1

Surge and Interactive Realignment in Presidential Elections, 1836–1964

Year	Presidential Candidates[a]		Democratic Vote		Republican Vote[b]	
	Democrat	Republican (or Whig)	Surge	Interaction	Surge	Interaction
1836	**Van Buren**	(3 Whigs)		5.65	*	*
1840	**Van Buren**	Harrison	−3.61		*	*
1844	Polk	**Clay**			*	*
1848	**Cass**	Taylor	−5.59		*	*
1852	Pierce	**Scott**			*	*
1856	**Buchanan**	Fremont			*	*
1860	**Douglas**	Lincoln		2.80	*	*
1864	McClellan	**Lincoln**		1.65	*	*
1868	Seymour	**Grant**	+6.09			
1872	Greeley	**Grant**				
1876	Tilden	**Hayes**	+1.45		−4.68	
1880	Hancock	**Garfield**				
1884	Cleveland	**Blaine**				
1888	**Cleveland**	Harrison				
1892	Cleveland	**Harrison**				
1896	**Bryan**	McKinley			+5.16	
1900	Bryan	**McKinley**				
1904	Parker	**Roosevelt**		1.14		
1908	Bryan	**Taft**				
1912	Wilson	**Taft**				
1916	**Wilson**	Hughes				
1920	**Cox**	Harding	−1.77		+7.73	
1924	Davis	**Coolidge**				
1928	Smith	**Hoover**		1.92		
1932	Roosevelt	**Hoover**	+16.28		−11.33	
1936	**Roosevelt**	Landon				1.20
1940	**Roosevelt**	Willkie				
1944	**Roosevelt**	Dewey				
1948	**Truman**	Dewey	−8.20	1.15		
1952	**Sevenson**	Eisenhower			+2.47	1.26
1956	Stevenson	**Eisenhower**				
1960	Kennedy	**Nixon**	+1.30			
1964	**Johnson**	Goldwater		2.06	−2.45	1.16

[a] The candidate of the incumbent party is in **boldface**.
[b] Values for the Republican party cannot be calculated before 1868.

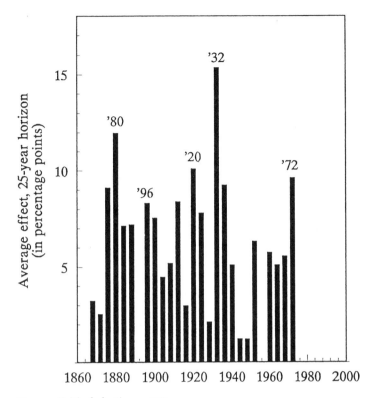

Fig. 4.1. Critical elections, 1868–1972

Long-Term Electoral Effects

Of help here are two exhibits—see Table 4.1 and Figure 4.1. These are two exceptionally interesting windows into American electoral history afforded by the work of other political scientists—Jerome M. Clubb, William H. Flanigan, and Nancy H. Zingale (hereafter CF&Z) in the case of Table 4.1, Larry M. Bartels in the case of Figure 4.1.[34] The exhibits are antiseptic in the sense that the authors prepared the underlying datasets innocent of the questions I am pursuing in this chapter. The authors cover different time spans—1836 through 1964 in CF&Z, 1868 through 1972 in Bartels—and their methodologies differ, but they address the same question: To what degree has each of the country's presidential elections (at least those during the stipulated time spans) been associated with realigning electoral change? That is, in the sense of voter coalitional patterns, to what degree has each election been a hinge-point separating the electoral past (a sequence of previous elections) from the electoral future (a sequence of succeeding elections)?

Of the statistical methodologies employed, suffice it to say that both authors use presidential election returns at the *state* level as their data base, and that both authors accommodate both *surge* and *interactive* electoral change (to use terms from CF&Z). For an intuitive sense of surge change, imagine a pattern in which each of the American states shifts 10 percent in a Democratic direction in election year B as compared to the previous election year A, and in which the earlier (A) result indexes the past and the later (B) result indexes the future. The durable Democratic party success of 1932 comes to mind. For a sense of interactive change, imagine a pattern in which half the states switch 10 percent in a Democratic direction and the other half 10 percent in a Republican direction, yet despite the considerable disruption in cleavage there is no (necessary) net national party percentage change between elections years A and B (and, again, each of the results indexes an extended past or future). In 1836, to cite an example, at a time when party identifications were early and fluid, the Democrats' nomination of the northerner Martin Van Buren to succeed the southerner Andrew Jackson (who had run in the three preceding elections) brought a major lasting regional reconfiguration of the vote without upsetting the overall party balance very much. That sort of pattern should arguably count as "realignment" too. In both the CF&Z and the Bartels analysis, any individual presidential election can be associated with various degrees of both surge and interactive change. One more set of guidelines is needed. Bartels provides a summary realignment value (he calls it "average effect, 25-year horizon") for each of his elections. These values are easily readable in the bar graph of 4.1. CF&Z, since they code separately for surge and interactive change, and also for each of the major parties (due to third parties, one major party's record is not just the mirror image of the other's), provide a potential *four* realignment values for each election—Democratic surge change, Democratic interactive change, Republican surge change, and Republican interactive change. For CF&Z, surge change can take a plus or a minus sign, whereas interactive change does not take a sign. Thus in Table 4.1, the FDR-Hoover election of 1932 is associated with a large positive Democratic surge (+16.28%) and a large negative Republican surge (−11.33%). The Van Buren election of

1836 is associated with sizable Democratic interactive change (5.65%). The CF&Z values listed in Table 4.1 are the ones the authors considered worth reporting.

Once past these complexities, Table 4.1 and Figure 4.1 are simple enough to read. Look for the high values—that is, let us say, the figures greater than 4.0 (whether preceded by a plus or a minus sign) in any of the columns of Table 4.1, and the eight tallest bars in Figure 4.1. From one exhibit or the other, and leaving aside rankings among the included instances, that winnowing yields the elections of 1848, 1868, 1876, 1880, 1896, 1912, 1920, 1932, 1936, 1948, and 1972. What explains the high realignment performances in these cases? Two general themes seem to emerge, both involving extended events. Depressions are one obvious theme. It was not only in 1932 that a presidential election followed three years of excruciating depression that had allowed an incumbent party to show its governing wares and line up for a prolonged voter penalty. That seems to have happened also—or at least it is a good part of the picture—in 1876 and 1896 following the downturns of 1873 and 1893—respectively the third and second worst depressions in American history. This American experience has not been unique. The slump of 1929 and also apparently that of 1893 brought electoral hinge-points elsewhere in the world.[35]

Depressions and recessions have also shaped the historical profile of congressional midterm elections. In party seat holdings, probably most —one exception is 1994—of the hinge-points in House midterm history have followed on economic slumps. Additional considerations have often figured in these instances, but economics has ranked high. In the wake of the economic crisis of 1857, the midterm of 1858 ushered in sixteen years of Republican control.[36] After the downturn of 1873, the midterm of 1874 ushered in a Democratic majority that prevailed for sixteen of the next twenty years.[37] The depression-ridden midterms of 1894 and 1930 each brought another sixteen-year string of, respectively, Republican and Democratic control—although, in a peculiar detour, the ruling New Deal Democrats lost eighty seats and effective *policy* control of the House in the midterm of 1938 following the sharp economic contraction of 1937–38— which was "in terms of speed if not duration . . . the most serious in the nation's history."[38] A cross-party conservative coalition ordinarily dominated the House for some sixteen years beginning in 1938. Finally, the midterm of 1958, held during a serious recession, brought major Democratic gains in seat holdings—both Senate and House—that greased that party's lawmaking enterprises later in the 1960s. The pattern in all the instances cited above—both presidential and congressional elections— is of a lasting negative electoral surge whacking the party holding the presidency.

To return to the high-value presidential elections, another theme seems to be wars—or, more precisely, wars combined with their often disruptive immediate aftermaths. In four of the instances drawn from Table 4.1 or Figure 4.1, a high-value realigning contest was the first presidential election to be held in the wake of a major war and its near aftermath—the 1848 election following the War with Mexico and its quickly resulting tension between North and South sparked by the Wilmot Proviso (would the newly acquired territories permit slavery?)[39]; the 1868 election following the Civil War and its aftermath of Reconstruction; the 1920 election following World War I and its ensuing strikes, red scare, and economic turmoil; and the election of 1948 following World War II.

Let it be admitted that this statistical pattern is not perfect. It *is* perfect in the case of the CF&Z analysis, where *all seven* of the especially high-value realigning elections between 1836 and 1964 (omitting the initial regional shakeup in 1836) succeeded either depressions (three instances) or wars (four instances). But the Bartels analysis offers only spotty support: It does not reach back to the election of 1848, and it does not highlight those of 1868 or 1948, although it does highlight that of 1920 and also that of 1972—the contentious Nixon-McGovern contest that occurred during the wind-down phase of the Vietnam War.

It is perhaps best to leave 1868 and 1948 to the realm of speculation. Yet note the existence of promising general logics that might animate any such speculation. That is, it is easy to imagine how wars and their aftermaths might crystallize new long-lasting voter coalitional patterns. Wars can trigger lasting policy changes that prove to be either popular or unpopular, in a general sense, or that beget both winners and losers (as with the North and South in 1865). Wars can engender lasting disagreement about whether they should have been fought in the first place (as with the Vietnam War). Wars can refashion electorates—as in the whirl of enfranchisement (of blacks) and disfranchisement (of southern whites) that followed the Civil War. Wars and their aftermaths are probably unexcelled breeders of "valence issues"—that is, issues centering on government competence and management. Little is deadlier for a ruling party than a reputation for poor performance, and it is a plausible bet that such stigmas can endure. Consider, although the example is not war-related, the

Hoover taint attaching to Republicans after 1932, or possibly the Carter taint attaching to Democrats after 1980.[40] Finally, wars can generate major new issues that cut electorates in new ways and that prove to be long lasting. Thus the War with Mexico ignited the controversy over slavery expansion. That new late-1840s discord, according to one interpretation, "marked the beginning of sectional strife which for a quarter of a century would subject American nationalism to its severest testing."[41] The Civil War brought a battery of enduring Reconstruction questions and issues. The experience of World War II, dramatizing as it did the hypocrisy of fighting racism abroad while accommodating it at home, lofted civil rights to prime issue status for the first time since the 1870s. Civil rights had not been a New Deal issue. At the electoral level, it became a leading postwar one courtesy of President Truman in 1946 and the Democratic national convention of 1948.[42] The experience of the Vietnam War injected a still evident hawk versus dove cleavage into American elections.

If lay-down cases exist for the idea that wars have spurred realigning change, these cases are probably the election of 1816 following the War of 1812 and that of 1920 following World War I. The 1816 instance has not entered the discussion yet, since it occurred at a time when elections were not yet producing returns suitable for modern datasets. But the case is strong. Here is the story. Four years previously, in 1812, and a few months into the War of 1812, the Federalist candidate had fallen only one state short of winning that year's presidential election through an able blend of position and valence appeals (the war shouldn't have been fought in the first place; why are the British occupying Detroit?). The Federalists were doing well.[43] But then they foot-dragged on the war effort to the point of near treason, the war closed in a surprising burst of victory and nationalistic enthusiasm, and the discredited Federalists performed dismally in the election of 1816 and never ran a candidate again.[44] They were "the most conspicuous casualty of the War of 1812."[45] A war, in short, can put a party out of business—which is one way to affect coalitional alignments.

As for the election of 1920, the disastrous defeat suffered by the ruling Democrats that year has been under-analyzed. Probably the leading interpretation is a dubious teleological case that the Democrats, that era's natural minority party, were *destined* to lose power somehow once the fluky Wilson presidency was out of the way. This view downplays not only the impressive Democratic gains of 1912 (the multi-party contest that produced Wilson) but also the preceding midterm landslide of 1910. But no matter. The destined/fluke interpretation ignores the magnitude and durability of the later Democratic slide: Never otherwise since 1789 has a major American party been bested by consecutive margins of 26, 25, and 17 percent as were the Democrats in 1920, 1924, and 1928.[46] It ignores events. The war itself and its explosive aftermath—strikes, international revolution, a red scare, a rocky economy, the League of Nations wrangle—brought a dream-world of position- and valence-issue material that an opposition party could dwell on for a long time. And it ignores the corresponding fates of parties or party systems elsewhere in the Allied Anglophone world. In Canada, farmer and labor uprisings in the wake of World War I seem to have permanently broadened that country's party system from two-party to multi-party.[47] In Australia, it is said that the burden associated with managing the war penalized the Labor party for a quarter century.[48] In Britain, that burden seems to have demoted the Liberal party from major-party status permanently.[49] It is as if they had been "run over by a bus."[50] It should be no surprise that the American Democrats suffered.[51]

Depression and war interpretations do not exhaust the high-value instances in Table 4.1 and Figure 4.1 (notably, the election of 1912 remains unaccounted for), but a word is in order on the ordinarily uncelebrated election of 1880 that spikes so high in the Bartels data. Events, albeit of a different sort, seem to have played a role there too. The crumbling of Reconstruction in the South in the 1870s took the form of, among other things, a sequence of events. The spasms of guerrilla violence that undercut the northern military occupation of Louisiana in 1874, Mississippi in 1875, and South Carolina in 1876 seem to have transfixed the country and fed into electoral patterns in the midterm of 1874 as well as the presidential elections of 1876 and 1880.[52] A national reaction amounting to Reconstruction fatigue apparently aided the Democrats, and, more directly, the surge to white supremacy in the Deep South affected voting patterns there. Yet at the presidential level the southern lunge toward immense Democratic majorities did not occur until 1880 in Florida, Louisiana, and South Carolina—the southern states where Army-fortified Republicans still controlled the count in 1876 and indeed swung the national result to Hayes that year by way of their counting. As well as possibly a complicated farewell to Reconstruction in general, the 1880 reading in the Bartels analysis picks up these extraordinary southern vote swings between 1876 and 1880. In general as regards that era, guerrilla uprisings could be consequential events, too.

Long-Term Policy Effects

I want to dwell on wars in this section, since the policy consequences of American depressions are relatively well-worked terrain, but I will start with depressions. Actually, that means largely *the* Great Depression of 1929, since no government before that time attacked a depression with anything like the policy ambition of the 1930s. The Democrats in power during 1893–94, for example, put strenuous effort into repealing the Sherman Silver Purchase Act of 1890 as an anti-depression move, and enacted a new income tax as government revenue plummeted, but did little else.[53] In the case of the Great Depression, a simple and convincing reading is: No depression, no New Deal. Absent the Great Depression, we do not know that anything like the New Deal would ever have happened in American history. A few years ago I attended a conference where the historian of the 1930s William Leuchtenburg speculated that in retrospect, at least in terms of its political economy, the New Deal may have been a "neomercantilist aberration."

For analytic purposes, it may help to sort the policy yield of the New Deal era into three categories.[54] The first category addresses policy innovations that proved to be *temporary* rather than long-term in their effects, but the boundaries here can be blurry and items like these should perhaps be mentioned since they are familiar. A plausible list of major innovations that had temporary effects, all of them relief or recovery moves, might be: the National Industrial Recovery Act (NIRA) of 1933, the Federal Emergency Relief Act (FERA) of 1933, and, in terms of agencies, the Reconstruction Finance Corporation (RFC) in 1932 during Hoover's presidency, the Public Works Administration (PWA) in 1933, the Civilian Conservation Corps (CCC) in 1933, and the Works Progress Administration (WPA) in 1935.

The second category addresses innovations that aimed at economic recovery, relief, the renovation of reeling institutions, or management otherwise of the depression emergency—their adoption would have been most unlikely absent such justifications—but which have stayed in effect permanently (in most cases with revisions) or at least through several succeeding generations after the 1930s. This list would likely include the Agricultural Adjustment Act (AAA) of 1933 inaugurating government crop supports, the Glass-Steagall Act of 1933 reorganizing the banking industry, the Federal Deposit Insurance Corporation (FDIC) of 1933 insuring bank accounts, the Federal Housing Administration (FHA) of 1934 insuring home mortgages, the Securities Act of 1933 and the Securities Exchange Act of 1934 regulating the discredited securities industry, the abandonment of the gold standard as documented in the Gold Reserve Act of 1934, and unemployment insurance and "welfare," as it later became known, as provisions of the Social Security Act of 1935. Possibly the list should include the Reciprocal Trade Agreements Act (RTAA) of 1934, this country's decisive shift away from high protective tariffs: "The legislative history shows that the State Department mainly sold the bill as something which would help recovery through the promotion of exports."[55] Also on the list would be major tax hikes of the early 1930s as the federal and state governments desperately strove to balance their budgets in the face of vanishing revenue. At the federal level, that meant the progressive-flavored Revenue Act of 1932 signed by Hoover—the principal federal tax increase of the decade. In the state of California, which has received recent study, it meant an emergency switch to highly elastic sales and personal income taxes that, in an unexpected turn, funded the immense expansion of that state's public sector during succeeding generations.[56]

Included in the third category are policy innovations that proved to be long-lasting but that do not seem to have been chiefly justified by reference to emergency depression conditions—or in fact to owe their adoption to any such justification. They came about mainly for a different reason. A political opening supplied by the depression made them possible. The business community was temporarily delegitimized. A traumatized public opinion was indifferent or amenable. Democratic party ranks soared above 300 in the House and as high as 75 in the Senate. Left-liberal interests and activists took up cherished causes that they would likely have pursued in virtually any economic context, given the chance. Here was the chance. Moves in this category would arguably include the Norris–La Guardia Act of 1932 curbing labor injunctions and outlawing yellow-dog contracts, the Tennessee Valley Authority (TVA) in 1933, the Wagner Act of 1935 prescribing collective-bargaining procedures in private industry,[57] the familiar pensions component of the Social Security Act of 1935, the Public Utilities Holding Company Act of 1935 breaking up the large utility empires, and the Fair Labor Standards Act (FLSA) of 1938 establishing a minimum wage.

As is well known, the New Deal years generated a formidable array of policy moves that stuck. Those documented here in categories two and three were depression-driven moves, through one causal route or another.

So far as one can tell: No depression, no moves. Certainly it is plausible that many of the included moves, or something like them, would have come about at some point since the 1930s somehow anyway. Pensions? Securities regulation? A break for the unions? A break for the farmers? These are good candidates, but we do not know when or in what form, and we really do not know whether.

As for American wars, they seem to be under-appreciated by political scientists—although not by economists or historians—as generators of major policy innovations that stuck.[58] Five general policy categories plus certain scattered items are worth mentioning. The first is taxes. The federal revenue system has been overwhelmingly a product of wars. The Civil War brought a high protective tariff—originating as an emergency revenue source in 1861—as well as duties on alcohol, tobacco, and certain luxuries that saw the government through half a century.[59] World War I brought serious progressive taxation—personal income tax rates in the high brackets that have never fallen anywhere near pre-1916 levels since that war, plus corporate and inheritance taxes.[60] World War II brought mass-based progressive taxation. The personal income tax was "dramatically expanded" in the early 1940s through widening its reach (the share of the workforce paying taxes rose from 7 percent before the war to 64 percent afterwards), raising marginal rates (the top bracket rate rose to 94 percent during the war), and pay-as-you-go withholding.[61] The Current Tax Payment Act of 1943, which established the pay-as-you-go procedure, must rank as one of the most lastingly consequential statutes ever enacted on any subject.[62] In general, the federal government has lived off World War II's lucrative tax design for the six ensuing decades. For a time, at any rate, there seems to have been a progressive redistributive effect, as was noted by Douglass C. North in 1966: "It is not at all clear that New Deal measures provided any significant redistribution of income. . . . The really significant fall [in income inequality] is clearly related to the high progressive tax rates imposed during World War II."[63] Taking American history as a whole, and leaving aside the special payroll withholding scheme associated with Social Security, which seems to enjoy wide approval as a contributory insurance device, there is little evidence that Americans have ever relished financing anything at the federal level except wars—and the wartime taxes have tended to stick.

A second category is the protective tariff. American trade policy has undergone endless variation, but three major duty-raising junctures involved wars—one at the outset of a war (the long-lived Civil War tariff has been mentioned), the other two in the wakes of wars. In a burst of nationalism following the War of 1812, Congress constructed a new high-tariff regime to shield industries nourished during that war, notably cotton textiles, that now fell vulnerable to British competition.[64] A similar burst of nationalism helped spur a record high tariff in the wake of World War I by way of the Emergency Tariff Act of 1921 and the Fordney-McCumber Tariff of 1922. War-nourished industries needed to be shielded again; this time they notably included a brand-new chemical industry. Metals and ores were now seen to need protection for defense reasons. A new array of assertive trade associations induced into existence by the government during the war now invested the national capital. Farmers signed on as postwar conditions ruined crop prices. In general, despite a good deal of wrangling over specifics in the legislative process of the early 1920s, "the necessity of protection was hardly challenged."[65]

A third category is suffrage expansion. It is well-known that the Civil War paved the way to the Fifteenth Amendment enfranchising African-Americans—a policy change that "stuck" in the northern and border states although of course the South was another matter. But there is more to be said. World War II brought another dose of small but real progress for southern blacks by way of the Soldier Voting Act of 1942 and a Supreme Court strikedown of the white primary in 1944 (indexing, it is said, the country's changing opinion on race during the war). In general, "The equilibrium [of black disfranchisement] in voting laws was decisively disrupted by World War II."[66] Later on, the Vietnam War left a deposit of teen-age voting.[67] Perhaps least appreciated is the role of World War I in the achievement of women's suffrage in 1920 by way of the Nineteenth Amendment. It is a surefire bet that women's suffrage would have won out in the United States sooner or later. A powerful movement was under way in the 1910s. The time seemed ripe. But movements can falter. Women in Switzerland had to wait until 1971. In fact, energetic contributions by American women to the wartime mobilization seem to have brought the proximate winning argument. Suffrage extension was "necessary to the successful prosecution of the war," President Wilson came to argue; "We have made partners of the women in this war."[68] The United States did not act alone. Women won the vote in many countries during World War I or its near aftermath, evidently through a logic of wartime contribution or various other democratizing impulses associated with war. The instances include Britain (for women over thirty), Canada, Germany, Austria, Czechoslovakia, Belgium, the Netherlands, and Sweden (the last two countries were neutrals, but the war could have spillover effects). Women in France, Italy, Hungary, and Japan had to wait until the close of World War II when apparently the same logics operated.[69] In general, in American history, wars have been a major engine of electoral democracy.

Related is a fourth policy category, race relations. In addition to the Fifteenth Amendment, it is of course fundamental that the Civil War levered the Emancipation Proclamation and the Thirteenth Amendment abolishing slavery as well as the Fourteenth Amendment guaranteeing individual rights against the states. World War II seems to have been critical to race policy in a different way. Immediately, it did not produce a great deal of policy change that proved durable (FDR's Committee on Fair Employment Practices, for example, did not survive the postwar environment). As noted earlier, however, the war and its aftermath raised the civil rights issue to prime status where it stayed and in time proved productive. Feisty returning African-American veterans were part of the picture.[70]

The fifth policy category is veterans' benefits—to which one's initial response might be: Well, yes, what else is new? Yet veterans' benefits have played a peculiarly important role in the history of American policymaking.[71] In the case of the Civil War, the benefits started small but grew into a large, ornate entitlements program in the late nineteenth century. They became an American version of a welfare state.[72] In the case of World War I, the payouts were also designed later: At least five veterans' bonus bills became law over the vetoes of Coolidge, Hoover, and Roosevelt. Surprisingly, those of 1931 and 1936 are good candidates for the most effective countercyclical spending moves by the government during the depression years.[73] Indeed, they probably merit inclusion as major relief moves along with the FERA and the WPA. In the case of World War II, the G.I. Bill of Rights, which was designed while the war was still on in 1944, funded higher education for over two million returning veterans, as well as providing home mortgages and other benefits. It brought another American version of a welfare state. According to one assessment of the G.I. Bill, "The transition toward a prosperous, middle-class society was accelerated by decades."[74]

In discussing depressions, I emphasized the "political opening" provided by the Great Depression of the 1930s. That logic can work in the case of wars, too. There are two particularly interesting instances. In the case of the Civil War, the enduring policy changes of that era did have, in general, emergency roots. But obviously, that is not all that was going on. In the realm of political economy, here was an all-time chance for the Whiggish legislative program that had lurked for decades without ever being satisfyingly accomplished. Now in 1861, the generally skeptical southerners had abandoned Congress. Coalitional opportunities improved. As in the 1930s, core interests and activists could spark the kinds of innovations they would have wanted anyway, war or no war. Hence, via at least this one path of the full causal story, the Morrill Tariff of 1861, the Land Grant College Act of 1862, the Pacific Railway Act of 1862 (an "internal improvement" in nineteenth-century terminology), the Homestead Act of 1862, and the National Banking Act of 1864.[75] We see here an updated version of Henry Clay's "American System"—the ambitious program that itself had come into existence to serve needs exposed by an earlier war, the War of 1812.[76] The other instance is from World War I. For something like the first half of the twentieth century, in the wake of the turn-of-the-century consolidation of nationwide U.S. corporations, a Progressive left-wing faction on Capitol Hill, composed mainly though not solely of Democrats, itched to push the rich to the wall through taxation. They got a chance to do that in the Revenue Acts of 1916, 1917, and 1918. Fortuitously, Progressive-oriented forces held key positions in Washington, D.C., when World War I came along, and their price for financing "preparedness" and then the war was stiff progressive taxation. In this sense, it was an emergency-driven accident that the modern American revenue system took on such a progressive cast.[77]

I have not tried to list the durable institutions spurred into existence by the wars, but there have been many. The Second Bank of the United States, for example—the one later undone by Andrew Jackson—was an answer to the near-bankruptcy, currency disorder, and debt brought on by the War of 1812.[78] The Bureau of Internal Revenue (the ancestor of the Internal Revenue Service) originated in the Civil War. The House and Senate Appropriations Committees, launched in 1865 and 1867, were an answer to the fiscal pressures of the Civil War,[79] as was the Bureau of the Budget in 1921 a response to those of World War I.[80] In the wake of the Espionage Act of 1917 and the Sedition Act of 1918, J. Edgar Hoover began compiling files on individuals in the newly created General Intelligence Division of the Federal Bureau of Investigation in 1919.[81] The Central Intelligence Agency (CIA) grew out of World War II's Office of Strategic Services (OSS). The National Science Foundation (NSF), although not formally established until 1950, grew from a new World War II–inspired blueprint for supporting basic scientific research.[82] There is a good case for the Council of Economic Advisers (CEA), launched in 1946: World War II had "institutionalized structural Keynesianism," showing that well-calculated deficit management could work.[83] Why not have more of it?

Finally, in a miscellaneous category, I found surprisingly good cases for war as a necessary cause of three of the leading *restrictive* innovations of American policy history—federal curbs on alcohol, immigration, and unions. The prohibition movement was a lively cause in the 1910s, but the Eighteenth Amendment and the Volstead Act might never have happened minus the World War I logics of a need to conserve grain, a "spirit of patriotic self-denial," and an association of alcohol with German-American culture.[84]

In general in American history, possibly no policy area has brought a greater mismatch between public opinion and government action than immigration. Not even during the high intake times around 1850, around 1900, and in the 1990s, all of which featured considerable discontent, has immigration been seriously curbed. Immigration has been a classic arena of veto-group politics.[85] The only major exceptions are East Asian exclusion starting in the 1880s and a sweeping cutback that accompanied World War I—by way of a literacy test and other barriers imposed in 1917, and, once those measures failed to produce a satisfying enough postwar cut, the imposition of national-origins quotas in 1921 and 1924. As animating causes, the war and its aftermath brought an intense fear of radicals, pressure for Americanization, and a discrediting of anti-restrictionist nationality groups that previously had been hard to beat—notably the German-American Alliance.[86] It is intriguing that the success of both prohibition and immigration restriction seems to have had something to do with German-American culture or influence. A player was subtracted from the policymaking table with the discrediting of the country's prominent German strain during World War I. In a lesser way, to be sure, it was something like the white South going home during 1861–65. Yet, as in the case of women's suffrage, World War I seems to have triggered many countries, not just the United States, to restrict immigration. In Britain, France, Switzerland, and Germany, immigration had remained "essentially uncontrolled" until World War I.[87] Canada, Argentina, Brazil, and Australia, which originated as neo-European ex-settler colonies like the United States, cut back on immigration in the 1920s "to prevent a worldwide flood of refugees from war-torn Europe."[88]

Labor unions, high-flying after the government's enabling moves of the mid-1930s, received their comeuppance during and after World War II.

Repeated, crippling strikes soured the public. An "almost hysterical hostility toward unions" greeted a rail walkout in 1946, for example. John L. Lewis of the Mine Workers became a national villain. Hence the pro-management revisions of labor law by way of the Smith-Connally Act of 1943 and the Taft-Hartley Act of 1947.[89] The essentials of the latter are still in effect today.

A Word on Assassinations

I have skimped on brief or short-term events, although there is no shortage of supremely important instances. In 1856, for example, crucial to the Republicans' emergence as the country's main opposition party were the so-called "Sack of Lawrence [Kansas]" by a pro-slavery mob and the caning of Senator Charles Sumner on the Senate floor. "These two acts, one on top of the other, traumatized the nation."[90] In the 1960s, key to the enactment of the Civil Rights Act of 1964 and the Voting Rights Act of 1965 were the Birmingham and Selma confrontations—the police dogs and the rest—that riveted national attention on deep-southern practices courtesy of the Reverend Martin Luther King, Jr., as impresario.[91]

But assassinations may deserve a special word. Not easily subjected to systematic treatment—they are nearly in a category with the Nicaragua and Mexico earthquakes—they have been neglected as causal factors. (Actually, a certain order has characterized them in the sense that many American assassins have *not* been randomly acting lunatics: It is sobering that President Lincoln, President McKinley, President Kennedy, Robert F. Kennedy, and the Reverend King were shot by, respectively, a southern nationalist, an anarchist, a defector to the Soviet Union, an Arab nationalist, and a white supremacist.)[92] I do not want to take up familiar speculations here on the order of: What if Lincoln had served out his full second term? I will stop at addressing two particularly energetic bouts of national policymaking—in fact, possibly the two most consequential exercises of American lawmaking since World War II.

One was the "Reagan Revolution" of 1981—that is, the Republicans' program of unprecedented tax and spending cuts enacted that year. A classic political opening prepared the way: The 1979 oil shock, double-digit inflation, and the Iran hostages crisis lofted the Republicans to power in 1980, enabling them to bill as an economic cure-all a program they no doubt would have been happy to pursue anyway. Yet as of March 1981 the plan seemed to be headed for the rocks on Capitol Hill. Then John W.

Hinckley, Jr., shot and nearly killed President Reagan. That brought on a "display of jaunty courage" by the president (as in his "Honey, I forgot to duck!"), which "turned Reagan into a national hero and immeasurably helped the passage of his fiscal program." His survey ratings soared. "The legislative payoff was dramatic": Moderate and conservative Democrats, hearing messages from home, signed on. The cuts were approved in a series of showdown votes that spring and summer.[93] All this is entirely believable. Without the assassination episode: no Reagan Revolution.

The other was the Great Society—or, more broadly, the extraordinary harvest of legislation enacted by a left-centered coalition on Capitol Hill during calendar 1964 and in the wake of the 1964 election during 1965. President Kennedy's legislative record had been so-so, but then he was assassinated in November 1963. The impact was enormous. "All that Kennedy had tried to do, all that he stood for, became in some sense sanctified." Lyndon Johnson took over the presidency with a "Let us continue" appeal: "We would be untrue to the trust he reposed in us, if we did not remain true to the tasks he relinquished when God summoned him."[94] As the new president, Johnson "possessed an enormous advantage that liberal predecessors had been denied since the late 1930s: a national mood so eager for strong presidential leadership that even Congress and interest groups had to take heed." That advantage owed chiefly to "the impact of Kennedy's assassination."[95] It helped make 1964 possibly the most productive legislative year since the 1930s.

But that was not all. Calendar 1965, following the election, was even more productive. An under-appreciated structural logic seems to have helped, although of course many other things were going on as always. It is a good bet that the assassination had one more effect—through the medium of augmenting Democratic congressional gains in the 1964 election. Here is the logic. We know from recent comparative work on presidential systems that congressional elections held *within* presidential terms tend to vary in their results according to when they are held. On average, the earlier in the presidential term, the better the presidential party does.[96] In the United States, we see just midterms. But if we had a quarter-term system, so to speak, one in which the interim congressional elections were held after just one year, we would likely have developed a popular and professional lore centering on "quarter-term bonus" rather than "midterm penalty." The effect in 1964 was that the Democrats lucked out. Not only did they enter the election season with a post-Kennedy aura: The election itself, due to timing, had the structural cast of a confirming plebiscite one year into the Johnson presidency. In the succeeding midterm of 1966, the Democratic congressional majorities came down with a thud, but by then the Great Society was on the books. All this having been said, it is certainly plausible that, given the strong impulse toward state expansion in the 1960s and 1970s in this country and elsewhere, much of the content of the Great Society would have found its way into American policy sooner or later anyway. But we cannot know how much or when, and quite possibly a good deal of it would not have.

Possible Implications

As a general matter, building on the above, it seems to me that we pay a considerable price as would-be explainers of politics by ignoring the following. First, events as causes. They deserve a place on the palette. Second, contingency. Many events are contingent, and in the real world unexpected happenings are powerful engines of political change. Third, counterfactuals. Once contingency is squarely looked at, alternative courses of political change are nearly impossible to block from one's mind, as many of my accounts above suggest. There is a case for deploying more professional resources into cautious (it is easy to be silly) counterfactual work. A good recent instance is Gary J. Kornblith's work speculating what would have happened if the close Polk-Clay election of 1844 had gone the other way. No War with Mexico? No Civil War? What happens to slavery?[97] Counterfactuals can help frame what *did* happen. Fourth, path dependence.[98] The consequences of contingent events earn a good deal of their interest because, for a multitude of reasons, they tend to stick. Hence, for example, the U.S. federal revenue system. Such stickiness is a powerful thing.

Beyond these general points, I see four implications for the study of American politics that are more particular.

First, it might be good to rethink the general explanatory apparatus of "underlyingness" that sees political change growing out of basic interests, enduring preferences, generation-long party platforms, and the rest. In fact, to employ statistical terminology, a great deal of the sweeping political change of American history has been due to *interaction* between any such "underlying" considerations and certain contingent events, notably depressions and wars, that allowed the "underlying" considerations to prevail. "Political openings" became available, as in the cases of the Whiggish economic program of the 1860s and the left-center New Deal thrust of the 1930s. Granted, it is possible for more or less event-free upwellings of policy change to occur—perhaps the Progressive era qualifies, although that is a complicated subject. Yet it is extremely difficult, given among other things the cast of this country's separation-of-powers system, to shake American policy out of whatever its existent equilibrium is. Party electoral sweeps taken alone have often failed as effective shakers: Consider the shifts to unified party control in 1948, 1952, 1960, 1976, 1992, and 2000 that brought only modest policy change. Events can be wonderful shakers, and the possible *interaction effect* between contingent events and programmatic drives is well-known to anyone who participates cannily in political life—consider, to take a best-case non-American example, Lenin idling in Switzerland in 1917. Such interaction has a place in the intellects of many political actors, and it might have more of a place in the explanatory equipment of political science.[99]

Second, in studying policy change we probably pay too much attention to elections. Granted, elections play a vital role. In the case of elections that *precede* policy change, they can often be said to cause it, in a proximate sense, or else, for one thing, to channel impulses or messages stirred by previous events such as economic crises that serve as more convincing distant causes—the medium for these transactions often being partisan electoral shifts. But a great deal happens *between* elections. Events can occur then, too. It is interesting to sift through American lawmaking history for significant enactments that arose from inter-election events—that is, instances where it is decisively credible that a successfully enacted measure would *not* have been enacted, absent a triggering event that occurred since the last biennial election (even if, yes, it is also true that the shape of the reaction to the event, or whether there was any reaction at all, owed at least partly to the propensities of the set of officeholders now in office yielded by that last election). The list might include the following:

- the Alien and Sedition Acts 1798 (there were troubles with France)
- the Embargo Act of 1807 (troubles with England)
- the creation of the Second National Bank in 1816
- the Force Bill of 1833 (reining in the South Carolina nullifiers)
- the First Reconstruction Act of March 1867 (spurred by events occurring in the South *after* the midterm election of 1866)[100]

- the First Ku Klux Klan Act of 1970 (troubles in the South)
- the repeal of the Silver Purchase Act in 1893
- the Aldrich-Vreeland Currency Act of 1908 (in the wake of a currency crisis)
- the style-setting Revenue Act of 1916[101]
- the Espionage Act of 1917
- the Sedition Act of 1918
- the Flood Control Act of 1928 (following the great Mississippi flood of 1927)[102]
- the Revenue Act of 1932
- the Emergency Banking Relief Act of March 1933 (the banking system was collapsing during the months *after* the election of 1932)
- the Burke-Wadsworth Selective Service Training Act of 1940 (with the Nazis on the march, an army might be needed)
- the Atomic Energy Act of 1946 (what to do with the new energy source?)
- the Marshall Plan in 1948 (troubles in Europe)
- the McCarran Internal Security Act of 1950 (following the Alger Hiss trials, the exposure of Klaus Fuchs as an atomic spy, and other events)
- the National Aeronautics and Space Administration Act of 1958 (after Sputnik)
- the National Defense Education Act of 1958 (also following Sputnik)
- the Kefauver-Harris Act of 1962 regulating pharmaceutical drugs (after the thalidomide scare)
- the Civil Rights Act of 1964 (after Birmingham)
- the Open Housing Act of 1968 (after the shock of Reverend King's assassination)
- the Rail Passenger Service Act of 1970 creating AMTRAK (after the Penn Central went bankrupt)
- the Federal Election Campaign Act of 1974 (after the Watergate revelations)
- the bailout of New York City in 1975
- the bailout of the Chrysler Corporation in 1979
- the bailout of the savings and loan industry in 1989
- the Persian Gulf Resolution of 1991 (Saddam Hussein had invaded Kuwait)
- the Use of Force Resolution of 2001 (after September 11)
- the USA Patriot Act of 2001

- the Corporate Responsibility Act of 2002 (following the collapse of Enron)
- the creation of the Homeland Security Department in 2002

To use the terms presented by Keith Krehbiel in *Pivotal Politics*,[103] it is not just elections that are capable of moving status quo policy outside the Capitol Hill "gridlock interval." Events, too, can shake up a preference distribution among the realm of elected officeholders to the point where presidential vetoes, Senate filibusters, and the rest cease to be a bar to action in some direction. Let me nail this down with an instance. On December 7, 1941, Pearl Harbor was attacked. On December 8, 1941, Congress and the president opted to abandon the American status quo policy of *not* waging war against Japan, and war was declared.

There is also a role for elections that *succeed* policy change, in which retrospective voter judgments come into play. That role is vital too, but it has limits. Commitments have been made—as with the Marshall plan in 1948. Vast enactment energy has been expended that is unlikely to be expended again—as with the Civil Rights Act of 1964. Veto-point politics would disallow a policy rollback—as with any number of enactments.[104] Moves have been authorized that cannot be undone—as in the case of the Persian Gulf Resolution of 1991 legitimizing a war. Most important, perhaps, events themselves have engineered new states of affairs that have entailed, as I argued earlier, new perceptions of problems, new causal stories, new ideas about what to do. *That* is where the explanatory focus should often go—on the social construction and management of events, rather than on the elections that bracket the events.[105]

A third point has to do with congressional studies. Room needs to be allowed for events and their consequences. In today's scholarship, not a great deal of room is allowed by possibly the most influential, and certainly a splendid, achievement in congressional studies of recent times— Keith T. Poole and Howard Rosenthal's charting of congressional roll call behavior since 1789 along chiefly one master dimension.[106] From the vantage point of events, I see four problems in this construction of history— or in an interpretation that is widely given it. First, events can have *cardinal* as well as ordinal-scale consequences. In 1859, for example, according to David M. Potter: "There was a revolution of opinion in the South within six weeks after [John Brown's raid on] Harpers Ferry."[107] Sectional tension heightened. Civil war loomed. No doubt there were relevant roll calls. An ordinal measure, which the Poole-Rosenthal scale basically is, may not pick up such cardinal widening.[108] Second, an event can instantaneously shift the entire membership of Congress along some important policy dimension—as with the members' change of mind about war with Japan on December 8, 1941, as opposed to on December 6, 1941. That kind of shift cannot be picked up by the Poole-Rosenthal scale. Third, a gripping event may provoke a unanimous or near-unanimous roll call or a voice-vote decision—as with the declaration of war against Japan in 1941 (one negative House vote was the only Capitol Hill opposition), the creation of the National Aeronautics and Space Administration in 1958 (voice-vote passage in both houses after Sputnik), the Kefauver-Harris drug regulation act of 1962 (voice-vote passage in both houses after the thalidomide scare), or the Use of Force Resolution in 2001 (the Pearl Harbor pattern was exactly duplicated). Virtually all roll-call analysis, including Poole and Rosenthal's, excludes results that are so one-sided. Yet policies arrived at so one-sidedly are not necessarily unimportant in a substantive sense (consider World War II), and one-sidedness can send its own kind of important signal: In real political life, 51 percent is not always the only verdict that is meaningful or worth aiming for on Capitol Hill. Finally, what does it mean if, as Poole and Rosenthal plausibly find, most congressional roll-call history maps onto a single dimension? It might mean that Congress is forever in the business of cataloguing a timeless distribution of dimensionalized interests or preferences that exists out there somehow naturally in the society. But this is unlikely.[109] There is too much chaos. Reality changes every day. Even if any such timeless distribution existed, we do not have anything like certain rules for mapping it onto a roll-call dimension. In fact, there is a place for events in the *creation* of a long-lasting dimension in roll-call voting. Somebody needs to process the chaos of the world into ideological order by decreeing that, for example, *this* is the left-wing solution to the savings-and-loan crisis or the Somalia mess and *that* is the right-wing solution. In one of its roles, the Capitol Hill community is a kind of collective Madame Defarge, weaving day after day an ideologically ordered tapestry out of whatever material comes in—including events.

For a fourth and last general point, American political science may tilt too much toward legislative politics as opposed to executive politics. Obviously, legislatures react to events, and they can also stage them: Consider the widely publicized Pecora hearings savaging Wall Street in 1932–33 that paved the way to banking and securities reform, or the Army-McCarthy hearings of 1954. But events are dominantly an executive realm. We like to think that we choose presidents to advance party programs, but, in fact, presidents once in office ordinarily focus on managing events. The Kennedy presidency, for example, hinged largely on addressing a series of trouble spots that included Berlin, Laos, Vietnam, Cuba (the Cuban missile crisis), Mississippi, and Alabama. In its historical importance, the Truman presidency was almost entirely an events presidency. I have not emphasized the point in this chapter, but chief executives can also obviously *create* events. The discretionary wars waged by both Bushes in Iraq and Clinton in Yugoslavia are recent cases in point. Such action is not an idiosyncrasy of the American presidential system: British prime ministers of both parties pursued policies identical to the American ones in all three of these instances. Rather, it reflects the enormous, risky leeway that inheres in executive power. No doubt publics have always known this. For American voters, the presidency has always been the main prize of the system, and that may owe chiefly to voter awareness of a president's power to manage and stage events.

NOTES

1. I am indebted to R. Douglas Arnold, John Ferejohn, Sonam Henderson, and Matthew Glassman for their helpful comments on this chapter.

2. Kramer, "Fluctuations." This and the entries in succeeding notes to this paragraph are intended as examples.

3. Stonecash, *Class.*

4. Green, Palmquist, and Schickler, *Hearts and Minds.*

5. Burnham, *Critical Elections.*

6. Hartz, *Liberal Tradition.*

7. Gerring, *Ideologies.*

8. Putnam, *Bowling.*

9. Whittington, *Construction.*

10. Matthews, *Senators.*

11. Polsby, Gallaher, and Rundquist, "Seniority"; Krehbiel, *Pivotal.*

12. Poole and Rosenthal, *Congress.*

13. Dahl, *American Constitution.*

14. Skocpol, *Soldiers and Mothers.*

15. Sundquist, *Politics and Policy.*

16. Stimson, *Public Opinion.*

17. Lazarsfeld, Berelson, and Gaudet, *People's Choice.*

18. Lazarsfeld, Berelson, and Gaudet, *People's Choice,* pp. xxviii, xxxiv, 17, 25, 60, 87.

19. There is a treatment of voters' "attitude toward the European war," but that approach has limits as a probe. Lazarsfeld, Berelson, and Gaudet, *People's Choice,* p. 35.

20. Lazarsfeld, Berelson, and Gaudet, *People's Choice,* p. 71.

21. Berelson, Lazarsfeld, and McPhee, *Voting.*

22. One good account by a historian is Divine, *Foreign Policy,* chs. 6, 7. See Divine's summary judgment at p. 275: "The Berlin blockade, as much as the liberal domestic program or any one ethnic group, gave Truman a priceless political asset when day after day he stood firmly against the Communists abroad without involving the nation in war."

23. For example, Bartels and Zaller, "Presidential Vote."

24. See, for example, Shaw, "Presidential Campaign"; Mueller, *War,* ch. 9.

25. Achen and Bartels, "Retrospection."

26. Kingdon, *Agendas,* pp. 99–105; Birkland, *After Disaster.*

27. To use a term from Fogel, "Problems," p. 216.

28. Alesina and Rosenthal, *Partisan Politics.*

29. On the impact of the passage of the Kansas-Nebraska Act, see for example Brady, *Critical Elections,* p. 172.

30. For a discussion, see Dray, *Philosophy,* p. 19.

31. See Dray, *Philosophy,* pp. 42–43; Nagel, *Structure,* pp. 582–83. These philosophers of science seem to scratch their chins about this historians' practice, but then they reflect, well, that is what historians do.

32. Fogel, "Problems."

33. McPherson, *Battle Cry,* pp. 770–76, 858, quotation at p. 774.

34. Clubb, Flanigan, and Zingale, *Partisan,* ch. 3, data from Table 3.1a at pp. 92–93; Bartels, "Continuity," pp. 313–17, data from Figure 8 at p. 315.

35. See the discussion in Mayhew, *Realignments,* pp. 77, 150, 164.

36. Huston, *Panic of 1857,* ch. 6. In particular, the Republicans scored dramatic, lasting gains in traditionally Democratic Pennsylvania in 1858. In the circumstance of economic difficulty, workers in the state's non-agricultural sectors seem to have bought into a Republican anti-free-trade ideology. Of course, North versus South issues figured in the late 1850s also.

37. On the depression of 1873, see Foner, *Reconstruction,* pp. 512–24 ("The Depression and Its Consequences").

38. Renshaw, "Keynesian," p. 344.

39. The 1848 election also seems to have brought one of the major realignments of congressional voting in American history. See CF&Z, *Partisan,* pp. 94–97.

40. Another example: It seems a reasonable bet, although the history has not been written this way, that many voters in the generation after 1893 saw the Democrats as simply bunglers. Given simultaneous control of the presidency, House,

and Senate during 1993–94 for the first time since 1858, the party, it could be surmised, proceeded forthwith to ruin the economy.

41. Potter, *Impending Crisis*, p. 17.

42. On the World War II roots of civil rights as an issue, see Klinkner and Smith, *Unsteady March*, chs. 6, 7; Keyssar, *Right*, 244–55; Hart, "Making Democracy"; Collins, "Fair Employment."

43. Risjord, "Election." Pennsylvania made the difference in the 1812 election.

44. Binkley, *Political Parties*, pp. 94–97; Watts, *Republic*, p. 282.

45. Turner, "Elections," p. 299.

46. Harding's percentage edge over Cox in 1920 is still the largest for any presidential election since the uncontested election of 1820.

47. Creighton, *Canada*, pp. 216–17; McNaught, *Canada*, pp. 230–31.

48. MacIntyre, *Australia*, p. 190.

49. Butler and Stokes, *Britain*, pp. 172–74; Wilson, *Downfall*. Another causal account goes: "Between 1914 and 1921 trade-union membership doubled and between 1918 and 1924 Labour displaced the Liberals as the largest anti-Conservative party, as a consequence of the Asquith-Lloyd George split [that is, the war-induced fracture of the Liberal party], the widening of the franchise in 1918, and the heightened class consciousness of British workers—all factors that could be attributed to the war." Stevenson, *Cataclysm*, p. 440.

50. Wilson, *Downfall*, p. 18.

51. It goes without saying that the costs of World War I rose far higher for Britain especially than for the United States. Still, even leaving aside the postwar turmoil of 1919–20, the war itself was not a minor enterprise for this country. It brought a government-directed economy, the country's "first real taste of truly large-scale government spending," restrictions on civil liberties vastly more serious than anything experienced since September 2001, repression approaching devastation of German-American culture, five million participants in the armed forces, two million troops (42 divisions) deployed in France, 114,000 war deaths (many from disease), and over 200,000 military wounded. See Cooper, *Pivotal*, pp. 279–80, 288–91, 297–305, quotation at p. 291; Stevenson, *Cataclysm*, pp. 405, 442; Luebke, *Bonds*. Note also that World War I could affect even resolute neutrals through spillover effects. Swedish politics seems to have been revolutionized in 1918 as the fall of Germany's monarchy sent a democratizing impulse across the Baltic. See Berman, *Social Democratic*, ch. 5 ("Sweden's Path to Democracy").

52. Foner, *Reconstruction*, pp. 550–52, 554–55 (on Louisiana), 558–63 (on Mississippi), 570–75 (on South Carolina). On South Carolina in 1876, see also Zuczek, "Last Campaign."

53. On the repeal of the Sherman Silver Purchase Act, see Faulkner, *Expansion*, pp. 147–51. On the income tax of 1894 as a remedy for falling revenue in depression circumstances, see Gordon, *Wealth*, pp. 273–74. The Supreme Court quickly struck down the income tax.

54. Sources on the era include Leuchtenburg, *Roosevelt*, chs. 3, 7, 10, 11; and Schwarz, *Interregnum*, pp. 88–98 and chs. 5, 6, 8.

55. Schlesinger, *New Deal*, p. 257. Still, the RTAA may fit better into category three here. By instinct and belief, the Democrats of that time were of course a low-tariff party.

56. Hartley, Sheffrin, and Vasche, "Reform." "The fiscal system enacted in California during the 1930s has persisted in its basic structure through today [1996]. These changes have allowed real per capita state expenditure to grow by a factor of approximately 10 from 1929/30 to 1989/90" (p. 658). This California revenue switch of the 1930s took place under Republican governors.

57. Yet the Wagner Act had an event-centered side, too. Among other things, the measure was a reaction to nationwide strikes during 1934 that amounted to "social upheavals." See Bernstein, *Turbulent*, ch. 6, quotation at p. 217.

58. Much of the factual material used in this section is used also in Mayhew, "Wars."

59. Bauer, Pool, and Dexter, *Business*, pp. 14–15; Brownlee, "Tax Regimes," pp. 44–48; Sylla, "Federalism," pp. 527–29; Porter, *War*, p. 260.

60. Brownlee, "Wilson"; Brownlee, "Tax Regimes," pp. 60–72; Brownlee, "Public Sector," p. 1030; Higgs, *Crisis*, ch. 7; Witte, *Tax*, ch. 4.

61. Wallis, "Finance," p. 73.

62. Murphy, "Child"; Brownlee, "Tax Regimes," pp. 88–101; Witte, *Tax*, ch. 6; Campbell and Allen, "Revenue."

63. North, *Growth*, pp. 178–79.

64. Bauer, Pool, and Dexter, *Business*, pp. 13–14; Baxter, *Clay*, ch. 2; Binkley, *Political Parties*, pp. 101–102.

65. Hicks, *Ascendancy*, quotation at p. 57; Kaplan and Ryley, *Prelude*, ch. 5; Eichengreen, "Smoot-Hawley," pp. 3–5.

66. Keyssar, *Right*, pp. 244–55, quotation at p. 244; Klinkner and Smith, *Unsteady March*, ch. 6.

67. Keyssar, *Right*, pp. 277–81.

68. The case for a causal connection between the war and women's suffrage is available in Kyvig, *Explicit*, pp. 226–39, first quotation at p. 234; Keyssar, *Right*, pp. 214–18, second quotation at p. 216; Cooper, *Pivotal Decades*, pp. 307–08; Wynn, *Progressivism*, pp. 148–52; Behn, "Conversion."

69. On the cross-national pattern of women's enfranchisement, see Lewis, "Winning," plus scattered sources on individual countries. As of the beginning of World War I, women had had the vote in New Zealand, Australia, Finland, Norway, and certain American states.

70. Klinkner and Smith, *Unsteady March*, chs. 6, 7; Keyssar, *Right*, pp. 244–53; Hart, "Making Democracy"; Collins, "Fair Employment."

71. See Campbell, "Invisible."

72. Skocpol, *Soldiers and Mothers*, ch. 2; Holcombe, "Veteran Interests."

73. Key, "Veterans"; Brown, "Fiscal," pp. 863–69; Lee and Passell, *View*, pp. 384–86.

74. Perrett, *Country*, quotation at p. 439; Olson, *G.I. Bill*, chs. 1–3.

75. See, for example, Bensel, *Yankee*.

76. Wiltse, *New Nation*, ch. 3; Baxter, *Clay*, ch. 2; Binkley, *Political Parties*, p. 101.

77. See the accounts in Brownlee, "Wilson"; Brownlee, "Tax Regimes," pp. 60–72.

78. Rockoff, "Banking," pp. 647–48; Watts, *Republic*, p. 278.

79. Wander, "Budget," pp. 25–28.

80. Farrar-Myers, Renka and Ponder, "Institutionalization," p. 1; Wander, "Patterns," pp. 31–35.

81. Goldstein, *Repression*, chs. 4, 5; Ungar, *FBI*, ch. 3.

82. Smith, *Science Policy*, pp. 1–3, 34–52; Polsby, *Innovation*, pp. 35–55.

83. Brownlee, "Public Sector," pp. 1050–51, quotation at p. 1050. See also Stein, *Fiscal Revolution*, chs. 8, 9.

84. The causal case is available in Kyvig, *Explicit*, pp. 218–26, quotation at p. 224; Kerr, *Prohibition*, p. 185; Cooper, *Pivotal Decades*, p. 307; Ferrell, *Wilson*, pp. 188–90.

85. See Tichenor, *Dividing Lines*.

86. Tichenor, *Dividing Lines*, pp. 138–46; LeMay, *Open Door*, pp. 70–72.

87. Kaufman, *Rise and Fall*, p. 56.

88. Graham, *Collision Course*, p. 47.

89. Patterson, *Mr. Republican*, quotation at p. 306; Lee, *Truman*, chs. 1–3; Amenta and Skocpol, "Redefining," pp. 114–16; Young, *Congressional Politics*, pp. 63–67; Sparrow, *Outside*, ch. 3; Wynn, *Progressivism*, p. 470.

90. Gienapp, *Origins*, pp. 295–303; Fogel, "Problems," pp. 227–29, quotation at p. 229.

91. Burstein, *Discrimination*, chs. 3–4, 8; Sitkoff, *Struggle*, chs. 5, 6.

92. For an interesting treatment, see Clarke, "Assassins."

93. Unger, *Recent America*, pp. 215–17. See also Barone, *Country*, p. 613; Brody, *Assessing*, pp.146–47; Brownlee and Steuerle, "Taxation," pp. 160–61. In the latter assessment, the assassination episode "had the effect of increasing popular support for the president and, by extension, whatever program he wanted. Congress found the pressure irresistible."

94. Matusow, *Unraveling*, p. 131.

95. Patterson, *Expectations*, pp. 530–31.

96. See Shugart, "Electoral Cycle," pp. 332–33.

97. Kornblith, "Rethinking." On counterfactuals, see also Fearon, "Counterfactuals."

98. See Pierson, "Path Dependence."

99. An interaction-effect argument of this sort addressing specifically bankruptcy legislation appears in Berglöf and Rosenthal, "Rejected," p. 6. During the

110 years through 1898, federal bankruptcy laws were enacted only when a) an economic panic had just occurred, and b) the Federalists, Whigs, or (post-1860) Republicans enjoyed unified control of the government.

100. See Donald, *Reconstruction*, pp. 56–57; McKitrick, *Andrew Johnson*, pp. 455–60, 473–85.

101. See Brownlee, "Wilson."

102. Pearcy, "Flood."

103. Krehbiel, *Pivotal*.

104. See, for example, Vogel, "Diffuse Interests," pp. 260–62, 266–68.

105. Political leaders, for example, in reacting to events, can often "frame" political contexts. See Arnold, *Congressional Action*, p. 96.

106. Poole and Rosenthal, *Congress*.

107. Potter, *Crisis*, p. 382.

108. For a similar comment, see Krehbiel, *Pivotal*, p. 74n.

109. See Converse, "Belief Systems."

BIBLIOGRAPHY

Achen, Christopher H., and Larry M. Bartels. 2004. "Blind Retrospection: Electoral Responses to Drought, Flu, and Shark Attacks." Paper presented at conference on "Knowledge, Problems, and Political Representation: Can Government Perform Better?" at University of Virginia, November 12–13.

Alesina, Alberto, and Howard Rosenthal. 1995. *Partisan Politics, Divided Government, and the Economy.* New York: Cambridge University Press.

Amenta, Edwin, and Theda Skocpol. 1988. "Redefining the New Deal: World War II and the Development of Social Provision in the United States." In *The Politics of Social Policy in the United States,* eds. Margaret Weir, Ann Shola Orloff, and Theda Skocpol. Princeton: Princeton University Press, 81–122.

Arnold, R. Douglas. 1990. *The Logic of Congressional Action.* New Haven: Yale University Press.

Barone, Michael. 1990. *Our Country: The Shaping of America from Roosevelt to Reagan.* New York: Free Press.

Bartels, Larry M. 1998. "Electoral Continuity and Change, 1868–1996." *Electoral Studies* 17, 301–26.

———, and John Zaller. 2001. "Presidential Vote Models: A Recount." *PS: Political Science and Politics* 34, 9–20.

Bauer, Raymond A., Ithiel de Sola Pool, and Lewis Anthony Dexter. 1963. *American Business and Public Policy: The Politics of Foreign Trade.* Chicago: Aldine Atherton.

Baxter, Maurice G. 1995. *Henry Clay and the American System.* Lexington: University Press of Kentucky.

Behn, Beth A. 2005. "Woodrow Wilson's Conversion Experience: The President, Woman Suffrage, and the Extent of Executive Influence." Paper presented at the annual conference of the Midwest Political Science Association.

Bensel, Richard Franklin. 1990. *Yankee Leviathan: The Origins of Central State Authority in America, 1859–1877.* New York: Cambridge University Press.

Berelson, Bernard R, Paul F. Lazarsfeld, and William N. McPhee. 1954. *Voting: A Study of Opinion Formation in Presidential Campaigns.* Chicago: University of Chicago Press.

Berglöf, Erik, and Howard Rosenthal. 2004. "Power Rejected: Congress and Bankruptcy in the Early Republic." Paper presented at History of Congress conference, Stanford University, March 2004, revised September 2004.

Berman, Sheri. 1998. *The Social Democratic Moment: Ideas and Politics in the Making of Interwar Europe.* Cambridge: Harvard University Press.

Bernstein, Irving. 1970. *Turbulent Years: A History of the American Worker, 1933–1941.* Boston: Houghton Mifflin.

Binkley, Wilfred E. 1962, 4th edition. *American Political Parties: Their Natural History.* New York: Alfred A. Knopf.

Birkland, Thomas A. 1997. *After Disaster: Agenda Setting, Public Policy, and Focusing Events.* Washington, D.C.: Georgetown University Press.

Brady, David W. 1988. *Critical Elections and Congressional Policy Making.* Stanford: Stanford University Press.

Brody, Richard A. 1991. *Assessing the President: The Media, Elite Opinion, and Public Support.* Stanford, Calif.: Stanford University Press.

Brown, E. Cary. 1956. "Fiscal Policy in the 'Thirties: A Reappraisal." *American Economic Review* 46, 857–79.

Brownlee, W. Elliot. 1985. "Woodrow Wilson and the Financing of the Modern State: The Revenue Act of 1916." *Proceedings of the American Philosophical Society* 129, 173–210.

———. 1996. "Tax Regimes, National Crises, and State-Building in America." In *Funding the Modern American State, 1941–1995,* ed. W. Elliot Brownlee. New York: Cambridge University Press, 37–104.

———. 2000. "The Public Sector." In *The Cambridge Economic History of the United States,* vol. III, *The Twentieth Century,* eds. Stanley L. Engerman and Robert L. Gallman. New York: Cambridge University Press, 1013–60.

———, and C. Eugene Steuerle. 2003. "Taxation." In *The Reagan Presidency: Pragmatic Conservatism and Its Legacies,* eds. W. Elliot Brownlee and Hugh Davis Graham. Lawrence: University Press of Kansas, 155–81.

Burnham, Walter Dean. 1970. *Critical Elections and the Mainsprings of American Politics.* New York: Norton.

Burstein, Paul. 1985. *Discrimination, Jobs, and Politics: The Struggle for Equal Employment Opportunity in the United States since the New Deal.* Chicago: University of Chicago Press.

Butler, David, and Donald Stokes. 1974. *Political Change in Britain: The Evolution of Electoral Choice*. London: Macmillan.

Campbell, Alec. 2004. "The Invisible Welfare State: Establishing the Phenomenon of Twentieth Century Veteran's Benefits." *Journal of Political and Military Sociology*, 32, 249–67.

Campbell, John L., and Michael Patrick Allen. 1994. "The Political Economy of Revenue Extraction in the Modern State: A Time-Series Analysis of U.S. Income Taxes, 1916–1986." *Social Forces* 72, 632–69.

Clarke, James W. 1981. "American Assassins: An Alternative Typology." *British Journal of Political Science* 11, 81–104.

Clubb, Jerome M., William H. Flanigan, and Nancy H. Zingale. 1980. *Partisan Realignment: Voters, Parties, and Government in American History*. Beverly Hills, Calif.: Sage.

Collins, William J. 2002. "The Political Economy of State-level Fair Employment Laws, 1940–1964." *Explorations in Economic History* 40:1, 24–51.

Converse, Philip E. 1964. "The Nature of Belief Systems in Mass Publics." In *Ideology and Discontent*, ed. David E. Apter. London: Free Press of Glencoe, 206–61.

Cooper, John Milton, Jr. 1990. *Pivotal Decades: The United States, 1900–1920*. New York: W. W. Norton and Co.

Creighton, Donald. 1959. *The Story of Canada*. Toronto: Macmillan.

Dahl, Robert A. 2003. *How Democratic Is the American Constitution?* New Haven: Yale University Press.

Divine, Robert A. 1974. *Foreign Policy and U.S. Presidential Elections, 1940–1948*. New York: New Viewpoints.

Donald, David. 1965. *The Politics of Reconstruction, 1863–1867*. Baton Rouge: Louisiana State University Press.

Dray, William H. 1964. *Philosophy of History*. Englewood Cliffs, N.J.: Prentice-Hall.

Eichengreen, Barry. 1989. "The Political Economy of the Smoot-Hawley Tariff." *Research in Economic History* 12, 1–43.

Farrar-Myers, Victoria A., Russell Renka, and Daniel Ponder. 2000. "Institutionalization in a Critical Period: Presidency, Congress, and the Development of the Executive Budget." Paper presented at the annual conference of the American Political Science Association.

Faulkner, Harold U. 1959. *Politics, Reform and Expansion, 1890–1900*. New York: Harper and Brothers.

Fearon, James D. 1991. "Counterfactuals and Hypothesis Testing in Political Science." *World Politics* 43, 169–95.

Ferrell, Robert H. 1985. *Woodrow Wilson and World War I, 1917–1921*. New York: Harper and Row.

Fogel, Robert W. 1992. "Problems in Modeling Complex Dynamic Interactions: The Political Realignment of the 1850s." *Economics and Politics* 4, 215–54.

Foner, Eric. 1988. *Reconstruction: America's Unfinished Revolution, 1863–1877.* New York: Harper and Row.

Gerring, John. 1998. *Party Ideologies in America, 1828–1906.* New York: Cambridge University Press.

Gienapp, William E. 1987. *The Origins of the Republican Party, 1852–1856.* New York: Oxford University Press.

Goldstein, Robert J. 1978. *Political Repression in Modern America: From 1870 to 1976.* Urbana: University of Illinois Press.

Gordon, John Steele. 2004. *An Empire of Wealth: The Epic History of American Economic Power.* New York: HarperCollins.

Graham, Hugh Davis. 2002. *Collision Course: The Strange Convergence of Affirmative Action and Immigration Policy in America.* New York: Oxford University Press.

Green, Donald, Bradley Palmquist, and Eric Schickler. 2002. *Partisan Hearts and Minds: Political Parties and the Social Identities of Voters.* New Haven: Yale University Press.

Hart, Justin. 2004. "Making Democracy Safe for the World: Race, Propaganda, and the Transformation of U.S. Foreign Policy during World War II." *Pacific Historical Review* 73, 49–94.

Hartley, James E., Steven M. Sheffrin, and J. David Vasche. 1996. "Reform During Crisis: The Transformation of California's Fiscal System During the Great Depression." *Journal of Economic History* 56, 657–78.

Hartz, Louis. 1955. *The Liberal Tradition in America.* New York: Harcourt, Brace.

Hicks, John D. 1960. *Republican Ascendancy, 1921–1933.* New York: Harper and Row.

Higgs, Robert. 1987. *Crisis and Leviathan: Critical Episodes in the Growth of American Government.* New York: Oxford University Press.

Holcombe, Randall G. 1999. "Veteran Interests and the Transition to Government Growth: 1870–1915." *Public Choice* 99, 311–26.

Huston, James L. 1987. *The Panic of 1857 and the Coming of the Civil War.* Baton Rouge: Louisiana State University Press.

Kaplan, Edward S., and Thomas W. Ryley. 1994. *Prelude to Trade Wars: American Tariff Policy, 1890–1922.* Westport, Conn.: Greenwood.

Kaufmann, Eric P. 2004. *The Rise and Fall of Anglo-America.* Cambridge: Harvard University Press.

Kerr, K. Austin. 1985. *Organized for Prohibition: A New History of the Anti-Saloon League.* New Haven: Yale University Press.

Key, V. O., Jr. 1943. "The Veterans and the House of Representatives: A Study of a Pressure Group and Electoral Mortality." *Journal of Politics* 5, 27–40.

Keyssar, Alexander. 2000. *The Right to Vote: The Contested History of Democracy in the United States.* New York: Basic Books.

Kingdon, John W. 1984. *Agendas, Alternatives, and Public Policies.* Boston: Little, Brown.

Klinkner, Philip A., and Rogers M. Smith. 1999. *The Unsteady March: The Rise and Decline of Racial Equality in America.* Chicago: University of Chicago Press.

Kornblith, Gary J. 2003. "Rethinking the Coming of the Civil War: A Counterfactual Exercise." *Journal of American History* 90, 76–105.

Kramer, Gerald H. 1971. "Short-Term Fluctuations in U.S. Voting Behavior, 1896–1964." *American Political Science Review* 65, 131–43.

Krehbiel, Keith. 1998. *Pivotal Politics: A Theory of U.S. Lawmaking.* Chicago: University of Chicago Press.

Kyvig, David E. 1996. *Explicit Authentic Acts: Amending the U.S. Constitution, 1776–1995.* Lawrence: University Press of Kansas.

Lazarsfeld, Paul, Bernard Berelson, and Hazel Gaudet. 1968, 3rd edition. *The People's Choice: How the Voter Makes up His Mind in a Presidential Campaign.* New York: Columbia University Press.

Lee, R. Alton. 1966. *Truman and Taft-Hartley: A Question of Mandate.* Lexington: University of Kentucky Press.

Lee, Susan, and Peter Passell. 1979. *A New Economic View of American History.* New York: W. W. Norton.

LeMay, Michael C. 1987. *From Open Door to Dutch Door: An Analysis of U.S. Immigration Policy Since 1820.* New York: Praeger.

Leuchtenburg, William E. 1963. *Franklin D. Roosevelt and the New Deal, 1932–1940.* New York: Harper and Row.

Lewis, Jone Johnson. 2004. "Winning the Vote: International Woman Suffrage Timeline." http://womenshistory.about.com/library/weekly/aa091600a.htm.

Luebke, Frederick C. 1974. *Bonds of Loyalty: German Americans and World War I.* De Kalb: Northern Illinois University Press.

MacIntyre, Stuart. 1986. *The Oxford History of Australia,* vol. 4, *1901–1942: The Succeeding Age.* New York: Oxford University Press.

Matthews, Donald R. 1960. *U.S. Senators and Their World.* Chapel Hill: University of North Carolina Press.

Matusow, Allen J. 1984. *The Unraveling of America: A History of Liberalism in the 1960s.* New York: Harper and Row.

Mayhew, David R. 2002. *Electoral Realignments: A Critique of an American Genre.* New Haven: Yale University Press.

———. 2005 "Wars and American Politics." *Perspectives on Politics* 3, 473–93.

McKitrick, Eric L. 1960. *Andrew Johnson and Reconstruction.* Chicago: University of Chicago Press.

McNaught, Kenneth. 1970. *The History of Canada.* New York: Praeger.

McPherson, James M. 1988. *Battle Cry of Freedom: The Civil War Era.* New York: Oxford University Press.

Mueller, John E. 1973. *War, Presidents and Public Opinion*. New York: John Wiley and Sons.

Murphy, Kevin. 1996. "Child of War: The Federal Income Withholding Tax." *Mid-America* 78, 203–29.

Nagel, Ernest. 1961. *The Structure of Science: Problems in the Logic of Scientific Explanation*. New York: Harcourt, Brace & World.

North, Douglass C. 1966. *Growth and Welfare in the American Past: A New Economic History*. Englewood Cliffs, N.J.: Prentice-Hall.

Olson, Keith W. 1974. *The G.I. Bill, the Veterans, and the Colleges*. Lexington: University Press of Kentucky.

Patterson, James T. 1972. *Mr. Republican: A Biography of Robert A. Taft*. Boston: Houghton Mifflin.

———. 1996. *Grand Expectations: The United States, 1945–1974*. New York: Oxford University Press.

Pearcy, Matthew T. 2002. "After the Flood: A History of the 1928 Flood Control Act." *Journal of the Illinois State Historical Society* 95, 172–201.

Perrett, Geoffrey. 1989. *A Country Made By War: From the Revolution to Vietnam—the Story of America's Rise to Power*. New York: Random House.

Pierson, Paul. 2000. "Increasing Returns, Path Dependence, and the Study of Politics." *American Political Science Review* 94, 251–67.

Polsby, Nelson W. 1984. *Political Innovation in America: The Politics of Policy Innovation*. New Haven: Yale University Press.

———, Miriam Gallaher, and Barry S. Rundquist. 1969. "The Growth of the Seniority System in the U.S. House of Representatives." *American Political Science Review* 63, 787–807.

Poole, Keith T., and Howard Rosenthal. 1997. *Congress: A Political-Economic History of Roll Call Voting*. New York: Oxford University Press.

Porter, Bruce D. 1994. *War and the Rise of the State: The Military Foundations of Modern Politics*. New York: Free Press.

Potter, David M. 1976. *The Impending Crisis, 1848–1861*. New York: Harper and Row.

Putnam, Robert D. 2000. *Bowling Alone: The Collapse and Revival of American Community*. New York: Simon and Schuster.

Renshaw, Patrick. 1999. "Was There a Keynesian Economy in the USA between 1933 and 1945?" *Journal of Contemporary History* 34, 337–64.

Risjord, Norman K. 1971. "Election of 1812." In *History of American Presidential Elections, 1789–1968*, vol. 1, ed. Arthur M. Schlesinger, Jr. New York: McGraw-Hill, 149–72.

Rockoff, Hugh. 2000. "Banking and Finance, 1789–1914." In *The Cambridge Economic History of the United States*, vol. II, *The Long Nineteenth Century*, eds. Stanley L. Engerman and Robert E. Gallman. New York: Cambridge University Press, 643–84.

Schlesinger, Arthur M., Jr. 1959. *The Coming of the New Deal.* Boston: Houghton Mifflin.

Schwarz, Jordan A. 1970. *The Interregnum of Despair: Hoover, Congress, and the Depression.* Urbana: University of Illinois Press.

Shaw, Daron R. 1999. "A Study of Presidential Campaign Event Effects from 1952 to 1992." *Journal of Politics* 61, 387–422.

Shugart, Matthew Soberg. 1995. "The Electoral Cycle and Institutional Sources of Divided Presidential Government." *American Political Science Review,* 89, 327–43.

Sitkoff, Harvard. 1981. *The Struggle for Black Equality, 1954–1980.* New York: Hill and Wang.

Skocpol, Theda. 1992. *Protecting Soldiers and Mothers: The Political Origins of Social Policy in the United States.* Cambridge: Harvard University Press.

Smith, Bruce L. R. 1990. *American Science Policy Since World War II.* Washington, D.C.: Brookings.

Sparrow, Bartholomew. 1996. *From the Outside In: World War II and the American State.* Princeton: Princeton University Press.

Stein, Herbert. 1969. *The Fiscal Revolution in America.* Chicago: University of Chicago Press.

Stevenson, David. 2004. *Cataclysm: The First World War as Political Tragedy.* New York: Basic Books.

Stimson, James A. 1999. *Public Opinion in America: Moods, Cycles, and Swings.* Boulder, Colo.: Westview Press.

Stonecash, Jeffrey M. 2000. *Class and Party in American Politics.* Boulder, Colo.: Westview Press.

Sundquist, James L. 1968. *Politics and Policy: The Eisenhower, Kennedy and Johnson Years.* Washington, D.C.: Brookings Institution Press.

Sylla, Richard. 2000. "Experimental Federalism: The Economics of American Government, 1789–1914." In *The Cambridge Economic History of the United States,* vol. II, *The Long Nineteenth Century,* eds. Stanley L. Engerman and Robert E. Gallman. New York: Cambridge University Press, 483–541.

Tichenor, Daniel J. 2002. *Dividing Lines: The Politics of Immigration Control in America.* Princeton: Princeton University Press.

Turner, Lynn W. 1971. "Elections of 1816 and 1820." In *History of American Presidential Elections, 1789–1968,* vol 1, ed. Arthur M. Schlesinger, Jr. New York: McGraw-Hill, 299–321.

Ungar, Sanford J. 1976. *FBI: An Uncensored Look Behind the Walls.* Boston: Little, Brown.

Unger, Irwin. 2002. *Recent America: The United States Since 1945.* Upper Saddle River, N.J.: Prentice-Hall.

Vogel, David. 1993. "Representing Diffuse Interests in Environmental Policymaking." In *Do Institutions Matter? Government Capabilities in the United States and Abroad*, eds. R. Kent Weaver and Bert A. Rockman. Washington, D.C.: Brookings Institution Press, 237–71.

Wallis, John Joseph. 2000. "American Government Finance in the Long Run: 1790 to 1990." *Journal of Economic Perspectives* 14, 61–82.

Wander, W. Thomas. 1982. "Patterns of Change in the Congressional Budget Process, 1865–1974." *Congress and the Presidency* 9, 23–49.

Watts, Steven. 1987. *The Republic Reborn: War and the Making of Liberal America, 1790–1820*. Baltimore: Johns Hopkins University Press.

Whittington, Keith E. 1999. *Constitutional Construction: Divided Powers and Constitutional Meaning*. Cambridge: Harvard University Press.

Wilson, Trevor. 1966. *The Downfall of the Liberal Party, 1914–1935*. London: Collins.

Wiltse, Charles M. 1985. *The New Nation, 1800–1845*. New York: Hill and Wang.

Witte, John F. 1985. *The Politics and Development of the Federal Income Tax*. Madison: University of Wisconsin Press.

Wynn, Neil A. 1986. *From Progressivism to Prosperity: World War I and American Society*. New York: Holmes and Meier.

———. 1996. "The 'Good War': The Second World War and Postwar American Society." *Journal of Contemporary History* 31, 463–82.

Young, Roland. 1956. *Congressional Politics in the Second World War*. New York: Columbia University Press.

Zuczek, Richard. 1996. "The Last Campaign of the Civil War: South Carolina and the Revolution of 1876." *Civil War History* 42, 18–31.

Chapter 5

Contingent Public Policies and Racial Hierarchy

Lessons from Immigration and Census Policies

Jennifer Hochschild and Traci Burch

This is not a revolutionary bill. It will not reshape the
structure of our daily lives or add importantly to our
wealth and power.
 —President Lyndon B. Johnson, October 3, 1965

Census 2000 will go down in history as the event that
began to redefine race in American society.
 —Kenneth Prewitt, January 2001

Individually or in combination, two federal policies have the potential to
transform the American racial and ethnic hierarchy more than any other
policy changes since the civil rights movement.[1] They are the Immigration
Act of 1965 and the introduction of the "mark one or more" instruction in
the race question on the 2000 census. Unlike the civil rights activities of
the 1940s through 1960s, the first change was not intended to overturn the
racial order and the second was a response to a process of transformation
already underway. Both were, and remain, highly dependent on the isolated choices of many people around the world, as well as strategies of political and business leaders and economic or other forces outside anyone's
control. Because the long-term effects of these policies have not played out
fully, their ultimate outcomes will remain unclear for a long time—but
they could be substantial.

This chapter[2] explores the design of each policy, their separate and possible joint consequences, and their potential long-term effects. Theoretically, we use these policies as vehicles to examine various kinds of political contingency such as unforeseen and thus unintended consequences, conditional individual acts by nonpolitical individuals, and unpredictable external shocks to a political system such as a terrorist attack or economic depression. We aim to demonstrate that contingency is much more important in understanding politics and policy-making than actors or analysts are usually willing to recognize, and that organizing a political narrative in terms of various kinds of contingency and degrees of likelihood of a contingent outcome gives coherence and structure to the analysis while retaining the necessary level of indeterminacy.

Why Focus on Contingency, and What Is It?

It is commonplace to observe that government policies may have unintended consequences, whether because policymakers fail to consider or predict accurately the impact of their choices or because the world changes in unpredictable ways after the policy is promulgated. It is also commonplace to observe that government actions can affect how people categorize themselves and others into races or ethnicities, which in turn can affect groups' privilege or disadvantage relative to others in society. But putting these two observations together yields some unexpected outcomes.

Consider first the role of contingency in politics. Analysts tend to ignore it, or to seek to explain it away. For example, the juridical commitment to originalism in interpreting the Constitution gives insufficient weight to the fact that policy designers in 1789 were not omniscient. Amendments to the Constitution, after all, show that later designers recognized unforeseen contingencies that needed to be addressed for the Constitution to remain viable; we have no grounds for assuming that by now the document is in its final, perfect form and should be interpreted only through the eyes of its authors. Functionalist arguments are similarly flawed because they ignore contingency. The presumption that policies or structures were designed to produce the effects that they actually have had, or that political actors can actually create institutions that correspond to their creators' interests, slights the possibility that policies and institutions were intended to do one thing but actually did another.[3]

Some theories of path dependency or incrementalism—the presumption that policy processes follow a more or less straight and predictable line from some (perhaps random) starting point—are equally blind to contingency. Most generally, the search for broad covering laws to explain political processes, institutions, and outcomes is predicated on the idea that contingent events are random, ultimately unimportant, or otherwise swamped by the power of the covering law. But unless one is prepared to argue that the Black Death of the 1300s had no impact on the history of Europe, or that the presidency of Abraham Lincoln was immaterial to the outcome of the American Civil War, this claim is implausible.

Political actors can be as loathe as political scientists to accommodate contingency in their efforts to make sense of the political arena. The outcome of an election may appear uncertain in advance, but every victorious politician claims that he or she won because of some identifiable virtue, policy stance, or experience. Passage of a law or outcome of a battle may seem similarly unpredictable ahead of time, but after the fact no floor leader or general will eschew a perfectly rational-sounding explanation for whatever outcome occurred.

If contingency matters, what is it? Many things, as Andreas Schedler shows in this volume. We focus on several components that correspond to aspects of the history of the 1965 immigration law and the 2000 census. Perhaps most important is the fact that "causal effects are not invariant, but context-dependent."[4] That is, how policies shape events that occur after they are implemented depends on whether the context of implementation resembles the context of passage or was correctly anticipated by policymakers. For the 1965 immigration law, those conditions did not hold.

A second form of contingency, which partly explains the first, is what Schedler calls conditional or uncertain individual action. That is, it is impossible to predict some external conditions or how particular conditions will motivate individual actions. Less abstractly, millions of people around the world decided after the mid-1960s that they preferred migration to staying at home, and many chose migration to the United States rather than elsewhere. (Even the terms "decided" and "chose" may be too volitional to explain some migratory paths.) Their choices, of course, were not completely autonomous; at the same time that people increasingly wanted to migrate, U.S. businesses would increasingly seek both skilled and unskilled labor, especially from relatively low-paying, non-white nations. Had these various individual actions and economic imperatives been different, the immigration law and its successors would not have had the unforeseen effects that did in fact ensue.

A third form of contingency results from the unintended effects of the 1965 immigration law. In Schedler's language, it corresponds most clearly with the intersection of normative, conceptual, and practical commitments. No one can confidently predict how the presence of millions of new immigrants and their children will affect racial and ethnic categorization and hierarchy over the next few decades. Immigrants might "become" white or black, thus reinforcing the extant racial order, or they might ally with American minority groups and disrupt the racial order, or they might remain as separate groups and complicate the racial order.

Contingency becomes even more evident, and more speculative, when one adds the possible effects of census 2000 to the current and possible future effects of the 1965 immigration law. The decision to permit people to "mark one or more" race does not demonstrate unintended consequences; supporters and opponents shared the expectation that permitting people to identify with more than one race on the census (and eventually on other governmental and nongovernmental forms) would lead to the blurring of group boundaries. What remains to be seen is whether this official recognition of racial mixture will have any substantial impact on the degree to which people actually choose to belong to more than one race, and whether such a choice will in turn have any effect on their affiliations and alliances.

All of this is highly contingent in the sense of Schedler's "individual action," and suggests as well two more forms of contingency—those of Schedler's "individual actor" and "catastrophic event." Individual political actors will have a big impact on the eventual effects of the 1965 immigration law on racial identity and coalitions, as well as on the effects of adding publicly legitimated multiracialism to those identities and coalitions. If political candidates run for office on the basis of a strong, single racial identity (David Duke for whites; Ron Dellums for blacks), these strategies will push coalitional politics in one direction. Conversely, if candidates campaign on the promise of incorporating immigrants into extant communities (Antonio Villaraigosa), or seek to use individual multiracialism to promote multiracial coalitions (Barack Obama), or promote nativism (Randy Cunningham), these platforms will push coalitional politics in a different direction. What individual actors will decide to do in the political arena over the next few decades is, in Schedler's terms, conditional and uncertain.

Finally, there is the possibility of a catastrophic event. If, for example, non-Americans make several more attacks like those of September 11,

2001, or if some other event permits nativist anxiety to culminate in a restrictive new immigration policy (as happened in 1924), then the combined effects of the 1965 immigration law and the 2000 census could move in yet another direction. In that case, we predict eventual stabilization of the current racial hierarchy, with immigrants assimilating into whiteness or blackness and multiracialism remaining the identity of a small number of liminal individuals.

Thus the concept of contingency, and the many particular forms that it can take, enables us to organize an otherwise bewilderingly complicated set of policies, trajectories, and possibilities. In the rest of this chapter, we focus on past rather than future contingencies, for the good reason that we have actual evidence about what has already happened. But we return intermittently to a discussion of various possible futures, since that is the arena in which the multiple types of contingency come into full view. In doing so, we use another simple but powerful theoretical typology, Paul Pierson's "time horizons of different causal accounts."[5] This chapter focuses on short-term causes, slighting his discussion of "slow-moving causal processes," but it uses his distinction between short-term and slow-moving outcomes. The former may be highly contingent, as we demonstrate for both immigration and multiracialism, but they can be understood as plausible or likely contingencies. Longer-term outcomes—caused by dynamics such as generational replacement, evolutionary selection, or accumulation of small changes[6]—are probably even more contingent; any predicted long-term outcome in the American racial order is best thought of as possible or even imaginable rather than likely or certain. That does not make questions about the long term less interesting, however, or less important.

The Immigration Act of 1965 and the Racial Order

The Laws

Prior to the 1965 Immigration Act, entry into the United States was largely governed by the provisions of the Immigration and Nationality Act of 1924. It enshrined in law the nativist and xenophobic sentiments that only northern and western Europeans should be welcome to join American society as citizens. The most recent substantial modification prior to 1965, the McCarran-Walter Act of 1952, preserved both national origins quotas and the limit on the number of immigrants admitted to the United States. Within the quotas, strong preference was given to those with needed job skills; after them came relatives of United States citizens or permanent resident aliens. The McCarran-Walter Act did permit spouses and unmarried minor children of citizens to immigrate without limits, and it abolished racial, gender, and marital prohibitions on becoming a naturalized citizen. It maintained a strong preference for northern Europeans and a relative or absolute disinterest in the rest of the eastern hemisphere. The McCarran-Walter Act continued the pattern of saying nothing about western hemispheric immigration.[7]

Although pressures to abolish the national origins quotas had persisted since 1924, the climate after World War II sharpened demands on the United States to modify its immigration policies in order to admit citizens from other parts of the world on an equal footing. As President Truman wrote,

> Long dormant questions about the effect of our immigration laws now assume first rate importance. What we do in the field of immigration and naturalization is vital to the continued growth and internal development of the United States—to the economic and social strength of our country—which is the core of the defense of the free world. Our immigration policy is equally, if not more important to the conduct of our foreign relations and to our responsibilities of moral leadership in the struggle for world peace.[8]

President Eisenhower also spoke urgently of the need for immigration reform in state of the union addresses, the Democratic Party included changing immigration policy in its platform, and President Kennedy spent much time trying to change the law. However, it took the shock of Kennedy's assassination, Lyndon Johnson's ascendance to the presidency, heightened Cold War anxieties, and the momentum of the civil rights movement and Great Society ambitions to finally get serious revisions. The Immigration and Nationality Law of 1965 (the Hart-Celler Act) included:

- More preference to immigrants with a close relative already in the United States;
- Preference to highly skilled workers in the arts and sciences;
- Limits on eastern hemispheric immigration of 170,000 per year;
- Elimination of discriminatory policies against Asian immigrants;
- Safeguards for American jobs through labor certification provisions;

- Provisions for admitting refugees; and
- New limits on western hemispheric immigration of 120,000 people per year.[9]

Country-specific provisions were eliminated, but immigration from any one nation in the eastern hemisphere was limited to 20,000 people per year. Immigration from the western hemisphere was not subject to country quotas.

The Hart-Celler Act has been substantially amended, most importantly in the Immigration Restriction and Control Act (IRCA) of 1986, the Immigration Act of 1990, and the USA Patriot Act of 2001. All three laws maintained the basic division between family- and employment-based selection criteria for each hemisphere, kept an overall quota on immigration, and exempted immediate family members of United States citizens from these restrictions. American immigration policy has thus resisted major changes since 1965.

Demographic Effects of the 1965 Law

The number of immigrants to the United States has historically varied according to factors ranging from potato-killing blights and murderous

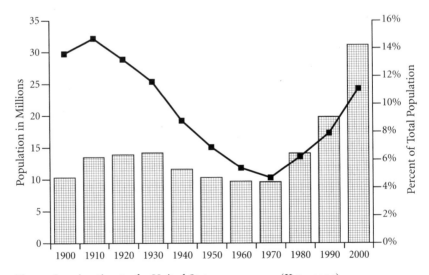

Fig. 5.1. Immigration to the United States, 1900–2000 (Katz, 2004)

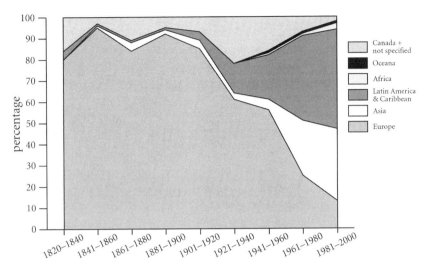

Fig. 5.2. Regions of immigration to the United States, 1820–2004 (author's analyses from *Yearbook of Immigration Statistics,* Department of Homeland Security).

pogroms to the need for labor created by industrialization and westward expansion. But laws are clearly associated with the level of flows, as figure 5.1 shows. In the decades after the 1924 immigration law took effect, immigration declined. However, World War II and the Cold War generated new populations of displaced people, creating demands that the United States open its doors to groups other than western Europeans. After 1952, congressional provisions often admitted refugees fleeing political persecution and natural disasters, as well as immigrants with distinct scientific or artistic skills. As a result, by 1965 overall levels of immigration were creeping upward, and only a third of immigrants actually came in under existing quotas.[10] Thus despite quotas, many immigrants arrived from Asia, Africa, Eastern Europe, and the Middle East.

Nevertheless, the short-term outcome of the Hart-Celler Act was powerful. Since it abolished national origins quotas, the source of immigrants shifted even more dramatically, as figure 5.2 shows. For most of the nineteenth and twentieth centuries, conflict had focused on which European or Asian nationalities were entering the United States and which should be permitted to do so. Immigration from Mexico and Latin America was first unregulated and largely ignored, then unregulated and sought by employers, then controlled (at least officially) through deportation and bracero programs. But by the 1970s, these old conflicts and employment policies were outmoded. Immigration from the "white" nations of Europe and Canada was replaced by immigration from the "non-white" nations of Latin America and Asia.[11] Moreover, these data understate the change since they do not include the rising and now large number of undocumented immigrants, mostly from non-European nations.

Put in terms of group membership, in 1970, whites (mostly native-born) comprised 83 percent of the United States population; blacks (almost all native-born) were 11 percent; Asians and Pacific Islanders (almost all foreign-born) were 1 percent; and Latinos (mostly foreign-born) were 4 percent. By 2000, the figures were, respectively, 69 percent, 13 percent, 4 percent, and 13 percent. If immigration policies are not changed, racial and ethnic minorities (as currently understood) will grow as a percentage of the nation until European Americans are less than half the population by roughly 2050. It seems astonishing that the citizens of the United States, most of whom want to maintain what they see as the traditional identity of their country, legislated themselves such a diverse population that the dominant race will soon become a minority.[12] Part of the explanation of that conundrum is that they did not deliberately choose to do so; the path toward this outcome was the unintended consequence of the decisions of millions of individuals responding to global economic, political, and demographic changes in the context of a law designed to do something else entirely.

The Intentions of Proponents

Proponents designed the Immigration Act of 1965 primarily as a symbolic gesture, aimed at various audiences. For American citizens, they expected passage of this act, along with the Civil Rights and Voting Rights Acts, to signal an end to government-sanctioned Anglo-Saxon supremacy in the United States. For people both inside and outside the United States, they wanted an act to reflect the country's growing "role of critical leadership in a troubled and constantly changing world," as the Secretary of State put it.[13] Given the Cold War and civil rights activity, the United States needed to be seen as a fair and meritocratic society, not one that judged people and nations through a lens of "bias and prejudice."[14] As Congressman Seymour Halpern (R-NY) said while opposing the "outrageously discriminatory" country quotas of the existing law, "Our immigration policy must dovetail with our foreign policy, if we expect to be successful in leading the free world."[15]

What they were all referring to was the fact that the extant law gave 70 percent of the immigration slots to residents of the British Isles, Ireland, and Germany, even though almost half went unused—leaving unfilled immigration spaces despite long waiting lists from other nations. Thus the national origins system, which constituted "overt statutory discrimination against more than one-half of the world's population,"[16] was the primary target of the bill's proponents.

Family reunification, the need for workers with specific skills, and humanitarian issues with respect to refugees were also targets for change. But Congress did not see the 1965 law as "a comprehensive revision" of the McCarran-Walter Act;[17] its purpose was merely to allocate visas so as to "choose fairly among the applicants for admission to this country without proposing any substantial change in presently authorized immigration."[18] After all, the law's drafters estimated, the increase in annual eastern hemispheric immigration would "not exceed 2,000."[19] Attorney General Nicholas Katzenbach, for example, assured a House Committee that the projected increase of 60,000 annual immigrants "would be nearly invisible" in a work force growing annually by three million people.[20] Secretary of Labor W. Willard Wirtz similarly testified that passage of the proposed change to the Immigration and Nationality Act would bring in only 24,000 new workers a year (along with perhaps 100,000 people outside the labor force such as housewives and children). In a workforce of about 86 million by 1970, working immigrants "would have no appreciable impact."[21]

Nor were legislators concerned about the loophole of family reunification, even though the proposed law would exempt more categories of family members from annual quotas. *Congressional Quarterly* cited a prediction of "30,000–40,000 immigrants annually . . . under these non-quota provisions."[22] Debates over changing the rules for western hemispheric immigration were much more intense and drawn out. President Johnson and his allies opposed any western hemispheric quotas in order to remain a "good neighbor" and retain the United States' "special relationship" with nations to the north and south. Likewise, Senator Jacob Javits (R-NY), for example, called the proposed western hemisphere ceiling "most unwise and improvident in terms of United States' relations with Latin America."[23] Conversely, labor unions, the American Legion, the American Coalition of Patriotic Societies, and other groups worried about too many

Latin American immigrants, whether because they would compete with native-born Americans for jobs or because they were of a disfavored race, ethnicity, or nation. Enough members of Congress feared that immigration from the western hemisphere was rising too rapidly and would continue to do so that they imposed a cap of 120,000. Since about 140,000 had immigrated in 1964 from Canada, Mexico, and the rest of Latin America, they expected the quota to decrease or at least curtail immigration from that stream. As the authoritative review article in *Congressional Quarterly* put it, the law "closed off the possibility of a very substantial increase in future immigration from the one area on which there previously had been no numerical restrictions. In this sense, the proposed change to the Immigration and Nationality Act could be described as a bill which . . . foreclosed any long-term upward trend in the number of immigrants."[24]

Supporters also did not expect abolition of national origins quotas to significantly change the origins of immigrants to the United States, except for a slight increase in southern and eastern Europeans.[25] Attorney General Robert Kennedy testified, "Mr. Chairman, 40 years ago the national origins system was adopted on the theory that immigration posed a threat to the ethnic composition of the United States. Today, even if one were to accept the assumption underlying that theory, as I do not, the idea that quota immigration could significantly affect our population is absurd."[26] To the claim that the bill would let in "hordes of Africans and Asiatics," Representative Emmanuel Celler (D-FL) responded:

> The bill would not let in great numbers of immigrants from anywhere at all.
> . . . [T]here will be some shift of immigration to countries other than the
> ones in Northern Europe which are now favored . . . but quota immigrants
> will have to compete and to qualify to get in, and quota immigration will
> not be predominantly from Asia and Africa. . . . Actually, many countries in
> Africa do not use their present quotas of 100.[27]

Projections by State Department officials and other experts supported these assertions. Norbert Schlei, an Assistant Attorney General, anticipated 5,000 Asian immigrants in the first year after abolishing the quotas —but then immigration from that source would "disappear."[28] Abba Schwartz, head of the State Department's Bureau of Security and Consular Affairs, predicted about 12,000 more Jamaican immigrants over the long run. He estimated only 820,000 newcomers from the eastern hemisphere in the five years after passage of the law, 82 percent of whom would be European.[29]

Judging by public opinion surveys, the American public agreed with supporters of the act in not expecting or wanting dramatic changes in this policy arena. According to the Roper Center for Public Opinion Research, 25 questions were asked on national surveys in 1964 and 1965 about immigration and immigrants.[30] On three of three questions, respondents overwhelmingly rejected increases in the overall level of immigration. On four others, respondents preferred quotas based on skill rather than nationality. On one question, they endorsed "admitting people who escape from Communism," and on another they agreed on the importance of an immigrant "having relatives who are American citizens with whom he can live." Respondents preferred that immigrants come from Canada, Great Britain, Scandinavia, or Germany—and not from Russia (sic), Asia, the Middle East, Mexico, or Latin America (the questions did not ask about Africa or the Caribbean).

Nor were Americans very interested in passage of the law itself. Barely 10 percent "felt bad because of U.S. strictness in limiting immigration" before it was passed; a majority knew nothing about American immigration policy; only a third knew that the law had in fact passed; and barely any found the law "important . . . personally" or deemed it one of President Johnson's major accomplishments. Had citizens been told that the immigration law of 1965 would have as much influence on American society as that era's civil rights laws or Great Society legislation, they would have been dumbfounded.

The Anxieties of Opponents

Opponents projected different effects of the bill. Representative Joe Skubitz (R-KS) thought it could raise unemployment and would "place . . . increased demands upon education, housing, health facilities, and transportation."[31] Senator Sam Ervin, Jr. (D-NC), feared it was "just one little hole in the dike for unrestricted immigration." (However, even Ervin predicted only 66,000 new job-seekers a year.)[32] The president of the Republican Committee of One Hundred Inc. warned that it would "enormously increase the number of immigrants permitted to enter the United States annually for permanent residence."[33]

Antagonists also predicted more accurately the effects of the proposed law on the United States' racial and ethnic makeup. The president of the Daughters of the American Revolution argued that "abandonment of the national origins system would drastically alter the source of our immigration."[34] The Greenwich Women's Republican Club also feared that the new bill "could change drastically the entire character of our Nation" since "the preponderance of immigrants . . . will begin to come more and more from Asia."[35] The spokesman for the Military Order of the World Wars believed that "the pending bills would discriminate against our own national origins, roots, and cultures and thereby produce radical changes in the homogeneity of our nation."[36] The president of the Republican Committee of One Hundred assumed that "we want to build a national population based on the predominantly northern and western Europe stock which discovered, explored and developed America, and which today so deeply cherishes our freedom and our ways of life," then asked rhetorically if instead "we [are] willing to permit the American population makeup to be based rather on the makeup of foreign lands whose natives can get in line fastest, in the greatest number, under a first-come, first-served scheme of entry."[37] These warnings went largely unheeded, however, whether because they were not believed or because of their taint of nativism and racism.

The Contingency of Individual Actions

Table 5.1 summarizes our analysis of the rationales used in all of the congressional hearings on the immigration bill. It confirms the qualitative analysis above, and suggests why the legislation passed. The final bill passed with a lopsided vote of 320–69 in the House and a voice vote in the Senate. President Johnson signed it, despite his dislike of western hemispheric quotas. Given that advocates, legislative supporters, and the President all did not intend or expect to destabilize the United States' demography, change how Americans thought about racial groups, or create new groups, why did those things happen?

Here is the first place in which contingency enters the analysis.[38] Proponents of the Hart-Celler Act were presumably not foolish or deceptive, and the legislative process was apparently neither corrupt nor misguided. Experts and lawmakers were acting on the best available information at the time. What happened, of course, is that circumstances changed in unanticipated ways. Immigration around the world began to increase in the 1960s and accelerated over the next few decades. The number of migrants rose from about 75 million in 1960 to about 190 million in 2005—from 2.5

TABLE 5.1

*Rationales for Support and Opposition to 1965 Immigration Act,
in 1964–65 Hearings of House of Representatives and Senate*

Rationale for Position	Favor Change (N = 184 speakers)	Oppose Change (N = 65 speakers)	No Stated Position (N = 20 speakers)
Concern about message that other nations are not good enough	24%	2%	5%
Desire to help neighbors and maintain good relations in western hemisphere	11%	0%	0%
Opposition to racism or racial discrimination	53%	5%	20%
Need for skilled workers—e.g., scientists, doctors	45%	0%	10%
Sends desired message to immigrants living in U.S.	21%	2%	10%
Endorse fairness to all nations	34%	3%	0%
Concern about backlogs in some countries	23%	0%	5%
Endorse family reunification	50%	0%	10%
Desire to help refugees from terror and disasters	26%	2%	5%
Concern about strain of immigrants on public services	16%	24%	5%
Concern about population growth throughout the world	0.5%	36%	0%
Concern about too many immigrants taking U.S. jobs	0%	42%	0%
Concern that immigrants can't assimilate	0%	40%	0%
Concern about urban unrest	0%	40%	0%
Desire to preserve Anglo-Saxon heritage	0%	18%	0%
Concern about exacerbating Communist threat by admitting subversives	0%	38%	0%
Fear that law permits unlimited immigration	0%	24%	4%
Makes pejorative comments about Africans	0%	17%	0%
Makes pejorative comments about Asians	0%	6%	0%
Makes pejorative comments about Latin Americans	0%	11%	0%
Average Prediction (scaled from "Expect no change in annual immigration" = 1 to "Expect 1 million or more annual immigrants" = 6)*	2.54	5.33	1

* When making predictions.

percent to 3 percent of the world population. The United States absorbed the highest proportion of immigrants by an order of magnitude; the United Nations estimates that the United States had received 38 million recent immigrants by 2005, compared with the Russian Federation at 12 million, Germany at 10 million, and the Ukraine, France, and Saudi Arabia at roughly 6 million each.[39] Legal immigration to the United States rose to over a million people a year in 2001 and 2002, with illegal immigration adding several hundred thousand more annually.

Furthermore, migration levels from what the United Nations identifies as less developed regions and least developed countries rose especially fast. In 2003, for example, the proportion of immigrants to the United States from Europe dropped to under 15 percent, the proportion from Asia reached a third of all legal immigration, and the fraction from Mexico, the Caribbean, and Central and South America reached over 40 percent. Illegal immigrants also came disproportionately from Latin America.

In short, people made and are still making the choice to move, for reasons that are perfectly explicable in retrospect but were not reasonably predictable in 1965. Contingency—that is, conditional and uncertain actions by unconnected individuals in many nations around the world—met a law, and the law, or at least its promulgators' intentions, gave way.

Consequences for the American Racial Order

Ramifications of the 1965 act will affect how Americans conceive of and experience race for much of this century. But the direction of the ramifications remains unresolved. Here are the third and fourth forms of contingency —the normative, empirical, and pragmatic choices of millions of individual actors, as well as the political calculations and commitments of identifiable political and social movement leaders. These multiple contingencies suggest several possible long-term consequences of immigration for the American racial and ethnic order.

On the one hand, immigration frequently exacerbates tensions between newcomers and native-born groups, especially when new groups challenge the existing distribution of social status, economic resources, and political power. The arrival of millions of eastern and southern Europeans in the late nineteenth century destabilized the category of "white," contributing to severe labor unrest, the flourishing of nativist and racist groups such as the Ku Klux Klan, and repression of African Americans as well as Asians and Native Americans.[40] Today, groups continue to racialize themselves, respond to others in racially nationalistic terms, and experience racialization by others, all in the context of competing for resources or fending off attacks. Some argue, for example, that Latinos should embrace a panethnic racial identity because "the assignment of racial boundaries arises in the form of social practices"—practices which include discrimination that has led to the subjugation of Latinos.[41] Others claim that Asians have been racialized and set up as targets by whites who seek to use them to justify subordinating purportedly inferior groups such as blacks.[42] Native- and foreign-born blacks frequently clash over elections, status, and jobs, resulting in tensions and negative stereotyping by both groups.[43]

Such tensions can be expected to increase as cities become more ethnically fragmented, as the proportion of immigrants in a given city increases, and as immigrants move into communities unused to demographic change.[44] Over the next few decades immigrant families and native-born Americans may well address these tensions by separating into distinctive communities, each with its own resources, centers of power, and vulnerabilities.

Alternatively, the presence of new groups may disrupt the extant American racial order, not merely add new groups into it. If new, non-white minorities perceive that they share an interest in dismantling white supremacy, they could form coalitions with existing minority groups in order to effect such a change.[45] Such destabilization is most likely to begin in states such as California, Hawaii, New Mexico, and Texas, where non-whites already constitute a majority of the population. Or perhaps immigrants will lead the way into a postmodern, highly contextualized structure in which Americans "experience race as a fluid, situational category that matters in some contexts but is irrelevant in others."[46]

On the other hand, immigrants might simply blend into and thereby strengthen the traditional American black-white binary. After all, most ethnic European immigrants "became white" by the mid-twentieth century,[47] thereby reinforcing old patterns of white supremacy and treatment of blacks as the ultimate out-group. A century later, many members of new groups are assimilating into mainstream American-ness by blurring boundaries through intermarriage, economic mobility, and acculturation.[48] According to this framework, even those who are not succeeding or are unable to enter mainstream society (a.k.a., "become white") are also assimilating, but into blackness—thereby once again reinforcing the classic racial order of the United States.[49]

There is sufficient evidence for all three possibilities to suggest that each is a reasonable prediction. Which ends up as the primary pattern, or whether something else entirely different comes to predominate (e.g., class- or religion-based politics?), depends on the normative, empirical, and pragmatic choices yet to be made by millions of individuals and hundreds of political leaders. It also depends on long-term forces such as generational replacement, evolutionary ecology, and the accumulation of many small changes. Just as the short-term outcome of the 1965 Immigration Act—rapid and substantial demographic change—was contingent in the sense of unanticipated, so the long-run outcome—shaping the United States' system of racial hierarchy—is contingent in the sense of unpredictable and uncertain at present.

Mark One or More: The Census, Racial Boundaries, and Racial Hierarchy

The new instruction to "mark one or more" race in census 2000 may further complicate the outcomes of the demographic changes wrought by recent immigration laws. The invitation to identify as multiracial has not yet had much impact on the American racial order, and it may never do so. Nevertheless, here too prediction is risky since the policy's eventual effect is contingent on individual actions and particular actors.

Unlike proponents and opponents of the 1965 Immigration Act, both supporters and detractors of the "mark one or more" instruction expressed similar predictions about how it would influence Americans' racial understandings; they differed mainly on whether these changes would improve or worsen the racial order. There was also a strange disjunction, unlike in the history of the Hart-Celler Act, between the issues on which most congressional testimony focused and the grounds on which policy makers and experts decided the change. Tracing these patterns can give us a handle on which long-term contingent outcomes seem plausible, possible, or fantastical.

The census' racial and ethnic categories have been about as malleable over time as any "objective" measure from a purportedly technical, nonpolitical agency can be. Across decades and sometimes within one census, the categories have mixed citizenship status, what we commonly understand as race, nationality, religion, and ethnicity. In 1850, the census had two racial categories—Black (slave or free) and Mulatto, with White as the unnamed other. By 1930 it identified ten groups—White, Negro, Mexican, Indian, Chinese, Japanese, Filipino, Hindu, Korean, Other mixed races—and by 2000 it offered an array of races, colors, nationalities, tribal possibilities, and ethnic identities, as shown in figure 5.3. The census first separately identified the ethnic category of Hispanic in 1970, but only in a sample of states; by 2000 the question on ethnicity had also effloresced into a list of Latin American or Caribbean nationalities asked of all respondents. Instructions to enumerators have consistently shown concern about how to tabulate people of mixed races, with the perennial goal of locating each person in his or her sole "real" racial group. Only in 2000 was racial mixture invited.

Even if the examples of nationalities on the census form are collapsed into the five major "races," allowing people to check more than one box produces 126 possible combinations of race and ethnicity. In 2000, about 7

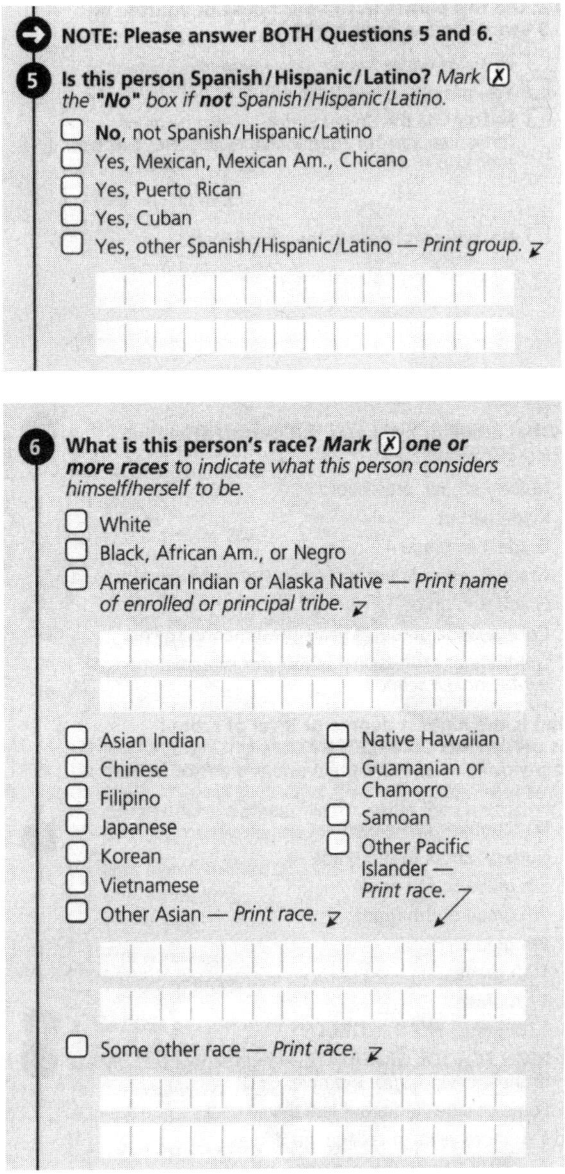

NOTE: Please answer BOTH Questions 5 and 6.

5 **Is this person Spanish/Hispanic/Latino?** *Mark* [X] *the* **"No"** *box if* **not** *Spanish/Hispanic/Latino.*

☐ **No**, not Spanish/Hispanic/Latino
☐ Yes, Mexican, Mexican Am., Chicano
☐ Yes, Puerto Rican
☐ Yes, Cuban
☐ Yes, other Spanish/Hispanic/Latino — *Print group.* ↙

6 **What is this person's race?** *Mark* [X] **one or more races** *to indicate what this person considers himself/herself to be.*

☐ White
☐ Black, African Am., or Negro
☐ American Indian or Alaska Native — *Print name of enrolled or principal tribe.* ↙

☐ Asian Indian   ☐ Native Hawaiian
☐ Chinese   ☐ Guamanian or
☐ Filipino   Chamorro
☐ Japanese   ☐ Samoan
☐ Korean   ☐ Other Pacific
☐ Vietnamese   Islander —
☐ Other Asian — *Print race.* ↙   *Print race.* ↙

☐ Some other race — *Print race.* ↙

Fig. 5.3. Ethnicity and race items on 2000 census.

million people—2.4 percent of the enumerated population—responded by marking more than one race (almost all chose two, but 823 chose six). Less than 3 percent is obviously a small fraction of the population, and if multiracial identification remains at that level, these individuals will be a conceptual anomaly and a headache for statisticians, but little more. However, although they disagreed on how, why, and to what effect, proponents, opponents, policy makers, and experts all agreed before the fact that officially recognizing multiracialism would deeply affect American racial categories and structures over the long run.

Purposes and Predictions of Multiracialism in the Census

By the early 1990s, advocacy groups were pressing for a category of "multiracial" to be added to the specified racial groups originally set in an OMB (Office of Management and the Budget) directive of 1977. In response to this and other concerns about the census' racial and ethnic categories, congressional committees held two sets of hearings. Also during the 1990s, the multiracial movement held a March on Washington, the census bureau conducted field experiments to test responses to various formats and wordings of the race and ethnicity items, and the National Academy of Sciences held a workshop that published an important report. In 1997 the OMB issued a revised standard that led to the instruction of "mark one or more" on the 2000 census.

Table 5.2 summarizes the rationales of those supporting and opposing a multiracial category who testified before Congress in the 1993 and 1997 hearings. As the table indicates, the hearings evinced a wide array of considerations. Some who testified noted that the existing system of racial categories no longer fit the changing demography of the United States. Representative Barney Frank (D-MA), for example, did not know what to make of the Cape Verdeans in his district: "People have a problem out there. Are they African-American? Are they Black? Are they Cape Verdean?"[50] Perhaps, it was suggested, a multiracial category would make him and others better able to classify and understand their new constituents. Representative Stephen Horn (R-CA) observed in his 1997 opening statement that "high rates of immigration and intermarriage between people of diverse racial backgrounds are rapidly changing the composition of our Nation's population."[51] An administrator from the OMB took no position on changes to the census, but similarly pointed out that "during the past

TABLE 5.2

Rationales for Support and Opposition to Multiracial Classification on 2000 Census,
in 1993 and 1997 Hearings in the House of Representatives

Rationale for Position	Favor Change (N = 19 speakers)	Oppose Change (N = 16 speakers)	No Opinion (N = 23 speakers)
Each person has the right to determine his or her own or child's identity	26%	0%	9%
Better form, or the next stage, of civil rights enforcement and/or Voting Rights Act enforcement	21%	6%	0%
Permits better medical research or treatment	21%	0%	4%
Step toward eliminating racial categorization or classification	5%	0%	0%
Better measure of actual demography of U.S. (or better measure of coming demographic changes in U.S.)	16%	0%	0%
May increase number of people who identify as multiracial	16%	0%	0%
Makes us better able to recognize and appreciate all ancestries —humanism	5%	0%	4%
Already being done by other organizations and/or states	21%	0%	0%
Will inhibit enforcement of civil rights/voting rights laws	11%	38%	0%
Will reduce number in a racial/ethnic group, so less federal or state funding for that group	5%	19%	4%
Way to escape blackness or other disadvantaged racial/ethnic group	0%	44%	4%
Other nations have tried "multiracialism," with bad results	5%	25%	0%
Too complicated or otherwise problematic statistically or logistically	21%	19%	4%
Makes pejorative comments about multiracials and/or about those endorsing the category	0%	0%	0%
Makes pejorative comments about opponents of multiracialism	0%	25%	0%

20 years, our country's population has become more racially and ethni-cally diverse, largely as a result of the growth in immigration and interra-cial marriages."[52]

Nevertheless, the intersection between immigration and multiracialism received more attention outside than within the congressional hearings. The report from the National Academy of Sciences' 1994 workshop noted that the Immigration Act was "changing the composition of the minority population" and that "population projections [along with other factors] . . . have led to the current debate about racial and ethnic populations and how they are classified."[53] The report predicted "increasing numbers of people with multiple ancestries, for whom future preferences for self-identification are unknown. . . . These factors raise questions about the usefulness of demographic analysis and population projections based on conventional assumptions of 'closed' ethnic groups with no exogamy." In an explicit recognition of contingency, the report observed in the next sentence that "the largest degree of consensus at the workshop was that any revision in the standard will itself need to be able to adapt to change."[54]

Scholars too had been regularly pointing to the connections among immigration, intermarriage, and instability in racial and ethnic categories. Hugh Davis Graham first described the unintended (in his word, "strange") interaction between immigration and the practice of affirmative action.[55] Kim Williams noted that the impact of "mark one or more" might be "most far-reaching, ultimately, in the ways in which it interacts with high levels of immigration."[56] Frank Bean and his co-authors discussed whether Latinos' and Asians' "high levels of intermarriage and multiracial reporting" signaled that "the long-standing black-white divide is breaking down"; they remained agnostic.[57] Sonya Tafoya showed the implications for intermarriage if immigration levels elsewhere came to match those in California.[58]

The OMB's revision of the census categories in 1997, which permitted "mark one or more" but not a category labeled "multiracial," accorded with these analyses. The agency again observed that the existing "minimum categories . . . do not reflect the increasing diversity of our Nation's population that has resulted primarily from growth in immigration and in interracial marriages."[59] In the formal language of the *Federal Register*, one can see officials struggling with the contingent consequences of the Immigration Act of 1965 and its successors. The Revision stipulated the social construction of race, asserted the need to "respect . . . individual dignity" by self-identification, and called for "reliable" and "meaningful" categories achieved through "appropriate scientific methodologies." It aimed, perhaps contradictorily, for racial and ethnic categories that are "comprehensive in coverage and produce compatible, nonduplicative . . . data"—and are "kept to a manageable size" as well as "understood by respondents and observers." In a final acknowledgement that current racial labels may be highly unstable, the OMB permitted "additional categories . . . provided they can be aggregated to the standard categories."

In contrast to the experts' focus, however, participants in the congressional hearings generally paid little attention to immigrants and their intermarriage. Political controversy lay elsewhere. Some advocates saw a multiracial option as a step toward eliminating all official racial and ethnic categories. Thus Speaker of the House of Representatives, Newt Gingrich (R-GA), stated that

It is wrong for some Americans to begin creating subgroups to which they have a higher loyalty than to America at large. . . . Ideally, I believe we should have one box on federal forms that simply reads, "American." But if that is not possible at this point, . . . allow[ing] them [i.e., Americans] the option of selecting the category "multiracial" . . . will be an important step toward transcending racial division and reflecting the melting pot which is America.[60]

Other proponents had a wholly different motivation: identification would permit multiracials to move under the umbrella of antidiscrimination laws and regulations. Thus, "it would be wrong to say that I would only be discriminated against because I am Korean or Asian American. . . . Sometimes people are discriminating against others just because they are multiracial—not because they are perceived to be one thing or another."[61]

Representative Horn's opening statement articulated a third reason for support, which also ignored immigration and demographic change: "An individual with parents from two different categories may not wish to choose one parental identity over the other. The children of two such individuals could conceivably belong to all of the current categories and feel that to choose just one is meaningless or offensive."[62] This was the grounds on which Representative John Conyers (D-MI) broke with the rest of the black congressional delegation: we "are becoming a more color-blind society, but we cannot guarantee equality for people of all races if we do not allow people to identify their complete racial background. We must not create a divide between multiracial people and other minority communities by denying multiracial people their right to stand up and be counted on the census."[63] Finally, arguments about the medical necessity of being able to know how many people there are of particular racial mixtures influenced the decision-makers of the OMB, even if those arguments lacked some of the rhetorical punch of other reasons for support.

Opponents of the multiracial designation offered a wholly different set of predictions about the likely effects of blurring racial boundaries. Most people of color who testified and almost all black legislators argued that multiracialism would inhibit, not expand, enforcement of civil rights laws. As Representative Danny Davis (D-IL) put it, "Until a process to collect meaningful, accurate or specific racial and ethnic data that remedies past, current and/or even prevent future discrimination is in place—I feel that the multiracial category could jeopardize the civil rights of many minorities as well as provide inconsistent and damaging effects on overall racial counts."[64] Representative Eleanor Holmes Norton (D-D.C.) was even more emphatic, casting a wide net in her explanation of why the temptation of multiracialism can mislead African Americans:

> At one point, blacks thought they might mitigate the effects of being black by claiming something else in their heritage. "Oh, I am black, but I am also American Indian. . . ." Oh, it was so pitiful. About the only thing that American racism did for us is saying no, you are one or the other. . . . So I sit here as a light skin black woman and I sit here to tell you that I am black. That people who are my color in this country will always be treated as black. . . . We who are black have got to say look, we are people of color, and we are readily identified. Any discrimination against one of us is discrimination against another.[65]

Policy Consequences

In sum, unlike the experts and policymakers, most of those involved in the congressional hearings on multiracialism paid relatively little attention to immigrants or immigration law. They focused instead on issues of personal identity and civil rights, especially for (implicitly native-born) blacks and whites, the two groups least affected by recent demographic change. The experts are clearly right about the links between immigration and intermarriage; nevertheless, a complete analysis of contingency requires asking also whether the long-run outcomes will speak to congressional hopes and fears.

Consider the short-term outcomes first. A third of the almost 7 million Americans choosing more than one race in census 2000 combined white and "some other race."[66] Most identified their second "race" as Hispanic or as a European or Middle Eastern nationality, suggesting that as immigration continues to rise, the number of people who think of themselves as only partly white will also rise.[67] Also, immigrants, young adults, and the relatively well educated were disproportionately likely to mark more than one.[68] That suggests that multiracials may set a trend or function as bellwethers of changes that are coming more slowly to the rest of American society.

Institutional changes also make it plausible that Americans will increasingly identify as multiracial. Federal agencies are required eventually to include the new instruction in their surveys and data collection; a few states mandate a multiracial or "mark more than one" option, and others have considered doing so. Universities are following suit, and hospitals are slowly moving in the same direction; other large institutions will arguably follow. Sooner or later, therefore, Americans may become familiar with the option of choosing more than one race.

Finally, inter-racialism as a literal fact is rising, as figure 5.4 shows. For whites and blacks, the base is very small so the overall numbers remain tiny, but the dramatic shift in the curve suggests a genuine and significant change. For other groups, especially Asians and Latinos, intermarriage rates are high in absolute terms and rising fast, especially among the young. Where racial intermarriage rises, so does the number of interracial children, as figure 5.5 shows for the black-white population. The result of all of these forces might be confirmation of Kenneth Prewitt's prediction with which we started, that "Census 2000 will go down in history as the event that began to redefine race in American society." If that turns out to be right, then the current racial and ethnic order may change significantly.

But all of this change is contingent on normative, empirical, and pragmatic choices of millions of individuals—many not yet living in the United States—so we must consider plausible alternatives. Some federal agencies and many private institutions are slow to incorporate "mark one or more" into their operations. A follow-up survey of those who chose more than one race in census 2000 showed great instability, with about equal proportions of people going back and forth between one race and more than one.[69] The 2004 American Community Survey showed a small but consistent decline in the proportion of people, in every social group, identifying with more than one race.[70] One of the United States' best demographers, Reynolds Farley, is even describing multiracialism as "a social movement that succeeded but failed."[71] In sum, even the short-term outcomes of changing the 2000 census are not yet clear; it is too soon to see how individual actions, and the choices of political actors, will settle out.

Still, the short-term contingencies seem reasonably constrained compared with the possible long-term implications of high and rising levels of immigration combined with official recognition of multiracialism. Perhaps those who testified that multiracialism will disrupt American racial categories and eventually undermine racial hierarchy itself will be proven correct. Or perhaps those who testified that it could undermine essential black solidarity will have their worst fears realized. Latinos describe their culture as one of *mestizaje*, racial mixture, regardless of any particular

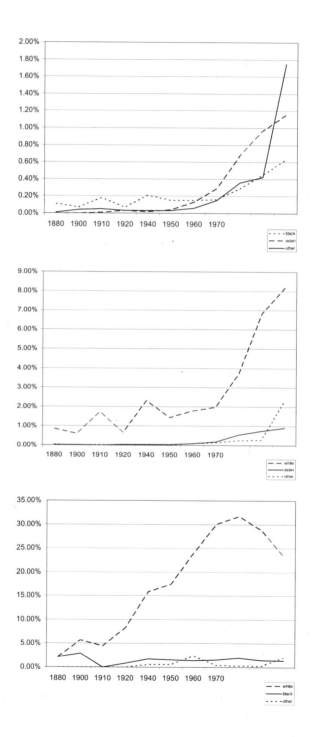

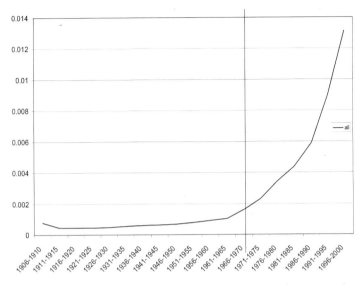

Fig. 5.4. (*opposite page*) Percentage of whites, blacks, and Asian Americans marrying out of their race, 1880–2000 (data and charts from Roland Fryer, Harvard University)

Fig. 5.5. (*above*) Percentage of black-white births, 1906–2000 (data and chart from Roland Fryer, Harvard University)

individual's family heritage. If current patterns of immigration and current birth rates persist, the Hispanic culture of racial mixture might come to pervade American society. Alternatively, people of Hispanic descent could be seen as a new monoracial group, thereby obscuring their ancestral diversity. Multiracials could provide crucial links between potential coalitional partners, or might develop a new coalition among themselves. If, say, a third of Americans identify with more than one race a few decades from now, race and ethnicity as we now know them will mean something very different personally, culturally, and politically—but that remains in the realm of speculation, not reasonable prediction.

The likelihood of these possible long-term consequences of the interaction between immigration and multiracialism depends, in part, on a final form of contingency, a catastrophic event that leads to the curtailment of immigration or the hardening of racial group lines. These possible outcomes are, in short, contingent in what Schedler identifies as the strongest sense of that term—indeterminate, conditional, and uncertain.

Conclusion

"Policies that start small may, if conditions are right for self-reinforcement or if unintended consequences are large, end up being extremely significant." Conversely, "policies that make a grand entrance may erode unless they possess characteristics that generate not just initial success but substantial resilience."[72] The outcomes of the 1965 immigration law and its successors illustrate the first point, and the eventual outcomes of the change in the 2000 census might—or might not —end up illustrating the second. Thus we find contingency in the future of group boundaries and racial hierarchy in the United States. The composition of the American population has been shaped by the unanticipated choices of millions of people around the world who used a law devised for other purposes; how we understand and practice race in the United States will be shaped by the choices of millions of Americans, old and new, over the next few decades. Contingency probably does not always rule politics, but sometimes it does.

NOTES

1. Our thanks to participants in the conference on "Contingency in the Study of Politics," Yale University, December 3–5, 2004, for helpful reactions and suggestions. Jennifer Hochschild also thanks the Guggenheim Foundation, Radcliffe Institute for Advanced Study, and Weatherhead Center for International Affairs at Harvard University for financial and intellectual support of the project of which this is a part. We are grateful to Abimbola Orisamolu and Sarah Talkovsky for research assistance, and to Suzann Evinger, Nancy Gordon, Susan Schechter, and Katherine Wallman for clarifying the roles of OMB and the census bureau. We are also grateful to Ian Haney López, David Hollinger, Kenneth Prewitt, and John Skrentny for valuable suggestions—some of which we actually took.

2. This chapter is part of a book-length project, written along with Vesla Weaver of the University of Virginia, on the possible political consequences of unstable racial and ethnic boundaries in the United States.

3. Pierson, *Politics*; see also Skocpol, "Bringing the State Back In."

4. Schedler, this volume.

5. Pierson, *Politics*, p. 81.

6. Ibid.

7. For a good political history of immigration laws, see Tichenor, *Dividing Lines.*

8. Truman, "Veto of the Immigration and Nationality Act."

9. Legislative History, "Immigration."

10. Ibid., p. 3331.

11. Reimers, *Still the Golden Door.*

12. To cite only one example, three-fifths of respondents to a 1995 survey would rather "encourage immigrants to blend into American culture by giving up some important aspects of their own culture" than encourage them to "maintain their own culture more strongly" Gallup/CNN/*U.S.A. Today*, "Poll."

13. Rusk, House, July 2, 1964.

14. Ibid.

15. *Congressional Quarterly*, "National Quotas for Immigration to End," p. 4

16. Rusk, House, July 22, 1964.

17. Legislative History, "Immigration," p. 3329.

18. Ibid., p. 3332.

19. Ibid., p. 3333.

20. Katzenbach, Feb. 10, 1965.

21. *Congressional Quarterly*, "National Quotas for Immigration to End," p. 474.

22. Ibid., p. 461.

23. Ibid., p. 478.

24. Ibid., p. 462.

25. That, indeed, was part of the point of the bill, since Democratic politicians were eager to maintain the support of white ethnics.

26. Kennedy, House, July 22, 1964.

27. Celler, June 16, 1964.

28. Schlei, House, July 23, 1964.

29. Schwartz, House, Aug. 3, 1964.

30. There were no other survey questions from 1960 to 1970. All evidence from this and the next paragraph comes from polls in the Roper Center database.

31. *Congressional Quarterly*, "National Quotas for Immigration to End," p. 473.

32. Ibid., p. 474.

33. Ibid., p. 476. Other opponents worried that immigrants would exacerbate racial strife or make blacks worse off, import a Communist threat, or worsen levels of organized crime. Overall, however, groups that had derailed immigration reform throughout the 1950s did not oppose the 1965 law because most accepted reassurances that the quotas would keep levels of immigration tolerably low. As *Congressional Quarterly* summarized, "Spokesmen for these organizations said one of their major goals had been achieved—imposing what amounted to an over-all world immigration quota and thus guaranteeing against an excessive number of immigrants. They pointed out that the net effect of the final bill was to limit immigration to about 320,000 persons a year" (*Congressional Quarterly*, "National Quotas for Immigration to End," p. 480).

34. Duncan, "Testimony."

35. Chapin and Gonzalez, "Testimony."

36. Fortier, "Statement."

37. *Congressional Quarterly*, "National Quotas for Immigration to End," p. 476.

38. The contingent factor of President Kennedy's assassination perhaps was also a necessary although not sufficient condition of passage of the Hart-Celler Act. We have no quarrel with that claim; it is simply outside the scope of our consideration.

39. United Nations, *Trends in Total Migrant Stock*.

40. Jacobson, *Whiteness of a Different Color*.

41. Haney López, "Race, Ethnicity, Erasure."

42. Kim, "The Racial Triangulation."

43. Waters, *Black Identities*; Rogers, "Race-based Coalitions."

44. Jones-Correa, "Structural Shifts"; Frey et al., "Tracking American Trends"; Zúñiga and Hernández-León, *New Destinations*.

45. Guinier and Torres, *The Miner's Canary*; Thompson, *Double Trouble*.

46. Kasinitz et al., *Becoming New Yorkers*, jacket description; Fernández-Kelly and Schauffler, "Divided Fates."

47. Jacobson, *Whiteness of a Different Color*; Roediger, *Working Toward Whiteness*; Gerstle, "The Working Class."

48. Alba and Nee, *Remaking the American Mainstream*; Perlmann, *Italians Then*; Smith, "Assimilation."

49. Waters, *Black Identities*; Portes and Rumbaut, *Immigrant America*.

50. Frank, House, July 29, 1993, p. 211.

51. Horn, "Statement on Federal Measures of Race and Ethnicity," p. 1.

52. Katzen, House, 1997, p. 45.

53. Edmonston, *Spotlight on Heterogeneity*, p. 6.

54. Ibid., p. 35.

55. Graham, *Collision Course*.

56. Williams, *Mark One or More*, p. 35.

57. Bean et al., *Immigration*, p. 26

58. Tafoya et al., *Who Chooses*.

59. Office of Management and Budget, *Revisions to the Standards on Race and Ethnicity*, p. 58782.

60. Gingrich, "Statement on Federal Measures of Race and Ethnicity."

61. Matt Kelley, quoted in Moore, "Census' Multiracial Option," p. 3 of internet version.

62. Horn, "Statement on Federal Measures of Race and Ethnicity," p. 4.

63. Conyers, "Statement on Federal Measures of Race and Ethnicity," p. 536.

64. Davis, "Statement on Federal Measures of Race and Ethnicity, p. 44.

65. Norton, "Statement on Federal Measures of Race and Ethnicity," p. 260.

66. Looked at in the opposite direction, about 2.5 percent of non-Hispanic whites, almost 5 percent of non-Hispanic blacks, 6 percent of Hispanics, and 14 percent of Asians chose more than one race.

67. Tafoya et al., *Who Chooses*.

68. Ibid.; Farley and Alba, "New Second Generation."
69. Bennett, *Exploring the Consistency.*
70. Farley, *Trends.*
71. Farley, "Multiple Races."
72. Pierson, *Politics,* p. 166.

BIBLIOGRAPHY

Alba, Richard and Victor Nee. *Remaking the American Mainstream: Assimilation and Contemporary Immigration.* Cambridge, MA: Harvard University Press, 2003.

Bean, Frank, Jennifer Lee, Jeanne Batalova, and Mark Leach. *Immigration and Fading Color Lines in America.* New York: Russell Sage Foundation and Population Reference Bureau, 2004.

Bennett, Claudette. *Exploring the Consistency of Race Reporting in Census 2000 and the Census Quality Survey.* San Francisco, CA: American Statistical Association, 2003.

Chapin, Mrs. Corneial, and Eleanor Gonzalez. Testimony. *Judiciary Committee, Subcommittee No. 1.* House of Representatives, 1965.

Celler, Emmanuel. Testimony. *Judiciary Committee, Subcommittee No. 1.* House of Representatives, 1964.

Congressional Quarterly. "National Quotas for Immigration to End." *Almanac: 89th Congress, 1st Session,* 1965 ed. Washington D.C., Congressional Quarterly Service 21, 1965: 459–482.

Conyers, John. Statement at *Hearings on Federal Measures of Race and Ethnicity and the Implications for the 2000 Census.* 105th Cong., 1st session, House, Committee on Government Reform and Oversight, Subcommittee on Government Management, Information, and Technology, 1997: 535–536.

Davis, Danny. Statement at *Hearings on Federal Measures of Race and Ethnicity and the Implications for the 2000 Census.* 105th Cong., 1st session, House, Committee on Government Reform and Oversight, Subcommittee on Government Management, Information, and Technology, 1997: 41–44.

Duncan, Mrs. Robert. Testimony. *Judiciary Committee, Subcommittee No. 1.* House of Representatives, 1964: 732–738.

Edmonston, Barry, Joshua Goldstein, and Juanita Lott. *Spotlight on Heterogeneity: The Federal Standards for Racial and Ethnic Classification.* Washington, D.C.: National Academy Press, 1996.

Farley, Reynolds. "Identifying with Multiple Races: A Social Movement That Succeeded but Failed?" *The Changing Terrain of Race and Ethnicity.* Ed. Maria Krysan and Amanda Lewis. New York: Russell Sage Foundation Press, 2004: 123–148.

Farley, Reynolds. *Trends in Identifying With More than One Race, American Community Survey: 2000 to 2004.* Ann Arbor, MI: University of Michigan, Population Studies Center, 2005.

Farley, Reynolds, and Richard Alba. "The New Second Generation in the United States." *International Migration Review* 36 (3), 2002: 669–701.

Fernández-Kelly, Patricia, and Richard Schauffler. "Divided Fates: Immigrant Children in a Restructured Economy." *International Migration Review* 28 (4), 1995: 662–689.

Fortier, Louis. Statement. *Judiciary Committee, Subcommittee No. 1.* House of Representatives, 1965.

Frank, Barney. Statement at *Hearings on the Review of Federal Measurements of Race and Ethnicity.* 103d Cong., 1st session, House, Committee on Post Office and Civil Service, Subcommittee on Census, Statistics, and Postal Personnel, 1993: 210–211.

Frey, William, Jill Wilson, Alan Berube, and Audrey Singer. "Tracking American Trends into the Twenty-First Century: A Field Guide to the New Metropolitan and Micropolitan Definitions." *Redefining Urban and Suburban America: Evidence from Census 2000,* vol. 3. Ed. Alan Berube, Bruce Katz, and Robert Lang. Washington, D.C.: Brookings Institution Press, 2006: 191–234.

Gallup/CNN/*U.S.A. Today.* Poll, 1995, from Lapinski, John, Pia Peltola, Greg Shaw, and Alan Yang, "Trends: Immigrants and Immigration." *Public Opinion Quarterly* 61, 2, Summer 1997: 356–383.

Gerstle, Gary. "The Working Class Goes to War." *Mid-America* 75 (3), 1993: 303–322.

Gingrich, Newt. Statement at *Hearings on Federal Measures of Race and Ethnicity and the Implications for the 2000 Census.* 105th Cong., 1st session, House, Committee on Government Reform and Oversight, Subcommittee on Government Management, Information, and Technology, 1997: 661–662.

Graham, Hugh. *Collision Course: The Strange Convergence of Affirmative Action and Immigration Policy in America.* Oxford: Oxford University Press, 2002.

Guinier, Lani, and Gerald Torres. *The Miner's Canary: Enlisting Race, Resisting Power, Transforming Democracy.* Cambridge, MA: Harvard University Press, 2002.

Haney López, Ian. "Race, Ethnicity, Erasure: The Salience of Race to LatCrit Theory." *California Law Review* 85, 1997: 1143–1211.

Horn, Stephen. Statement at *Hearings on Federal Measures of Race and Ethnicity and the Implications for the 2000 Census.* 105th Cong., 1st session, House, Committee on Government Reform and Oversight, Subcommittee on Government Management, Information, and Technology, 1997: 1–5.

Jacobson, Matthew. *Whiteness of a Different Color: European Immigrants and the Alchemy of Race.* Cambridge, MA: Harvard University Press, 1998.

Jones-Correa, Michael. "Structural Shifts and Institutional Capacity: Possibilities for Ethnic Cooperation and Conflict in Urban Settings." *Governing American Cities: Interethnic Coalitions, Competition, and Conflict.* Ed. Michael Jones-Correa. New York: Russell Sage Foundation Press, 2001: 183–209.

Kasinitz, Philip, John Mollenkopf, and Mary Waters, eds. *Becoming New Yorkers: Ethnographies of the New Second Generation.* New York: Russell Sage Foundation Press, 2004.

Katz, Bruce. "Redefining Urban and Suburban America." September 30, 2004. Retrieved November 7, 2004, from www.brook.edu/metro/speeches/20040930_nthp.htm.

Katzen, Sally. Statement at *Hearings on Federal Measures of Race and Ethnicity and the Implications for the 2000 Census.* 105th Cong., 1st session, House, Committee on Government Reform and Oversight, Subcommittee on Government Management, Information, and Technology, 1997: 45–48.

Katzenbach, Nicholas. Testimony. Senate *Subcommittee on Immigration and Naturalization.* Washington, D.C.: March 4, 1965.

Kennedy, Robert. Testimony. *Judiciary Committee, Subcommittee No. 1.* House of Representatives, 1964.

Kim, Claire. "The Racial Triangulation of Asian Americans." *Politics and Society* 27 (1), 1999: 103–136.

Legislative History. "Immigration and Nationality Act-Amendments." *Congressional Record,* 1965, p. 111.

Moore, Solomon. "Census' Multiracial Option Overturns Traditional Views," *Los Angeles Times,* March 5, 2001.

Norton, Eleanor Holmes. Statement at *Hearings on Federal Measures of Race and Ethnicity and the Implications for the 2000 Census.* 105th Cong., 1st session, House, Committee on Government Reform and Oversight, Subcommittee on Government Management, Information, and Technology, 1997: 259–261.

Office of Management and Budget. *Revisions to the Standards for the Classification of Federal Data on Race and Ethnicity.* Washington, D.C.: Executive Office of the President, OMB Office of Information and Regulatory Affairs, 1997.

Perlmann, Joel. *Italians Then, Mexicans Now.* New York: Russell Sage Foundation Press, 2005.

Pierson, Paul. *Politics in Time: History, Institutions, and Social Analysis.* Princeton, NJ: Princeton University Press, 2004.

Portes, Alejandro, and Rubén Rumbaut. *Immigrant America: A Portrait.* Berkeley: University of California Press, 1996.

Reimers, David. *Still the Golden Door: The Third World Comes to America.* New York: Columbia University Press, 1992.

Roediger, David. *Working Toward Whiteness.* New York: Basic Books, 2005.

Rogers, Reuel. "Race-based Coalitions among Minority Groups: Afro-Caribbean Immigrants and African-Americans in New York City." *Urban Affairs Review* 39 (3), 2004: 283–317.

Rusk, Dean. Testimony. *Judiciary Committee, Subcommittee No. 1.* House of Representatives, 1964.

Schlei, Norbert. Testimony. *Judiciary Committee, Subcommittee No. 1.* House of Representatives, 1964.

Schwartz, Abba. Testimony. *Judiciary Committee, Subcommittee No. 1.* House of Representatives, 1964.

Skocpol, Theda. "Bringing the State Back In: Strategies of Analysis in Current Research." *Bringing the State Back In.* Ed. Peter Evans, Dietrich Rueschemeyer, and Theda Skocpol. Cambridge, England: Cambridge University Press, 1985: 3–41.

Smith, James. "Assimilation across the Latino Generations." *American Economic Association Papers and Proceedings* 93 (2), 2003: 315–319.

Tafoya, Sonya. "Mixed Race and Ethnicity in California." *The New Race Question: How the Census Counts Multiracial Individuals.* Ed. Joel Perlmann and Mary Waters. New York: Russell Sage Foundation, 2002: 102–115.

Tafoya, Sonya, Hans Johnson, and Laura Hill. *Who Chooses to Choose Two?* New York: Russell Sage Foundation and Population Reference Bureau, 2004.

Thompson, J. Phillip III. *Double Trouble: Black Mayors, Black Communities, and the Call for a Deep Democracy.* New York: Oxford University Press, 2005.

Tichenor, Daniel. *Dividing Lines: The Politics of Immigration Control in America.* Princeton NJ, Princeton University Press, 2002.

Truman, Harry. Veto of the Immigration and Nationality Act. *Essential Documents in American History,* 1952. Retrieved 2 Nov. 2004 from http://www.wiv.edu/users/wat100/masultra/docs.htm.

United Nations. *Trends in Total Migrant Stock: The 2005 Revision.* New York: United Nations, Population Division, 2006.

Waters, Mary. *Black Identities: West Indian Immigrant Dreams and American Realities.* Cambridge, MA: Harvard University Press, 1999.

Williams, Kim. *Mark One or More: Civil Rights in Multiracial America.* Ann Arbor, MI: University of Michigan Press, 2006.

Zúñiga, Victor, and Rubén Hernández-León, eds. *New Destinations: Mexican Immigration in the United States.* New York: Russell Sage Foundation Press, 2005.

Chapter 6

Region, Contingency, and Democratization

Susan Stokes

Recently,[1] Robert Dahl noted that the challenges facing the world's roughly 200 countries vary, from the *transition* to democracy in non-democracies, to the *strengthening* or *consolidation* of democracy in newly democratized countries, to the *deepening* of democracy in older democracies.[2] As we grapple toward an understanding of transitions to democracy and of its consolidation and deepening, we frequently try to discover general laws of cause and effect, ones that operate in the same way over time and space. With a few exceptions, we have ignored the role of contingency in encouraging or impeding democratization. Yet mounting evidence points toward spatial unevenness in democratization and in the consolidation of democracy. And this spatial unevenness can be the result of contingent choices and chance events.

The dictionary definition of contingency is something that is likely but not certain to happen, happens by chance, or dependent on something else. In this chapter I define a contingent cause or outcome as one that depends on choices or events whose probability of occurring is low. After discussing contingency in general and offering some examples of political phenomena that are subject to contingent causation, I focus on contingencies related to spatial location. I examine the role of *region* in democratization. In so doing, I hope to clarify what we mean by regional effects in politics, and to specify whether, and which kinds of, regional effects represent a form of contingency.

What Is Contingency?

Political outcomes may be contingent in at least three senses. A potential cause may have its effect only in the presence of some background condition or additional cause, and the fact that an interaction is required makes the event unlikely (interactions). Or an outcome may appear *ex ante* unlikely because it depended on two or more factors that had to occur in a particular temporal sequence (sequence). Or it may rely on a choice by an actor who might have made another choice (choice). All of these senses of contingency have been discussed at length in recent scholarship.[3]

Interactions

In interactions, *A* and *B* cause *C*; with only *A* or only *B*, *C* does not occur. Unless both *A* and *B* are certain to occur, then, according to probability theory, the fact that they both have to occur makes the outcome *C* less likely than it would be had only *A* or only *B* been required. Almond and Verba's *The Civic Culture* contains an example.[4] They find that, in advanced democracies, people who trust government also participate more in politics. But in developing countries trust does not cause participation. If trust is *A* and development—the necessary background condition—is *B*, and if participation is *C*, then *A* and *B* together cause *C*, but *A* alone or *B* alone does not.

Kalyvas offers an example in which the chance simultaneity of two causally unrelated events has an effect that would have been absent had the two events not coincided.[5] In England in the early 1970s and France and early 1980s, leftist governments came to power and instituted policies of nationalization. In both countries major economic crises followed these nationalizations, crises that were caused by events that had little to do with the nationalizations. The chance near-simultaneity led, in the minds of the mass publics of both countries, to "the association of nationalization with economic crisis and the subsequent rejection of nationalization by public opinion."[6] If nationalization is *A* and economic crisis *B*, then had either *A* or *B* not occurred, the discrediting of nationalization (*C*)—and, indeed, according to Kalyvas, a broader collapse of a Keynesian economic hegemony—would also not have occurred. Indeed, had these events not unfolded in the particular order that they did—for instance, had economic crises preceded nationalizations—then *C* would not have followed. Kalyvas's example leads us nicely, then, into a consideration of *sequence* and contingency.

Sequence

A must happen before *B* in order for *C* to occur; if *B* happens before *A*, *C* does not occur. In addition to Kalyvas's example, here are two more. First, where the habit of political contestation among opposing elites preceded mass electoral participation, Dahl explains, the emergence of democracy was smooth; where the two emerged simultaneously, it was turbulent.[7] Second, if, in Western European countries, constituencies favoring bureaucratic autonomy came into existence before the franchise was extended, then parties were induced to mobilize voters by using programmatic appeals and by providing public goods. If mass enfranchisement took place before a constituency emerged that favored state autonomy, then the outcome was patronage politics.[8]

Note that "sequences" can be nearly simultaneous, and do not necessarily entail processes that unfold over long periods of time. Kalyvas's example, where economic crisis followed quickly after nationalization, is a sequence that unfolded quickly. The sequences that Kalyvas describes happen to be temporally compact. Sequences will also tend to be temporally compact in cases of policy innovation. But to the extent that policy innovators are aware of the importance of proper sequencing, this sequencing is *ex ante* probable and hence the sense of contingency is reduced.

Consider economic liberalization, which the governments of many developing countries have undertaken in the past two decades. It is now the conventional wisdom among practitioners and scholars that trade liberalization (*A*) has the desired effect of increasing consumer welfare (*C*) only when it follows domestic relative-price adjustment (*B*). If internal price structures are out of whack, a flood of cheap goods from abroad will destroy many efficient domestic firms along with inefficient ones. A similar sort of sequencing should take place in financial-sector liberalization. If reform is to produce an efficient financial system, the privatizing of banks must succeed a process by which lenders learn how to price risk. The opposite sequence occurred in Mexico in the mid-1990s, and it resulted in a catastrophic string of bank failures and a generalized economic crisis.

Choice and Chance

Often in the social sciences what we mean by an outcome being contingent is that, for it to happen, some actor has to make a choice, or take a particular action, and it is not unimaginable that he or she would not have made that choice or taken that action. Had X not taken action A, B would not have happened. This is indeterminacy: in Schedler's framework, "things could have been different."[9] The lower the probability, *ex ante*, that X would do A, the more contingent the outcome. Fearon cites the example of the Brazilian coup d'etat of 1964, as analyzed by Stepan.[10] Had Joao Goulart not responded to an earlier uprising of junior officers with leniency, Stepan contends, there was a high probability that the coup would not have taken place. His leniency caused discontent among military leaders and produced a "winning coalition" for a coup, a coalition that had been elusive just weeks earlier.[11] And Goulart might not have taken the action that he did: the evidence is that he debated in his own mind between leniency and a tougher response, one that would have mollified the senior officers. Goulart's (X's) action (A), which was not obviously more likely than a different action (not-A), produced B, a highly contingent outcome.

Transitions to democracy, like transitions to dictatorship, have been attributed to chance events. Having found no link between economic development and transitions to democracy, Przeworski and his associates posit that chance events—the death of a dictator, a leader's absorption of Christian-democratic ideology—can cause democratization. "Some dictatorships have fallen in the aftermath of the death of the founding dictator, such as a Franco, uniquely capable of maintaining the authoritarian order. Some have collapsed because of economic crises, some because of foreign pressures, *and perhaps some for purely idiosyncratic reasons*."[12]

In sum, in common social-science usage, outcomes are contingent if an interaction of factors or a specified sequence of factors is required to bring them about, or if a particular choice or action is required. The smaller the probability, *ex ante*, that the interaction, sequence, or choice or action would occur, the greater the sense of contingency.

What Is a Regional Effect?

I define a region as a contiguous and compact space constituted by a set of countries in the world or by an area within a country. Whether a contiguous and compact space constitutes a region is largely a matter of convention and public perception, as is the definition of a given region's borders. Natural features frequently define the borders of conventional regions: the oceans around the African continent define the boundaries of the region we call "Africa." Natural features shared by countries can create a region:

the location within their borders of segments of the Andes mountains define the "Andean region" just as the shared location of segments of the Appalachian mountains define the "Appalachian region." A given geographic territory can simultaneously belong to different regions. Alvarez, Cheibub, Limongi, and Przeworski offer two coding schemes for the world's regions, one more coarse-grained, the other more fine-grained. Hence in one scheme, Tunisia (for example) is located in a region called "Africa," in the other it is located in a region called "Middle East/North Africa."[13]

Scholars are likely to identify regional effects of four sorts. (1) *A* is a factor operative in a region and *A* causes *B*. But it is not regional location but *A* that causes *B* (*spurious regional effect*). (2) A vector of causes *A* is operative in a given region. The same vector would have the same effect in any region, but the probability of the vector appearing elsewhere is small, and this small probability creates a particular link between the region and the outcome (*regional vector*). (3) Structural factor *A* is present in a region. *A* causes *B*, but its effect on *B* is a negative function of the spatial distance from *A* (*proximity-dependent regional effects*). Finally (4), some quality of a region as a whole, or the dynamics within it—diffusion, persuasion, learning—change the behavior of units within that region, in comparison with the behavior they would exhibit were they located in a different (*regional dynamics proper*).

Spurious Regional Effects

Many ostensibly regional effects are really not regional at all; the effect of region is spurious. Indeed, when we think about why regions differ politically from one another, our first instinct may be to offer explanations in which region itself plays little part. That is, we treat the effect of region as a spurious stand-in for some other factor.

Consider, for example, the effect of region on the types of political regimes of the countries located in it. A randomly chosen country in Western Europe in the period 1950–1990 had a 95 percent chance of being a democracy, whereas a randomly chosen African country had only a 7 percent chance.[14] Pressed to explain this cross-regional difference, we might say that Africa is highly economically unequal and that inequality discourages democratization.[15] But if this is true, then it is inequality, not Africa, that impedes democracy. Call this the *spurious* explanation of regional effects.

Spurious causes may be either contemporary or historical. Continuing with the African example, we might note that African countries were subjected to European colonial rule. Colonial administrations invented tribal distinctions and sometimes stoked tribal antagonisms, and these distinctions and antagonisms militated against democracy. Here not Africa but a particular legacy of colonialism impeded democracy. But there is a reasonable sense in which region really is a cause in this case, more so than in the example just discussed. Although any region that had undergone the same kind of colonial rule would be equally prone to dictatorship, if no other region did experience the same form of colonialism, with the same relevant features that would later discourage democracy, it is not unreasonable to call this a regional effect.

Regional Vector of Causes

Historically driven regional effects of this sort are like the interactions discussed earlier. A combination of factors is required if a given outcome is to occur, and these factors are uniquely present in a certain region. Strictly speaking, were this same combination of factors in place elsewhere, the same outcome would occur. But their co-occurrence is unlikely: it reflects the region's particular history and defines it as a region. Arend Lijphart's discussion of the factors that need to be in place for "ethnofederal" institutional arrangements to succeed is a case in point.[16] Ethnofederalism means the sharing of executive powers among representatives of distinct ethnic or linguistic groups, as well as quotas for their bureaucratic representation. Such schemes will work, Lijphart contends, in places where an array of factors is in place—indeed, he lists nine such factors. Cumulatively, the list sounds like a description of Belgium.[17] Although Lijphart identifies other countries (Canada, Malaysia) where ethnofederalism works, one suspects that a "Belgian" context is really required.

Another example is the American South, a region that is politically distinct from the rest of the country. Perhaps we want to explain why a white southerner in the early twenty-first century is more likely to vote for the Republican Party than is a similar person in the Northeast. The list of factors that we would need to mention would read like the history of the South. It would be quite true that, were the factors to appear together in some other region, we would expect the same results: it is not Southern soil, in a literal sense, that must be present for the outcome to occur, but the various factors and forces that define the South's story. Because we are unlikely to find such a combination of factors elsewhere, we would be overly fastidious if we objected to the notion of Southern regional effects.

Regional Dynamics

If these regional effects are not, strictly speaking, regional, what form might a truly regional effect take? Pure geographic location is a factor that one encounters rarely in the social world. We would be skeptical of the claim that being located, as Africa is, between 35 degrees north and 40 degrees south longitude and 60 degrees east and 20 degrees west latitude discouraged democracy. If Norway were to become dislodged from Scandinavia and float southward until it reached the West African coast, but remained in all other ways the same, we would not expect it to fall prey to coups and dictatorship. Geographic features, by contrast, do sometimes influence social phenomena. Mountainous terrain, for instance, is claimed to help insurgencies.[18] Yet this is not a regional effect for the same reason that inequality is not: a country in the heart of Western Europe with big volcanoes would presumably be just as prone, all else being equal, to insurgencies (and hence just as inhospitable to stable democracy) as are countries with big volcanoes elsewhere in the world.

In considering spatial unevenness in relations of cause and effect, we need to distinguish two phenomena: (1) causes that operate over a politically defined jurisdiction, and (2) dynamics of mutual influence or persuasion that dissipate over space, and that hence operate over a region, whether conventionally or politically defined. I consider each in turn.

POLITICAL JURISDICTIONS

When compact and contiguous spaces are not merely conventional regions but also political jurisdictions, spatial location can have powerful effects. I mentioned earlier the example of countries that share the Andes mountains and hence are known conventionally as the "Andean region." Countries of the Andean region joined in 1969 in the Andean Pact, a multilateral organization with an attendant bureaucracy. Agreements governing trade within the Andean Pact have force within its borders but not outside them, creating spatial unevenness over a series of social and economic phenomena. An even starker example is the convention of "North America," which brings to mind the United States and Canada more readily than it does Mexico: school children in all three countries have to be taught that Mexico is part of North America as well as being, more obviously, part of Latin America. The signing in the 1990s of the North American Free Trade Agreement transformed a loose convention into a legal and bureaucratic reality, creating enormous spatial effects.

From the vantage point of someone residing close to the border between jurisdictions, these jurisdictions can appear to create big contingencies. Imaginary lines separate places where economic opportunities, political regimes, legal structures, and opportunities of many sorts are vastly
different. One of the effects of political jurisdiction, in addition to creating
boundaries for the operation of laws, is that they define the sphere of action of political actors such as parties and candidates. Later in the chapter
I illustrate the impact that this separation of physical space into spheres of
political action can have, even in a sense by accident, on the beliefs and
worldviews of the people living there.

DYNAMIC INTERACTIONS, INFLUENCES, OR PERSUASIONS
THAT DISSIPATE OVER SPACE

Many causal factors in politics rely for their effect on spatial proximity.
We know, for instance, that a person's friends, family, and acquaintances
influence his or her political opinions and voting behavior, and one's
friends, family, and acquaintances tend to live nearby.[19] The power of persuasive communications is an inverse function of distance. All else being
equal, a person's family and friends will exert less influence over her if she
moves to a distant place; her views will shift to some degree in the direction of those of people in her new milieu.

If a large proportion of proximate countries have chosen a particular
political regime, the preponderance of this regime type may exert pressure
on other countries in the same region to choose this same regime. The advantages of doing so may lie in *network externalities*, which explain why
computer buyers select brands that many other users have chosen (e.g.,
they anticipate that service will be better for a popular than for a seldom-
used brand).[20] By the same logic, to the extent that democracies prefer to
trade with other democracies, a rash of democratizations in neighboring
countries will make democratization more attractive for holdout dictators. Such network externalities are more often cited as explaining clusters
in time than in space. In the case of computer purchases this is particularly so: computer networks are less dependent on spatial proximity than
are other sorts of interactions. But trade is less costly and hence (*ceteris
paribus*) more intensive the closer two partners are to one another. Hence
a wave of democratizations in nearby trading partners exerts a more powerful effect than such a wave on distant shores. Network externalities related to trading patterns among like political regimes will therefore produce spatial-proximity effects on regime choice.

Elster suggests that spatial contiguity is always required in causal relations. *Local causality* means that "action at a distance is impossible. If a cause is said to have an effect distant from it in time or space, we assume that there must be a continuous chain from cause to effect, with no unbridgeable gaps in it."[21] For example, educational investment encourages economic growth. But without the constraint of local causality we would expect educational investment in Alaska to stimulate development in Papua–New Guinea.

What Elster's formulation misses is that causal factors rely *to varying degrees* on spatial proximity. Even in the area of political influence and persuasion, one effect may rely on face-to-face interactions whereas another can race across large spaces with dizzying speed. The age of computers and electronic communications challenges a literal interpretation of local causality. Educational investment in Alaska really might stimulate development in Papua–New Guinea if the training materials were available on the state's website.

Weakliem and Biggert document substantial differences in political opinion among people living in different regions of the United States, and explain that these differences come in part from regional identities.[22] They contend that regional identities can function like other identities—religious, ethnic—and structure the interactions that a person experiences and hence the influences that he or she absorbs. A white Protestant southern man, for example, can be expected to oppose abortion or favor the death penalty with a higher probability than would a sociologically identical person from New England, and the difference reflects communication and mutual persuasion among people living in each region.

In voting behavior, another classic example is offered by Butler and Stokes.[23] They show that in Britain of the 1960s, working-class voters who lived in predominantly middle-class resort communities (middle-class suburbs), where the Conservative Party was dominant, voted for Conservatives at much higher rates than did working-class voters who lived in mining towns, where Labour was dominant. Ninety-one percent of working-class voters who lived in districts that contain mining communities voted for Labour, against only 48 percent who lived in resorts. The reverse was also true. Middle-class voters in resorts voted for Conservatives at higher rates (93%) than did their counterparts who lived in mining seats (64%). Butler and Stokes cite as plausible explanations voters' perception and conformity to local political norms, and "the persuasive influence of informal contacts on the shop floor, in the public house, and other face to face groups of the elector's world."[24]

In the context of an argument that in American politics these sorts of location or regional effects are small, Gary King offers a hypothetical example that is helpful in illustrating what regional effects on Americans' voting behavior would look like:

> [C]onsider two voters. Both are conservative, poor, white men who identify with the Republican Party, prefer more defense spending and insist that the federal government balance the budget immediately. They are each afraid that someone will take their guns away, hope to end welfare as anyone knows it, and think Rush Limbaugh should be president. The only difference is that, after being raised as twins in Utah, they were separated. One moved to Lancaster County, Pennsylvania, amidst many other voters like himself. The other settled in Brookline, Massachusetts, with Michael Dukakis and many other Liberal Democrats. Now suppose Bill Clinton runs for re-election against Phil Gramm in 1996. Both voters would obviously vote for Gramm.[25]

Were this not the case—were the Massachusetts twin likely to vote for Clinton—we would conclude that a regional effect was at work. (King's refutation of such an effect is not entirely persuasive. One suspects that the regional effect of living in Brookline would be to inculcate a Democratic Party identity, a preference for gun control, and a distaste for Rush Limbaugh, and any tendency to vote for Democrats would flow from these regionally shaped preferences.)

Should we expect regional effects on the probability of transitions to democracy? For a hypothetical example of such an effect, assume that Region 1 encompasses the set of countries A, B, and C. Region 2 is made up of countries D, E, and F. Assume, furthermore, that the countries in the regions and the regions themselves are identical in all respects except their regional location: A, B, and C are located in conventionally recognized Region 1, D, E, and F in conventionally recognized Region 2. Suppose that all six countries were dictatorships at the outset and that, for exogenous reasons, A, B, and D democratized. International donors who wanted to encourage democratization observed these events. They inferred that the democratization of D was a fluke but that the democratization of A and B was a trend. They therefore showered resources on A and B. C, observing the shower, also democratized. But the donors ignored D, and neither E

nor *F* democratized. In this example, the shared regional identity of *C* with *A* and *B* is the only factor distinguishing *C* from *E* and *F*; the cause of democratization of *C* was its regional location.

One could object that the example is contrived because it involves international donors who assume some sort of regional contagion of democracy, an assumption that then creates just such a regional contagion. (Still, as Weakliem and Biggert showed in the context of regional effects on political views in the United States, regional identity can in itself constitute a powerful political force.) Why might such intra-regional influence occur, even without the self-realizing assumption of regional contagion? It might be a result of learning, with information disseminating more readily to spatially proximate places or within a region and less fully to distant ones and to other regions. Let's say that *A* democratizes and, rather than sending the former dictator to jail, *A*'s newly elected leaders send him to a comfortable exile abroad. The news travels quickly to *B* and the fate of *A*'s dictator is highly salient to the ruler of *B*, who, anticipating a comfortable retirement, also steps down and makes way for elections. But the news of events in *A* arrives slowly to *D* and is less salient to *D*'s dictator, who remains in office. If the greater geographic distance between *A* and *D* explains the lesser salience in *D* of events in *A,* then this is an example of a proximity-dependent effect. If the fact that the two are located in different regions explains the lesser salience, then we have an example of regional location as cause of democratization.

Of course one could state the effect in non-regional terms: the anticipation of a luxurious retirement for dictators increases the probability of democratization.[26] But if a dictator will tend to anticipate such a retirement when a neighboring dictator (and not a distant one) or a dictator in his own region (and not one in another region) has been treated this way, then the effect will be, respectively, proximity-dependent and region-dependent.

Regional effects also appear under circumstances of network externalities, at least when these externalities distribute themselves in a spatially uneven manner. Elkins notes the political benefits of being a member of a crowd, rather than an outlier. "In terms of norms, the predominant benefit is reputational. Joining a growing majority of other actors confers a degree of legitimacy or, in the case of a negatively valenced practice, *cover* from criticism."[27] And the comparison set, the units that either offer cover or turn the unit in question into an outlier, will tend to be either countries that are spatially proximate or countries that are in the same region.

The cover that large numbers of fellow dictatorships provide, and the added pressure to democratize once that cover is lifted, helps explain the apparent contagion in the most recent round of Latin American democratizations. When the first military government fell in the region—Ecuador's in 1979—this event probably put little pressure on dictators in other countries in the region. But a decade later Chile was the only holdout: the cover was gone. All else being equal, it was more costly for the Chilean regime to remain in power in a region where nearly every other country was a democracy than it had been while the Chilean military's Brazilian, Argentine, and Uruguayan counterparts were also still in power.[28] The prediction follows that, if regional contagion of this sort is at work, democratization should accelerate: we should observe ever-shorter gaps in time between each subsequent fall of a dictatorship.

I have distinguished among spurious regional effects—causes or outcomes that are prominent in a region but that are explained by non-regional or non-spatial factors; regional vectors of causes—causes that are uniquely jointly present in a given region—and regional dynamics proper. Among regional dynamics proper I have distinguished the effects of political jurisdictions from dynamics of influence and persuasion among people who live in a region, whether politically or conventionally defined. As the next section shows, we have growing evidence of the regional unevenness of democratization and of the consolidation of democracy across regions in countries. Some apparently regional effects on national democratization are spurious, but others are suggestive of regional dynamics of persuasion and influence. And intra-national regional effects on democratic consolidation illustrate the power of contingent choices of actors to speed or obstruct this consolidation.

Regional Effects on Transitions to Democracy

What region of the world a country is located in has a big effect on the probability that it will democratize. Perhaps because our grasp on the mechanisms that produce spatial unevenness is weak, we have only begun to study these apparent regional effects. Przeworski and his colleagues find that, among countries at the same income level as Latin America's, "[b]eing in Latin America makes democracy 12 percent more likely . . . than elsewhere."[29] But they offer no explanation for this apparent regional dynamic.

Acemoglu, Yared, and Robinson also study democratization cross-nationally.[30] To control for countries' economic institutions—institutions which, they contend, can either promote or inhibit democratization—they organize cross-national pooled time-series data as a panel. This procedure is equivalent to including a dummy variable for each country in the sample. In effect they are positing that each country's economic institutions, the influence of which extends only to its borders, affect the probability of a transition to democracy. The authors indeed find that being, say, Portugal rather than being any other country influences the probability that Portugal will democratize. We cannot know whether the country-specific effects that they model really reflect economic institutions, or whether they reflect some other differences among the countries. That is, what they have discovered may be regional effects in the sense that I am using the term: countries are jurisdictional regions, and their jurisdictional-spatial discreteness may be what influences their probability that they will undergo a transition to democracy.

Mainwaring and Pérez-Liñán go more deeply into regional effects on the probability of a transition to democracy and on the quality of democracy.[31] They define regions as I have defined them, as conventionally recognized compact and contiguous spaces. Regions are "geographically bounded parts of the world that are commonly viewed as occupying the same large part of the world. In this understanding, Latin America, Europe, Africa, the Middle East, and Asia are regions of the world."[32] They find that Latin American and Middle Eastern regions powerfully shape the probability of a transition to democracy, as well as the quality of the democracy once it has been established. Within Latin America, Mainwaring and Pérez-Liñán find that per-capita Gross Domestic Product (GDP) has no effect on the level of democracy (as measured in the Polity IV dataset)[33] whereas it does affect the quality of democracy if one extends the analysis to all countries or to all non–Latin American countries with incomes in the Latin American range. This implies that, for development to influence the quality of democracy, it must interact with a country's being located outside of Latin America. Mainwaring and Pérez-Liñán also show that the shape of the function relating income to the level of democracy is very different in Latin America than in the rest of the world. And they show that the shape of the function relating income to the probability of a *transition* to democracy is very different than in the rest of the world. Finally, they find that the only factor significantly influencing the probability of transitions among dictatorship, democracy, and semi-democracy in

Latin American countries is the number of other countries in the Latin American region that were democracies at the time. This final result is suggestive of the contagion examples I offered earlier.

Mainwaring and Pérez-Liñán's explanations include both true regional effects, as I defined them, and some spurious ones. In fact, the role of the Catholic Church was both spurious and truly regional. After Vatican II, "change in the Catholic Church affected prospects for democracy in other regions, but Latin America is the only overwhelmingly Catholic region of the world, hence change in the Church affected Latin America more than other regions."[34] In this instance, not location in the Latin American region, but the presence of the Catholic Church, encouraged democratization. One would expect the post–Vatican II Church to have favored democratization in the Philippines, say, just as strongly as it did in Latin America.

But Mainwaring and Pérez-Liñán also point toward true regional dynamics. They point toward interactions among factors, interactions that were unlikely to be repeated in other regions. They write, "although the Catholic Church is global in scope, it has regional specificities that stem from a combination of responding to some regionally specific opportunities and challenges, a regional leadership organization (the Latin American Bishops' Conference), and regional communication among theologians, priests, religious [leaders], and bishops."[35] Not just Catholicism in general but Catholicism as it interacted with other conditions specific to Latin America encouraged democracy. The more such factors that needed to interact, or to be jointly present, to produce the effects that we observe in a region—Catholicism and inequality and non-European populations and proximity to the United States—the more contingent—the smaller the *ex ante* probability of—the effect on democratization. Mainwaring and Pérez-Liñán also hint at regional dynamics of communication and persuasion. They explain that the "dissemination of norms and ideas frames the way political actors within countries perceive political regimes and their own interests and political preferences."[36]

I have discussed both spurious and true region effects on democratization where regions are contiguous groups of countries. Although one might describe these effects as contingent in the sense that they depend on regional location and influences, this is not contingency in a strong sense. After all, the location of a country in one region of the world or another is hardly a low-probability fact or one that could easily have turned out differently. And the kinds of chance events Przeworski and his coauthors point to certainly are contingent but they are not unevenly distributed across regions. Although I have offered several examples of regional effects on democratization, both real and hypothetical, the only one that has the air of contingency about it is the shift in the role of the Catholic Church after the Second Vatican Council—an event which, under a different ecumenical leadership, might never have occurred.

In the next section I illustrate another kind of regional effect, this one related not to democratization but to the consolidation of democracy. My research in Argentina demonstrates true regional dynamics, where strategic choices made by key actors in some regions helped consolidate democracy, whereas other choices by other actors in other regions hampered it. These are regional dynamics: they depend on intra-regional processes of persuasion and influence. And they are contingent regional dynamics in the sense of contingency explained earlier: if actors (in this case, leaders of political parties) had made choices other than the ones they did make, the outcome would have been different, and the choices they did make were, *ex ante,* not the only ones imaginable.

Within-Country Regional Effects on the Consolidation of Democracy

In many countries the consolidation of democracy varies across regions. The Italian south was dominated through the 1960s by clientelism and inefficiency, whereas in the north local governments were relatively clean and efficient.[37] In India, communal violence is endemic in some localities but absent in others.[38] In the nineteenth-century United States, New York, Cincinnati, and Philadelphia were notorious machine towns, whereas Detroit and San Francisco were relatively free of patronage and graft.[39] And such regional differences persist: even today one would be less surprised by a major municipal corruption scandal in New Orleans than in Minneapolis. In Latin American countries, parties effectively compete for office and act accountably in some regions, whereas competition is muted and governments escape accountability in others.[40]

Some of this cross-regional variation can be attributed to structural differences from one region to the next in economic development, income equality, or levels of education. But, as in cross-national variation in democratization, structural factors leave much of the variation in the degree of consolidation unexplained. In this section I illustrate this cross-regional unevenness with data from one new Latin American democracy, Argentina. I demonstrate that many of the structural differences one might expect to cause regional differences do cause them, and yet even when one takes structural factors into account, regional differences persist. In part this persistent regional variation is the product of contingent political choice.

Regional Unevenness in the Consolidation of Democracy in Argentina

In 1983, in the wake of a disastrous war against the United Kingdom, the military leaders who had ruled Argentina since a coup d'etat 10 years earlier were driven from power. The jubilation that many Argentines felt in the first years of democracy inevitably faded as national governments failed to solve basic problems or even to keep the country from chaos. Argentina is a federal system, and politics in the provinces had dynamics of their own. Some provinces were the feudal domains of ruling families, and national leaders attempting to carry out reforms had to co-opt or entice recalcitrant governors.[41] In other provinces electoral competition prompted violent clashes. In contrast, in some provinces and locales, a creative political leadership found innovative ways to improve public policy and enhance citizen participation.

Cleary and Stokes studied a subset of Argentine regions where local political practices and local political cultures varied. Our regions were jurisdictional: they were provinces or districts governed by local and provincial governments. We studied the district (*partida*) of General Pueyrredón, in the province of Buenos Aires, where the seat of government was Mar del Plata, a city of half a million inhabitants; the rest of the province of Buenos Aires, heavily dominated demographically and economically by the federal capital and the Greater Buenos Aires urban area; the province of Córdoba, which encompasses more than 600 cities, towns, and *comunas,* including the city of Córdoba, Argentina's second largest; and finally Misiones, a small, poor, and rural province in the northeast, bordering Brazil and Paraguay. Drawing on secondary literature and our own research, we found Mar del Plata and Misiones to occupy poles in a ranking of the four regions by levels of democratic consolidation. Buenos Aires and Córdoba fell in between. *Regional quality of democracy* is an independent variable, and these four cases represent distinct magnitudes on this variable.

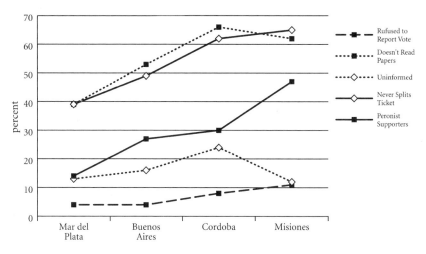

percent

| Rufused to Report Vote |
| Doesn't Read Papers |
| Uninformed |
| Never Splits Ticket |
| Peronist Supporters |

Fig. 6.1 Political behaviors by region

Although they live at most a few hundred miles apart, people in these distinct Argentine regions engage in strikingly different political behaviors.[42] The Peronist party is Argentina's most clientelistic party, the one most similar to U.S. political machines.[43] Our surveys revealed that more than three times as many people in Misiones as in Mar del Plata supported the Peronists (see Figure 6.1). Almost twice as many voters in Misiones as in Mar del Plata reported that they never split their ticket, a practice that Almond and Verba associate with less-developed democracies and less-reflective electorates.[44] About half as many people in Misiones as in Mar del Plata got their news from newspapers. And nearly three times as many in Misiones refused to tell our interviewers how they had voted—a sign, again according to Almond and Verba, of a closed and fearful political culture. Among the measures reported in Figure 6.1, only in their subjective sense of being informed about politics did we find no difference between residents of the two polar regions. The regions that we studied are located in the same country. The people in these regions lived through the same national political history, sustained the same set of political parties, and had basically similar political institutions. Yet people living only a few hundred miles apart participated in sharply different regional political cultures and had very different ways of thinking about politics.

They displayed striking differences in their implicit theories of responsive government. In a series of questions, we posited that governments are sometimes responsive and asked people to choose among explanations for this responsiveness. In each case, we asked them to choose between a personalistic response—governments are responsive when they are staffed by good people—and an institutional or interest response—governments are responsive because their leaders want to be reelected or because they want to avoid being sanctioned by the courts or the press. Table 6.1 shows responses to two of these questions by region, with the regions listed in declining order of consolidation. The table shows a monotonic decline in the numbers of respondents, from the most- to the least-consolidated region, who said that governments provide good services when they are under the watch of the courts, the congress, or the press. It shows a near-monotonic increase in the numbers who said that governments provide good services when they are staffed by good people. But one might well ask whether these are really *regional* differences. The more-consolidated regions, after all, are also wealthier and have a more equal distribution of income than the less-consolidated ones; apparent regional effects could be spurious. The surveys confirm, for instance, that Mar del Plata has the smallest percentage of poor people and the largest percentage of middle-income peo-

TABLE 6.1
Responses to Questions about Responsive Government, by Region

	Mar del Plata	Buenos Aires	Córdoba	Misiones	Total
Services					
When governments provide good services to the people, is this because					
they are under the watch of the courts, congress, or the press	65% (311)	56% (268)	48% (232)	40% (192)	52% (1003)
they are good, committed people	30% (142)	40% (192)	40% (194)	53% (256)	41% (784)
no answer	6% (27)	4% (20)	11% (54)	7% (32)	7% (133)
Attention					
When politicians really pay attention to people like you, is this because					
they want to be reelected	85% (410)	80% (386)	78% (365)	78% (365)	81% (1546)
they really care	12% (55)	17% (83)	16% (76)	18% (87)	16% (301)
no answer	3% (15)	2% (11)	6% (29)	4% (18)	4% (73)

TABLE 6.2
Logit Models of Responses to Questions about
Government Responsiveness

Dependent variable	(1) Service		(2) Attention	
Income	−0.057	(0.043)	−0.105	(0.054)
Education	0.041	(0.037)	−0.060	(0.043)
Housing	−0.006	(0.076)	0.018	(0.094)
Gender	**−0.318**	(0.102)	−0.062	(0.119)
Age	**−0.013**	(0.004)	−0.006	(−0.004)
Peronist supporter	**−0.230**	(0.116)	**−0.420**	(0.150)
Radical supporter	−0.058	(0.144)	0.045	(0.226)
Log Population	0.006	(0.037)	0.031	(0.046)
Buenos Aires	**−0.408**	(0.184)	**−0.438**	(0.214)
Córdoba	**−0.618**	(0.187)	−0.313	(0.255)
Misiones	**−1.080**	(0.229)	**−0.517**	(0.247)
Constant	**1.605**	(0.528)	**2.664**	(0.742)
N observations	1920		1920	

NOTE: These and all subsequent regressions draw on five datasets with imputed values for missing data, generated with the *Amelia* program described in King et al. (2001) and implemented in Honaker et al. (2001). **Boldface** indicates coefficients where p < 0.001; the numbers in parentheses are robust standard errors.

ple; Misiones, by contrast, has the largest number of poor people and the fewest middle-class people. Intuition leads us to expect that wealthier people and those living in more equal regions would be more likely to hold an institutional theory of government responsiveness and be less trusting of unmonitored politicians.

Multivariate analysis, reported in Table 6.2, confirms some of these intuitions. Some, however, are not confirmed. Income, education, and housing quality had no significant effect on the probability that a person would attribute good service and responsiveness to politicians' desires to avoid sanctions and to be reelected. Younger respondents and men were more likely to offer institutional explanations for responsiveness. But what matters here is that the regional effects remain, even in the presence of controls. Respondents from all three other regions were less likely than those from Mar del Plata to offer institutional answers to all three questions.

In fact region shaped people's interpretations of government responsiveness more powerfully than any other factor. Simulations are useful in illustrating how much more.[45] Consider the factors that influence the probability of a respondent's saying that governments provide good services when they are "under the watch of the courts, the congress, or the press" and not when "they are staffed by good, committed people" (see Table 6.1). Figure 6.2 reports the simulated predicted probabilities of this

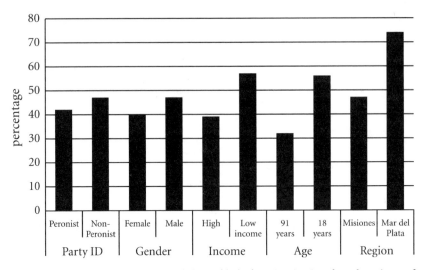

Fig. 6.2. Simulated expected probability of beliefs in institutional explanations of government responsiveness. Simulation executed with *Clarify* program (see note 44). Independent variables held at their sample means.

answer, conditional on a whether a person supported the Peronist party or did not, was male or female, had high or low income, was 91 years old or 18 years old (the oldest and youngest in our samples), and whether the person lived in Misiones or in Mar del Plata. Holding all other factors at their sample means, the regional effect predicts a 27 percent increase in the probability of the institutional response, a larger effect than any other and much larger than all others but age. If one wished to predict whether a randomly selected person held a personalistic or an institutional view of government responsiveness, the most valuable piece of information is what region he or she lived in.

In short, we find strong regional differences in political behaviors and in ways of thinking about politics—differences in what one might call *regional political cultures*. Later I present statistical evidence that these regional cultures are not reducible to structural differences among the regions, but instead are at least partly the product of the contingent choices of political parties and party leaders. The inventive choices of political leaders in one region, Mar del Plata, helped to define good performance by local governments in terms of the provision of public goods, the enactment of sound public policy, and the soliciting of public opinion in matters of common concern. This style of leadership stood in stark contrast to that of leaders elsewhere, who relied on the private payoffs of clientelism to mobilize voter support. Hence in some regions politicians took actions that speeded the consolidation of democracy, whereas in others they slowed this process. Although in some measure politicians' choices were driven by the underlying characteristics of their respective electorates, their actions went beyond mere responsiveness to these characteristics.

To get a feel for some of these choices, one might consider alternative ways that parties can mobilize electoral support and how these strategies of mobilization varied across regions. Among other strategies, parties can offer private benefits as *quid pro quos* for the votes of individuals, a strategy known as clientelism. Or they can use programmatic appeals and promises to provide public goods. We shall see that parties' choices of strategies are in some measure explained by the underlying characteristics of the populations they seek to mobilize. In poor and economically unequal regions, parties have an incentive to use clientelism; in wealthier and more equal regions they have an incentive to adopt universalistic and programmatic appeals.

Yet even when we control for these underlying characteristics of regional electorates, we find persistent regional differences. Mar del Plata, for instance, has a relatively affluent electorate and is less pro-Peronist than voters in other regions. These structural characteristics of the region lead us to expect less clientelism, but not as much less as we actually find.

To explain this absence of clientelism and the region's tilt toward programmatic politics, we must take into account the nature and actions of the district's political leadership. This leadership was exemplified in the mid-1990s by Mayor Elio Aprile, a philosophy professor on leave from the local branch of the National University. Aprile dreamt up a scheme at the outset of his first term that would allow his administration to undertake an ambitious program of community infrastructural development—everything from tree-plantings to road paving to streetlight installation. To pay for the program, which he called *Mar del Plata 2000,* he held a referendum in which voters would decide whether to impose on themselves a special tax over a period of eight years. Everything about Aprile's effort was innovative. No city had used the device of a referendum to raise its own taxes; in fact, the Mar del Plata administration had to deploy a team of lawyers to navigate around Buenos Aires provincial law, which barred binding referendums. The debate about the proposed special tax, and about using a popular referendum to make this decision, was lively and attracted national attention. Most remarkable, the referendum was approved, and people in a poor country where politicians were suspected of graft agreed to turn substantial amounts of money over to their political leadership for the purpose of securing public goods.

Statistical analysis shows results that are consistent with the interpretation that contingent political innovation and not merely structural factors explain regional differences in the quality of democracy in Argentina. Had parties and leaders chosen different strategies—strategies that one could have imagined them choosing—the cross-regional unevenness in the consolidation of democracy would have been muted.

Our surveys confirm regional differences in styles of electoral mobilization and in voter-party linkages. Across regions, people's linkages to political parties differed sharply. And their perceptions of other people's linkages to parties also differed. We asked which party was most popular in the respondent's neighborhood and then asked why people supported this party, whether because it "gave out favors" or because it was "concerned about everyone." In effect, the question asked people to assess the prevalence of clientelism versus a more universalistic politics in their neighborhoods. Less than half the number of respondents in Mar del Plata than in any other region attributed party strength to clientelism (see Table 6.3).

In themselves these regional differences in party strategy are not particularly surprising. Regional differences in the characteristics of electorates would lead us to expect that parties would vary their messages and tactics from place to place in a country. For example, consider a party that was active in a country where people in region A were wealthy and people in region B poor. Given the diminishing marginal utility of income and given the greater ease of monitoring votes in low-income places, we might expect the party to attempt to garner support in region A with program-

TABLE 6.3
Views of Reasons Why Neighbors Support Locally Prominent Party, by Region

	Mar del Plata	Buenos Aires	Córdoba	Misiones	Total
Favor					
Do people support this party because					
it has done them some favor	16%	45%	37%	35%	29%
	(77)	(215)	(175)	(166)	(564)
it is concerned for everyone	52%	42%	43%	45%	69%
	(250)	(200)	(204)	(217)	(1330)
no answer	32%	14%	21%	20%	22%
	(153)	(65)	(101)	(97)	(416)

Poverty ⟶ Clientelist strategy ⟶ Regional prominence of clientelism

Fig. 6.3. Party strategy of clientelism as an intervening factor between regional poverty and the regional prominence of clientelism

matic appeals and in region *B* with personal handouts.[46] In a relatively middle-class community like Mar del Plata, we would expect parties to try to attract support with innovative programs and public goods, such as Mayor Aprile's *Mar del Plata 2000*. The relationship between *B*'s poverty, the party's strategy there, and the consequent regional concentration of clientelism might be as depicted in Figure 6.3. The party's strategic choice becomes an intervening factor between the region's poverty and the prominence of political clientelism there. In statistical terms, apparent regional differences in clientelism should disappear in the presence of controls for income: at a given income level, we expect the same strategy and the same probability of clientelism. Or, to the extent that not the poverty of individuals but the proportion of poor people living in their community promotes clientelism, then controlling for characteristics of communities should suppress any apparent effect of region on clientelism.

But cross-regional differences do not disappear in the presence of controls for individual and regional poverty, and Figure 6.3 is therefore not an accurate portrayal of the causal relations involved. The irreducibility of region is brought out by the regressions in Table 6.4. All five are logit models of the probability that a respondent would say that clientelism explains the popularity of the most popular party in his or her neighborhood. Model 1 shows that perceptions of clientelism are more likely in Buenos Aires, Córdoba, and Misiones than in Mar del Plata (the omitted region). This is true despite controls for the income, education, gender, age, and party preference of the individual respondent, and despite a control for the size of the municipality in which the respondent lives. The next four models in Table 6.4 control for other features of the communities in which respondents lived, features that might explain parties' strategic choices. Models 2 and 3 control for the proportion of poor people in the municipality with two measures (measures which are highly collinear): the proportion of people in the respondent's municipality who live in poor-quality housing, and the proportion whose income falls below a poverty line and hence leaves them with "unsatisfied basic needs." A measure of municipal public expenditures per capita in 1998 (models 4 and 5) allows me to control for level of economic development of the municipality.

TABLE 6.4

Logit Models of the Probability of Respondents Reporting that Campaign
Handouts Explain their Neighbors' Support of Locally Popular Party

	(1)	(2)	(3)	(4)	(5)
Income	−0.056	−0.050	−0.042	−0.051	−0.049
	(0.038)	(0.038)	(0.038)	(0.044)	(0.037)
Education	0.039	0.034	0.036	0.035	0.034
	(0.041)	(0.041)	(0.041)	(0.041)	(0.041)
Housing	−0.009	−0.007	−0.001	0.013	0.011
	(0.102)	(0.103)	(0.004)	(0.104)	(0.104)
Gender	0.013	0.021	0.029	−0.001	0.004
	(0.107)	(0.107)	(0.107)	(0.106)	(0.105)
Age	−0.001	−0.001	−0.001	−0.001	−0.001
	(0.004)	(0.004)	(0.004)	(0.004)	(0.004)
Peronist	**−0.557**	**−0.563**	**−0.583**	**−0.597**	**−0.594**
	(0.156)	(0.156)	(0.156)	(0.155)	(0.155)
Radical	**−0.671**	**−0.705**	**−0.690**	**−0.695**	**−0.705**
	(0.186)	(0.185)	(0.186)	(0.185)	(0.185)
Log population	−0.030	0.008	−0.007	−0.065	−0.047
	(0.041)	(0.043)	(0.040)	(0.045)	(0.053)
Buenos Aires	**1.387**	**1.319**	**1.233**	**1.067**	**1.080**
	(0.216)	(0.220)	(0.227)	(0.268)	(0.271)
Córdoba	**1.100**	**1.127**	**1.115**	**0.972**	**0.997**
	(0.257)	(0.255)	(0.256)	(0.270)	(0.271)
Misiones	**1.746**	**1.428**	**1.305**	**1.163**	**1.117**
	(0.258)	(0.318)	(0.315)	(0.380)	(0.381)
Poor-quality housing		0.014			0.005
		(0.008)			(0.009)
NBI (poverty measure)			**0.045**		
			(0.017)		
Municipal expenditures per capita				**−0.002**	**−0.002**
				(0.001)	(.001)
Constant	−0.975	**−1.582**	**−1.858**	0.296	−0.080
	(0.595)	(0.645)	(0.645)	(0.798)	(1.041)

These municipal-level factors have the expected effect: poverty and in-equality encourage clientelism, and municipal economic development discourages it. But they fail to eliminate the effect of region. Hence the continuing statistical significance of the coefficients on the province dummy variables, despite all of the individual and municipal controls.

Figure 6.4 displays the joint effects of region and poverty on expectations of clientelism. When we assume a resident of a Misiones municipality with that province's highest rate of poverty (poor-quality housing =

71%), the expected percentage of clientelist responses is 69 percent. When we assume a resident of a Misiones municipality with that province's lowest rate of poverty (17%), the probability of a clientelist response drops to 52 percent. When we assume a Misiones municipality with Mar del Plata's rate of poverty (8%), the probability of a clientelist response drops to 48 percent. And when we assume a resident of Mar del Plata (and a poverty rate of 8%), the probability of a clientelist response drops to 18 percent.[47]

My inability to make regional effects go away, even in the presence of controls for factors that differ by region and that influence party strategy, suggests that they are not spurious stand-ins for characteristics of individuals that also vary by region; nor are they spurious stand-ins for structural features of communities. They represent *choices* that political leaders have made, choices that are not, in turn, explained—or at least not entirely explained—by the distinctive characteristic of regional electorates and hence the distinctive regional incentives that regional parties face. These are choices that might have gone differently. Mar del Plata, for instance, might not have elected a mayor who turned out (somewhat to the electorate's surprise) to be the activist and innovator that he was. In this sense, the

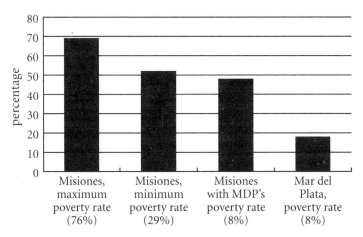

Fig. 6.4. Simulated expected percentages who say their neighbors support parties because of clientelist inducements, in Misiones and Mar del Plata, under varying poverty rates (housing quality). Simulated expected percentages generated by *Clarify* (see note 44). The simulations assume a male Peronist sympathizer who in all other respects is typical of our sample (i.e., other independent variables held at their sample means).

outcomes—political mobilization via particularistic rewards and vote-buying in one region, via programmatic appeals and public goods in another—are contingent.

Conclusion

Outcomes are contingent when they are the product of interacting factors, or a sequence of events, or the choices of actors, and when these interactions, sequences, and choices are far from inevitable. Regions can have contingent effects on political outcomes, and regional differences can themselves be contingent outcomes.

I have distinguished between contingencies and non-contingencies, and between regional effects and effects that are not regional. Table 6.5 reviews examples offered in this chapter of democratization and democratic consolidation that fall in the four categories suggested by these two distinctions. The upper-left-hand cell offers the example of the encouraging effect of equality on democratization. The causal force that equality has on democracy thus approaches more closely than the other examples in Table 6.5 a universal effect: it is non-contingent and equally powerful across regions. The equality effect is empirically well documented and stands on firm theoretical grounds (i.e., the more equal the distribution of resources, the less upper-income actors fear being expropriated under democracy).[48] And empirical evidence of its existence comes from all regions of the world. The lower-left-hand cell offers the example, drawn from the writings of Przeworski and his coauthors, of democratization as a non-regional chance event. The death of a dictator (among other possi-

TABLE 6.5
Examples of Contingent and Non-Contingent Effects, and Regional and Non-Regional Effects, on Democratization

	Non-Regional Effect	Regional Effect
Non-Contingent Effect	Equality on democratization (African example)	Diffusion and contagion (Chile pressured to democratize after other Latin American dictators have fallen)
Contingent Effect	Chance events— e.g., death of dictator	Party leaders choose strategies that either promote or inhibit regional democratic consolidation (Argentina)

ble contingencies) produces a chance opening for democratization, but there is no regional unevenness in the mortality rates of dictators. In the upper-right-hand cell, diffusion and contagion exemplify dynamics that are regional—differentially effective within and outside of a region—and yet non-contingent. It is *ex ante* highly probable that holdout regimes will be under more pressure, or perceive themselves to be under more pressure, to democratize than are early democratizers.

The lower-right-hand cell, finally, offers an example of democratization where both regional effects and contingency are at work. A party leadership chooses a strategy for mobilizing voters. Its choice diffuses through its regional constituencies ideas and practices that encourage or impede democratic consolidation. That other leaders in other regions choose other strategies, and that these choices cannot be reduced to structural differences among the regions, underscores the contingency of the regional unevenness in consolidation.

A heightened sensitivity to specific regional dynamics of democratization and democratic consolidation, and to the contingency sometimes entailed in these dynamics, may help counterbalance the determinism and universalism of some earlier accounts of democratic transitions. Chance interventions can help consolidate regional democracy, just as chance events can lead countries to democratize. Of course chance interventions and low-probability choices can undermine democracy and encourage dictatorship, as we saw they did in Brazil. And recent U.S. policy in the Middle East cautions us to pay attention to what may be very real structural limitations for democratic transitions. This policy also reminds us that we must understand the role of regional particularities in making democratization more or less likely. Understanding just how far structural determinants take us in explaining democratization, and how much more is due to contingency, chance, and choice, can only improve social science and public policy.

NOTES

1. This paper draws on research carried out in collaboration with Matthew Cleary and supported by the Russell Sage Foundation's Program on Trust. I am grateful to Cleary, as well as to Jennifer Bair, Andrew Schrank, and Zachary Elkins for their comments

2. Dahl, *On Democracy,* p. 2.

3. See Pierson, *Politics in Time*; Elster, *Explaining Technical Change*; and Giddens, *Central Problems in Social Theory*.

4. Almond and Verba, *The Civic Culture*.

5. Kalyvas, "Hegemony Breakdown."

6. Ibid., p. 335.

7. Dahl, *Polyarchy*.

8. Shefter, "Party and Patronage"; see the discussion in Pierson, *Politics in Time*.

9. Schedler, "Mapping Contingency," this volume.

10. Fearon, "Counterfactuals and Hypothesis Testing," pp. 184–185; Stepan, "Political Leadership."

11. Stepan "Political Leadership," p. 129

12. Przeworski et al., *Democracy and Development*, p. 89, emphasis added.

13. Alvarez et al., *ACLP*.

14. Calculated from Alvarez et al., *ACLP*.

15. Boix, *Democracy and Redistribution*; Acemoglu and Robinson, *Economic Origins of Dictatorship and Democracy*. Countries in the African region have the second highest average Gini index in the world (44), second only to Latin America's (50). Calculated from the ACLP database.

16. Lijphart, "The Power-Sharing Approach."

17. Of his nine conditions, seven are present in Belgium.

18. Fearon and Laitin, "Ethnicity, Insurgency, and Civil War."

19. Berelson, Lazarsfeld, and McPhee, *Voting*.

20. See Katz and Shapiro, "Network Externalities," and Elkins, *Democracy and Diffusion*.

21. Elster, *Explaining Technical Change*, p. 28.

22. Weakliem and Biggert, "Region and Political Opinion."

23. Butler and Stokes, *Political Change in Britain*.

24. Ibid., p. 184. Butler and Stokes implicitly assume that workers who live in resorts are not systematically different from workers who live in mining seats in ways that would influence their voting behavior. They implicitly make the same assumption about middle-class Britons who live in mining seats. Recent U.S. elections make one wonder whether the suppression of turnout and partisan vote counting, quite apart from differences in party choice among similar voters in different regions, might have contributed to local partisan hegemony.

25. King, "Why Context Should Not Count," p. 160.

26. Yet the example of former dictators being provided with a comfortable retirement may also encourage would-be dictators to instigate coups against elected leaders. That the treatment of former dictators creates opposing incentives, one for them to step down once they are in power, the other for them to grab power when they are out of it, makes this treatment a perennial topic of debate among democratizers (a debate that has parallels in other areas of action of new demo-

cratic regimes, for example whether and what sorts of prosecutions former dictators should be exposed to, whether and what sorts of truth commissions ought to be held, and so forth). Ideally one would want to quantify, or at least loosely weigh, the countervailing effects and compare their magnitude.

27. Elkins, *Democracy and Diffusion*, p. 9, emphasis in the original.

28. Paraguay had still not democratized when, in 1988, Pinochet lost the plebiscite that would have allowed him to remain as president until 1997. But Paraguay is a country whose events are not closely watched around the region, or the world. Its long-time dictator, Alfredo Stroessner, undoubtedly felt pressure from regional democratization, but the fact that he was still in power in 1988 would not have been terribly salient in Chile and hence of little comfort to Pinochet.

29. Przeworski et al., *Democracy and Development*, p. 87.

30. Acemoglu, Yared, and Robinson, "Income and Democracy."

31. Mainwaring and Pérez-Liñán, *Why Regions of the World Are Important*.

32. Ibid., p. 4.

33. Polity IV is a database that contains information on political regimes, ethnic conflict, and other characteristics.

34. Mainwaring and Pérez-Liñán, *Why Regions of the World Are Important*, p. 34.

35. Ibid.

36. Ibid., p. 31.

37. Chubb, "The Social Bases of an Urban Political Machine"; Putnam, *Making Democracy Work*.

38. Varshney, *Ethnic Conflict and Civic Life*; Wilkinson, *Votes and Violence*.

39. Gimpel, "Reform-Resistant and Reform-Adapting Machines."

40. Cleary and Stokes, *Democracy and the Culture of Skepticism*.

41. Remmer and Wibbels, "The Subnational Politics of Economic Adjustment"; Gibson and Calvo, "Federalism and Low-Maintenance Constituencies."

42. The analysis in this section draws on sample surveys we conducted in early 2002 in the four regions. We used multistage cluster sampling procedures, based on census tracks. The margin of error was 4.5 percent.

43. Auyero, *Poor People's Politics*; Levitsky, *Transforming Labor-Based Parties*.

44. Almond and Verba, *The Civic Culture*.

45. I generated the simulations using the *Clarify* program (Tomz, Wittenberg, and King). *Clarify* draws simulations of parameters of statistical models (in this case, logit regressions) from their sampling distribution and then converts these simulated parameters into expected values, such as expected probabilities of an answer to a survey question, given hypothetical values of explanatory variables. *Clarify* software and documentation are available from Gary King's website at http://Gking.Harvard.edu.

46. See Dixit and Londregan, "The Determinants of Success of Special Interests," and Stokes, "Perverse Accountability."

47. Simulated expected probabilities produced by *Clarify*. I assume a male Peronist sympathizer who in all other respects is average for the sample.

48. See Boix, *Democracy and Redistribution*, and Acemoglu and Robinson *Income and Democracy.*

BIBLIOGRAPHY

Acemoglu, Daron, and James A. Robinson. *Economic Origins of Dictatorship and Democracy.* New York: Cambridge University Press, 2006.

Acemoglu, Daron, Pierre Yared, and James Robinson. *Income and Democracy.* Typescript, Massachusetts Institute of Technology, 2005.

Almond, Gabriel A., and Sidney Verba. *The Civic Culture: Political Attitudes and Democracy in Five Nations.* Princeton, NJ: Princeton University Press, 1963.

Alvarez, Michael, José Antonio Cheibub, Fernando Limongi, and Adam Przeworski. *ACLP Political and Economic Database Codebook,* 1999. Available at http://www.ssc.upenn.edu/~cheibub/data/ACLPCodebookPDF

Auyero, Javier. *Poor People's Politics: Peronist Survival Networks and the Legacy of Evita.* Durham: Duke University Press, 2000.

Bernard Berelson, Paul F. Lazarsfeld, and William N. McPhee. *Voting: A Study of Opinion Formation in a Presidential Campaign.* Chicago: University of Chicago Press, 1954.

Boix, Carles. *Democracy and Redistribution.* New York: Cambridge University Press, 2003.

Butler, David, and Donald E. Stokes. *Political Change in Britain: Forces Shaping Electoral Choice.* London: Macmillan, 1969.

Chubb, Judith. "The Social Bases of an Urban Political Machine: The Case of Palermo." *Political Science Quarterly* 96(1) 1981: 107–125.

Cleary, Matthew, and Susan Stokes. *Democracy and the Culture of Skepticism: Political Trust in Argentina and Mexico.* New York: Russell Sage, 2006.

Dahl, Robert. *On Democracy.* New Haven, CT: Yale University Press, 1998.

Dahl, Robert. *Polyarchy: Participation and Opposition.* New Haven, CT: Yale University Press, 1971.

Dixit, Avinash, and John Londregan. "The Determinants of Success of Special Interests in Redistributive Politics." *Journal of Politics* 58(4) 1996: 1132–1155.

Elkins, Zachary. *Democracy and Diffusion: Concepts, Mechanisms, and Consequences.* Prepared for presentation at the "Centennial Conference on Democracy in the 21st Century: Prospects and Problems," University of Illinois, October 24–26, 2004.

Elster, Jon. *Explaining Technical Change.* New York: Cambridge University Press, 1983.

Fearon, James. "Counterfactuals and Hypothesis Testing in Political Science." *World Politics* 43:2 (1991): 169–195.

Fearon, James, and David Laitin. "Ethnicity, Insurgency, and Civil War." *American Political Science Review* 97 (2003): 75–90.

Gibson, Edward, and Ernesto Calvo. "Federalism and Low-Maintenance Constituencies: Territorial Dimensions of Economic Reform in Argentina." *Studies in Comparative International Development* 35(3) (2000): 32–55.

Giddens, Anthony. *Central Problems in Social Theory: Action, Structure, and Contradiction in Social Analysis.* Berkeley, CA: University of California Press, 1979.

Gimpel, James G. "Reform-Resistant and Reform-Adapting Machines: The Electoral Foundations of Urban Politics, 1910–1930." *Political Research Quarterly* 46 (1993): 371–82.

Honaker, James, Anne Joseph, Gary King, Kenneth Scheve, and Naunihal Singh. *Amelia: A Program for Missing Data* (Windows version). Cambridge, MA: Harvard University, 2001, http://Gking.Harvard.edu/

Kalyvas, Stathis. "Hegemony Breakdown: The Collapse of Nationalization in Britain and France." *Politics and Society* 22(3) (1994): 316–48.

Katz, Michael, and Carl Shapiro. "Network Externalities: Competition and Compatibility." *American Economic Review Papers and Proceedings* 75 (1985): 424–40.

King, Gary. "Why Context Should Not Count." *Political Geography* 15(2) (1996): 159–64.

King, Gary, James Honaker, Anne Joseph, and Kenneth Scheve. "Analyzing Incomplete Political Science Data: An Alternative Algorithm for Multiple Imputation." *American Political Science Review* 95(1) (2001): 49–69.

King, Gary, Michael Tomz, and Jason Wittenberg. "Making the Most of Statistical Analyses: Improving Interpretation and Presentation." *American Journal of Political Science* 44(2) (2000): 341–55.

Levitsky, Steven. *Transforming Labor-Based Parties in Latin America: Argentine Peronism in Comparative Perspective.* New York: Cambridge University Press, 2003.

Lijphart, Arend. "The Power-Sharing Approach." In Joseph V. Montville, ed., *Conflict and Peacemaking in Multiethnic Societies.* Lexington, MA: Lexington Books, 1990, pp. 491–509.

Mainwaring, Scott, and Aníbal Pérez-Liñán. *Why Regions of the World Are Important: Regional Specificities and Region-Wide Diffusion of Democracy.* Working Paper #322. Notre Dame: The Helen Kellogg Institute for International Studies, 2005.

Pierson, Paul. *Politics in Time: History, Institutions, and Social Analysis.* Princeton, NJ: Princeton University Press, 2004.

Przeworski, Adam, Michael E. Alvarez, José Antonio Cheibub, and Fernando Limongi. *Democracy and Development: Political Institutions and Well-Being in the World, 1950–1990.* New York: Cambridge University Press, 2000.

Putnam, Robert. *Making Democracy Work: Civic Traditions in Modern Italy.* Princeton, NJ: Princeton University Press, 1993.

Remmer, Karen, and Eric Wibbels. "The Subnational Politics of Economic Adjustment: Provincial Politics and Fiscal Performance in Argentina." *Comparative Political Studies* 33(4) (2000): 419–51.

Shefter, Martin. "Party and Patronage: German, England, and Italy." *Politics and Society* 7 (1977): 403–52.

Stepan, Alfred. "Political Leadership and Regime Breakdown in Brazil." In Juan Linz and Alfred Stepan, eds., *The Breakdown of Democratic Regimes.* Baltimore, MD: Johns Hopkins University Press, 1978.

Stokes, Susan C. "Perverse Accountability: A Formal Model of Machine Politics with Evidence from Argentina." *American Political Science Review* 99(3) (2005): 315–25.

Tomz, Michael, Jason Wittenberg, and Gary King. *Clarify: Software for Interpreting and Presenting Statistical Results.* Version 2.0. Cambridge, MA: Harvard University, June 1, 2001. http://gking.harvard.edu

Varshney, Ashutosh. *Ethnic Conflict and Civic Life: Hindus and Muslims in India.* Princeton, NJ: Princeton University Press, 2002.

Weakliem, David L., and Robert Biggert. "Region and Political Opinion in the Contemporary United States." *Social Forces* 77(3) (1999): 863–886.

Wilkinson, Steven I. *Votes and Violence: Electoral Competition and Ethnic Riots in India.* New York: Cambridge University Press, 2004.

Part III

What Is to Be Done?

Chapter 7

Contingency, Politics, and the Nature of Inquiry
Why Non-Events Matter

Gregory A. Huber

Contingent events are probabilistic.[1] They manifest or do not manifest because of some uncertainty about the future that is unknown or unknowable to human participants. A simple toss of a coin, for example, will produce an observed outcome of "tails" about half of the time. The contingent outcome "tails" following a coin toss is, prior to the toss, a contingency. How should political science incorporate the fact that important political interactions are embedded in situations where outcomes are unknown prior to their occurrence?

The problem political scientists face in confronting contingency is particularly difficult for two reasons. First, rarely are we interested in contingent events for their own sake. Whether a political leader survives an assassination attempt is interesting, in most lines of political inquiry, because we believe that who leads matters and not because the continued persistence or death of that particular leader is itself of interest. We as political researchers are therefore interested in the downstream effects of potential and realized contingencies. In contrast, in gambling or operations research, one might care only about the contingent event itself (does the coin come up heads, or how frequently do we need to test a product to ensure that it is of high quality 99.95% of the time?). Political scientists must therefore incorporate contingency as a mediating factor in the political outcomes they study.

Second, political actors are strategic. As such, manifestations of contingencies as contingent outcomes are shaped by the choices of political actors and themselves shape the behavior of strategic actors in anticipation of potential contingent events. For example, political leaders in parliamentary systems may call elections now rather than in the future if the economy is doing well and they fear the contingent outcome brought about by the combination of a surprise future economic downturn and retrospective voting behavior. Thus, elections may be more likely to take place during good economic times than bad ones. Similarly, wise leaders avoid starting wars with enemies much more powerful than themselves. While there is uncertainty about the contingent outcome of any military interaction, strategic actors nonetheless anticipate the likely contingent outcome (defeat) and plan accordingly. In contrast, those studying the behavior of coins or the quality of production can safely assume that their subjects do not change their behavior strategically. Human decisions, unfortunately, are substantially more complicated.

If one accepts the basic notion that contingencies matter, both because they shape subsequent outcomes and anticipatory behavior, what should political science do to grapple with and manage this uncertainty? My argument here is twofold. First, not all contingencies are the same. In particular, there are some events that are fundamentally unforeseeable ex ante. These events are rare, however, and it is my contention that they should not be the focus of our research. Rather, political science should make primary those foreseeable contingencies around which strategic political actors maneuver. Foreseeable events, like unforeseeable events, are fundamentally probabilistic. Nonetheless, they matter because political actors have beliefs about the probabilities that they will manifest, and these beliefs shape the strategic interactions among political actors.

Consequently, my second argument is that political science already has the capacity for incorporating this second form of contingency, knowable uncertainties, into analysis of strategic behavior. The way to account for this form of contingency, however, is not to study the observed probabilistic manifestations of contingent outcomes, but instead to study how strategic actors behave in light of those potential contingencies. The most useful tool for understanding the effects of these foreseeable contingencies on political interactions is the formal and informal analysis of strategic behavior in the face of uncertainty through the use of game theory.

The remainder of this chapter is organized as follows. I first review different types of contingency and make the case for focusing on those contingent events about which strategic political actors may maneuver. Next, I demonstrate why and how the analysis of anticipatory strategic behavior should lie at the heart of the study of contingency in politics. Third, I identify the limitations of using observed contingent events to understand the role of contingencies in politics and suggest that analysis of anticipatory strategic behavior has implications for the allocation of research resources across many topics of interest to political scientists. Finally, I conclude by addressing several potential counter-arguments to my position.

Forms of Contingency and Their Study

All contingencies are not the same. In particular, it is analytically useful to distinguish those contingencies about which we know something, anything, and those of which we are unaware.[2] A useful label for the latter category is unknowable and unnatural disasters—things that are so out of the ordinary that we do not even believe they could occur. (An extreme example would be the universe simply ceasing to exist. A more realistic example is of a hurricane striking in the time before weather forecasting and the maintenance of historical records.) Because these events are fundamentally external to our immediate cognitive environment, they cannot affect, ex ante, our strategic behavior.

Clearly these types of contingencies matter—an unforeseeable hurricane kills many people. But because these events are not even considered by strategic actors prior to their occurrence, generalizing about the effects of unexpected hurricanes or other fundamentally external influences on human behavior is difficult and of limited value. Unforeseeable events are singular occurrences. In societies with written records, a hurricane is only an unforeseeable event once. Thereafter individuals could choose to alter their behavior in anticipation of a hard-to-predict surprise storm. Unforeseeable events are also generally rare and unique, so inferring from them the effect of other unique events is difficult. In short, the first flood is likely to have different effects than the first hurricane, etc.

Three objections might be raised to the argument that unforeseeable contingencies are best avoided by political science. One might claim, for instance, that if we are really interested in how humans behave in response to becoming aware of new contingencies, realized unforeseeable contingencies are interesting. The experience of the French Revolution, for example, has large effects on subsequent democratization efforts. But once the contingency of mob rule manifests the first time, it become foreseeable and is best approached in the manner described below. (Alternatively, one could go further and argue that strategic participants knew about the risk of mob rule, but simply revised upward their belief about its likelihood after observing it in the French case.)

Alternatively, one might state that there are many interesting circumstances in which some of the participants in a strategic interaction have knowledge of contingencies but others do not. In insider stock-trading cases, for example, corporate insiders might know that a company is about to be purchased whereas ordinary stockholders do not. These are not really examples of unforeseeable events, however. Instead, they are cases in which there are ordinary informational asymmetries. These example abound, as when individuals who have better knowledge of their own ideology and competence run for office before voters who know relatively little about the candidates.

Finally, one could argue that unforeseeable events are common and important. In designing public policy, for example, there are numerous instances of "unintended consequences" that have yielded dramatically different outcomes from those sought by policymakers. My argument, however, is that few of these cases are actually unforeseeable contingencies. Rather, strategic policymakers generally make decisions that yield outcomes that were considered, but were dismissed as unlikely to occur. Of course, it is interesting that policymakers make decisions that are, ex post, clearly badly informed. But, to presage the argument below, it is my claim that these sorts of strategic decisions are where political scientists should focus their attention rather than beginning with an analysis of the effects of these decisions. (Furthermore, as is explained below, if one does not consider the strategic sources of bad decisions, empirical analyses of the effects of these decisions are likely to be biased.)

So, if we instead focus our research efforts on foreseeable events, what are the implications for the study of politics? Prior to addressing this question directly, it is useful to note that even relatively rare events may influence strategic human behavior and thereby the outcome of realized contingencies. For example, serious earthquakes are rare in San Francisco, but the city has nonetheless chosen to impose stringent building codes. Earthquakes are even more rare in Chicago, but they still occur. In the event of a major earthquake in either city, however, individual buildings in Chicago are likely to fare less well because the city has not adopted stringent building codes to protect its citizens from the realized contingency of an earthquake. That is not because earthquakes are unknown, but because mandating earthquake-proof buildings is not seen as worth its relative cost (wisely or not). Similarly, six inches of snow in Atlanta brings the city to its knees while Hartford shrugs because it has invested in the technology necessary to cope with the more frequently anticipated contingency of snow. Preparing (or not) for earthquakes and snow are strategic decisions in anticipation of foreseeable contingencies.

Whether to prepare for natural disasters is representative of the numerous cases in which individuals make strategic choices in light of their beliefs about the likely effects of these choices on desired outcomes. This, I claim, is the realm where political science is likely to find the most success in building generalizable models of human interaction. Rather than asking what effect did the assassination of Yitzhak Rabin have on the Middle East, a far more useful endeavor is to focus on the more general question of what the problem of potential assassinations has on the behavior of government leaders.

How to Confront Contingency: The Power of Anticipatory Action

In this line of reasoning, it is a short step from being assassinated to losing an election. Both outcomes matter (and not only for the incumbent). How should political science internalize these contingencies? Here, I answer this question by way of an extended discussion of a particular area of political science research. One of the fundamental questions of politics is how the practice of selecting government officials alters their behavior. Taking this question more narrowly, one area of ongoing research focuses on debates about the appropriate method for selecting judges. If one is to make arguments about the (in)appropriateness of judicial elections, however, it is necessary to have a theory that links judicial behavior to systems of judicial selection. How should one do this?

One approach is to seek out what appear to be interesting "contingencies" surrounding judicial elections. In other words, one might look for historical events where the practice of electing judges appears to matter. One might imagine that such an approach to this topic could lead one to discover the following (hypothetical) historical narrative:

Judge Smote ascended to the bench after beating the incumbent, Judge Light, in a bruising electoral contest that focused on Judge Light's earlier sentencing behavior. Judge Smote's campaign advertisements focused on a case in which Judge Light sentenced David Randall, who was convicted of indecent exposure, to a probationary sentence in lieu of time in prison. While on probation, Mr. Randall was arrested for exposing himself to a young child. In an indecent exposure case now before the court, Judge Smote assigned the defendant John Davis the maximum prison sentence allowed by law.

One could ask many different questions in light of this incident, but for my purposes I wish to focus on one potential question and how it reveals the limitations associated with using realized contingencies as explanations for politically relevant outcomes. Specifically, one could imagine political scientists interested in the effects of judicial elections raising the question of "What explains the harsh sentence given to the Mr. Davis?" Taking as given Mr. Davis' decision to commit the crime for which he was convicted and the process that led to his conviction, one explanation for Mr. Davis' sentence is the presence of Judge Smote rather than Judge Light on the bench. Analytically, it follows that this line of inquiry now requires us to explain why Judge Smote, and not Judge Light, was sentencing on that particular day.

Thus, we must explain the outcome of the electoral contest between Judges Light and Smote. Given the narrative above, we might attribute Judge Light's defeat to her lenient sentence for Mr. Randall, combined with his decision to commit a crime while on parole. We might then conclude that the harsh sentence given to Mr. Davis is the product of a pair of realized contingencies given the institution of judicial elections: Judge Light's lenient sentence and Mr. Randall's recidivism.

What are the potential limitations of this explanation that are internal to the logic of the explanation itself? (That is, putting aside any concerns about the generalizability of the inferences that can be drawn from this single episode.) Foremost, we must establish that Judge Smote and Judge Light would have sentenced Mr. Davis differently. At first glance, this is a trivial matter (assuming the two cases are, on the merits, actually alike). After all, Judge Light sentenced an earlier defendant convicted of the same crime to a lenient sentence. But would Judge Light, if she had never been challenged or had won reelection, been similarly lenient? Alternatively, absent her successful campaign against Judge Light, would Judge Smote have been so punitive? Consider in turn three revisions to the above story.

First, suppose that Judge Smote never challenged Judge Light in the first place. In facing the Davis case, Judge Light might nonetheless have sentenced more punitively because of her experience in the Randall case. When sentencing Mr. Randall, Judge Light was uncertain about the probability he would recidivate. The realized contingency of Randall's recidivism could have led her to revise upward her beliefs about the appropriate sentence necessary to prevent this recidivism.

Second, imagine that Judge Light had managed to hold off Judge Smote in a close election. Facing the Davis case with the experience of having nearly lost office on the basis of decision that was perceived as too lenient, she might then have sentenced more punitively to inoculate herself in the next election against the criticism of being too liberal.

Third, what if Judge Smote had not obtained the bench as a result of beating Judge Light but had instead been appointed to the bench because of Judge Light's untimely accidental death? In this instance, Judge Smote would face the Davis case without the experience of knowing that the lenient sentencing of an individual convicted of the relatively minor offense of indecent exposure could become the flashpoint of a successful campaign against an incumbent judge. If so, she might have sentenced Mr. Davis as leniently as Judge Light did in the Randall case.

In the first alternative account for the observed sentence given to Mr. Davis, the institution of judicial elections is irrelevant. Rather, fundamental uncertainty about the nature of recidivism explains the different sentences in the Randall and Davis cases. In the latter two accounts recidivism is also important, but it is important solely because of the institution of judicial elections. More fundamentally, however, judicial elections explain the more punitive sentence for Mr. Davis, but this more punitive sentence will occur regardless of whether Judge Light is defeated by Judge Smote. Rather, it is the institution of judicial elections and the potential defeat of judges who assign lenient sentences that leads judges to sentence more punitively than they would otherwise.

The problem political analysts face in explaining the single case outlined above is that these four competing explanations are all potentially valid. Skilled researchers might bring secondary evidence to bear to establish that Judge Smote is indeed more punitive than Judge Light (even apart from the need to posture to gain office), but these efforts do little to address the core question for political scientists about the role of judicial elections in explaining judges' decisions. This is precisely because, by focusing on observed "contingencies," one can miss the enormous power of strategic behavior in anticipation of those contingencies and attribute to events, rather than strategic behavior, important political outcomes.

To illustrate this point more fully, let me return to the simple question: How do judicial elections shape judicial behavior? The above narrative suggests that lenient sentencing coupled with recidivism can result in incumbent judges losing office. Very few incumbent judges lose office, however, despite persistent claims of judicial liberalism. Why not? One explanation is that judicial elections don't affect judicial behavior (perhaps voters are so uninformed that judges pay elections no heed). But another potential explanation is that judges are perfectly aware of the possibility of having their sentencing revealed as inappropriately lenient and, ex ante, adjust their sentencing behavior in response.[3] Thus, the realized contingency of lenient sentencing and recidivism may not manifest because judges do not sentence leniently when they anticipate politically costly recidivism.

At the very least then, an analyst searching only for instances of observed judicial leniency (a sentence is "too" lenient when recidivism occurs) would understate the effects of judicial elections on incumbent behavior. We might even wrongly interpret that elections have little effect on judicial behavior. Furthermore, if judges do account for the potential publicity costs of lenient sentencing in their initial decisions, those instances of judicial leniency that do manifest in recidivism are likely to be unrepresentative of the cases where judges feel most constrained by the institution of judicial elections. (All judges might recognize that sex offenders are likely to recidivate, but not realize that one of the many drunk drivers they see in their courtrooms is going to get drunk and cause an accident involving a school bus.)

Fortunately, political science is relatively well equipped to deal with these impediments to direct inference from observed outcomes. The primary tool is the use of models of strategic interaction under the rubric of non-cooperative game theory. While many formal game theoretic analyses are expressed mathematically, the logic of strategic action in the face of uncertainty translates broadly and can be expressed rather informally. The critical insight of this approach is that we can understand how contingency (uncertainty) affects behavior by causing actors to anticipate outcomes before they occur.

Before applying this approach to the question at hand, consider a very simple example from the world of academia: Why don't teachers in large lecture courses assign the same exam question about the most important topic covered in a course each time they teach the class? The answer is simple: because students, who presumably have access to past tests, would learn exactly what they had to study to get an A and would study nothing more. Randomizing examination questions forces students to anticipate a range of examination topics. Presumably this serves the professor's interest in encouraging students to learn all of the material relevant for a given class, even at the cost of not getting to probe students' knowledge about the single most important topic covered. In other words, professors anticipate students' strategic studying and construct exams accordingly. Given that professors think some topics are more important than others and also have other things to do with their time, they may not write entirely new exams each semester, but the exams will incorporate enough new questions and variation in topics to keep students on their toes.

Applying the same logic to the question of judicial elections, consider the following highly simplified model of this important political interaction. There are three strategic "players": a voter, an incumbent judge, and a (potential) challenger to the incumbent judge. The voter, like most people, is busy and would prefer not to spend his time monitoring the minutia of judicial decision-making. The incumbent judge enjoys being a judge and is willing to give up some of her potential judicial sentencing authority to retain that esteemed office. Finally, the potential challenger would like to someday become a judge, but would prefer to experience the costs of a campaign only if she has a reasonably good chance of defeating the incumbent.

In an active campaign, the challenger can seek to publicize incidents of judicial "malfeasance" by the incumbent such as taking a bribe, presiding over a case in which the judge has an interest, or simply assigning a sentence the public doesn't like. Because it is easier for the public to understand the reasons that a convicted felon deserved a harsh sentence than the mitigating circumstances that warrant a more lenient one, however, challengers will have an easier time communicating to the public cases of apparent excessive judicial leniency than cases of excessive judicial punitiveness. Busy voters will rely on claims by challengers (perhaps skeptically) to evaluate incumbent performance, in effect allowing the challenger to "audit" the incumbent's performance on their behalf. In anticipation of this behavior, incumbent judges have an incentive to become more punitive in order to reduce the number of cases a challenger could use to advertise the incumbent's apparent judicial leniency, thereby reducing the probability the potential challenger will actually enter the race in the first place.

The point then is that judicial elections can "matter" by leading incumbent judges to become more punitive *even though* there are few, if any, cases of judges losing office because of sentencing too leniently. From an incumbent judge's perspective, the relevant contingency is whether or not a given sentencing decision will later be portrayed as excessively lenient. If challengers are highly effective at uncovering instances in which the public might perceive judicial leniency, judges must be concerned about leniency in all of their cases. Alternatively, if the claim of under-punishment is persuasive only when accompanied by realized recidivism, then judges must weigh the probability of recidivism against their own sentencing preferences. Ex ante, however, whether a convicted felon will recidivate is unknown (although judges might have a good sense of which convicts are most at risk). The judge, therefore, cannot strategize knowing if the contingency will manifest, but has to behave as if it might manifest. Thus, the possibility of a contingent event occurring alters the sentencing behavior of incumbent trial court judges in the presence of judicial elections.

Implications: Guidance for Research and Resources

So far, this essay has argued that manifestations of contingencies may reveal relatively little about the important implications of contingency for the strategic behavior of political actors. The aforementioned case of judicial selection, however, may appear too narrow for some political scientists. Does the logic of strategic action in light of contingency travel to other areas of research—for instance, debates about the role of events as causes or the process of democratization? The answer put forth here is that analysis of strategic action in light of uncertainty is not only appropriate to this diverse body of topics, but also essential if political science as a discipline is to allocate its scarce resources to understanding the political world.

How can analysis of strategic behavior help political science in identifying the appropriate allocation of scarce disciplinary resources? Assume that one is interested in the effect of political campaigns on voter turnout. One common approach to studying this topic is to use existing survey instruments and data collection projects to analyze the covariation between campaign contact and voter turnout. The problem, of course, is that campaigns do not target a random sample of potential voters. Rather, campaigns seek to mobilize voters who would otherwise not vote in the absence of their activity and tend to ignore those who would vote or not vote regardless of the campaign.

Estimating the general effect of campaigns on turnout from campaigns that are targeted at those most likely to be affected by the campaign is therefore nearly impossible. Instead, the knowledge that ordinary professional campaigns are targeted has spurred calls for field experiments to randomly campaign and then observe the effect on turnout. The results of incorporating the realization of strategic behavior by campaigns into empirical research on this topic are stunning. Using National Elections Survey data, Wielhouwer and Lockerbie estimate the effect of campaign contact on turnout at 23.6%.[4] In a more recent study, Hillygus estimates that campaign contact increases the probability of turnout by 40% among those who do not already intend to vote.[5] In a randomized field experiment that removes the bias introduced by targeted campaigning, however, Gerber and Green find a much more modest effect of personal contact of about 7%.[6] At best, given strategic behavior, "there is an illusion of learning from observational research."[7] At worst, however, political science as a discipline is investing in uninformative projects *at the expense of* potentially more revealing forms of inquiry. (For example, administering the National Election Survey, which provides the data used in the Weilhouwer and Lockerbie article, has an annual cost of about 1 million dollars. The Gerber and Green experiment cost less than $50,000.)

But what about "larger" questions, like the conditions that lead to the solidification and consolidation of democracy?[8] Is strategic behavior really relevant for understanding the contingencies that manifest in successful democratic consolidations and those that result in returns to military rule or authoritarianism? Here again, it is my contention that focusing too much on the success or failure of observed efforts at democratization may overlook the strategic interactions that explain when and how autocratic leaders or exclusionary regimes choose to experiment with democratization in the first place.

Consider Chile, where the possibility of the resurgent democratic state turning on the remnants of the Pinochet regime led those actors to enact constitutional measures giving persistent powers to interests of the old regime. The constitutional provisions, in anticipation of a contingency that nearly manifested anyway (witness Pinochet's near extradition), have had profound effects on the practice of Chilean democracy.[9] Or consider the fears of property expropriation that may lead minority regimes with immobile assets to be unwilling to experiment with democratization for fear of having those assets expropriated by the newly powerful majority.[10] In short, a great deal of the "action" in democratization may take place prior to the decision to experiment with democracy and may also determine the form that the experiment will take. By looking only at observed institutions and the relative success or failure of democratic regimes, however, we risk attributing to those institutions success and failure without realizing that the institutions themselves are fundamentally rooted in prior political conflict.[11] In short, contingent events within new democracies matter, but what chance events are likely to occur (and whether they will matter) is shaped by the institutional choices that precede the trial of democratization.

One might accept my contention that institutions, rules, and practices are themselves the contingent outcome of larger political conflict, but still maintain that contingencies internal to these systems matter in determining political outcomes. That events—particularly wars and depressions—are causes of political outcomes is the fundamental contention in Mayhew's essay.[12] Clearly wars and depressions matter; the critical question, however, is why do they matter? The Japanese surprise attack on Pearl Harbor plunges the nation into World War II and gives the Roosevelt administration great latitude to pursue its interests in allying with European countries against the Axis. Critically, what makes the event such a powerful "cause" is that it is external to the behavior of the Roosevelt administration. Americans do not blame Roosevelt or the Democrats for Pearl Harbor, and if anything, the Democrats subsequently succeed in making political hay out of Republican insistence that isolationism would protect American interest over the long run from "Europe's war."

In contrast, consider the events of late August 1998. At that time, the Clinton administration ordered a military assault on alleged terrorist facilities in Sudan and Afghanistan. One key target of the attack was Osama bin Laden, the head of a terrorist organization alleged to be acting to threaten the United States. At the time, President Clinton stated the attacks were necessary to "counter an immediate threat." Skeptics were quick to suggest that Al Qaeda was not a real threat to the United States and that the motivation for the attack was to distract the nation from the growing domestic crisis Clinton faced because of his relationship with a former White House intern, Monica Lewinsky. (The attack took place three days after Clinton first addressed the nation regarding this relationship.) How then did the public react to this critical event? Was the president justified in going after bin Laden, or was he an invented enemy who posed little threat to the United States? At the time, a CNN survey found that more than one third of Americans thought Clinton ordered the attacks partly to divert attention from the Monica Lewinsky sex scandal.[13]

This episode helps understand how we should approach the problem of contingency in studying politics for two reasons. First, strategic actors must consider the sources of seemingly external events. In this case, Americans disagreed about whether Clinton had obtained new information that led him to stage an attack abroad (and which might warrant rallying to the flag to support his leadership in a time of crisis) or was trying to pretend that he had obtained such information even as he was instead acting simply for political preservation. Those who opposed Clinton had a strong interest in convincing the public that the attack was unjustified. On the other hand, supporters of Clinton sought to do otherwise. This point may seem obvious, but it is important because it suggests that in strategic situations actors will consider carefully the motives of those who claim to have access to "private" information about "exogenous" contingent events that explains their actions.

Second, the manifestation of the attack provides further insight into the nature of contingency as a source of non-events. Clinton ordered the attack despite the realization that some skeptics would doubt his motives. Imagine if he had not, despite the clear evidence (at least in the post-9/11 world) that bin Laden posed a real threat. One could easily have seen him arriving at this conclusion precisely because the public would doubt his motives. (Clinton did not take more extreme action, such as invading Afghanistan or substantially increasing pressure on Pakistan to end its alliance with the Taliban, perhaps because of the broad skepticism that would have surrounded such an aggressive move during the Lewinsky scandal.) That is, Clinton's range of feasible political activity was limited because of the public's uncertainty about the merits of claims of private knowledge. This suggests that political inquiry must also consider how the fact that strategic actors evaluate claims of externally driven contingent events skeptically shapes *inaction*. Overall, political actors might not take desirable action precisely because of ex post negative evaluation of their actions, even though outside political actors would, if completely informed, endorse the move.[14] (This is precisely the logic underpinning Canes-Wrone, Herron, and Shotts' model of pandering in presidential leadership.[15]) It is not surprising therefore that a great deal of real political conflict concerns debates about which events are unforeseen contingencies and which are altogether unforeseeable. Political actors have an incentive to take credit for unforeseeable good contingencies by portraying them as products of good leadership. They also have an incentive to prevent bad foreseeable contingencies or to distance themselves from these unfortunate events by claiming they were unforeseeable and beyond their control. (Voters, for their part, sometimes seem able to distinguish who is "at fault" in different contexts. For example, Ebeid and Rodden show that gubernatorial election outcomes are less tied to local economic condition in states vulnerable to international market forces [e.g. commodity price swings] than in more insulated states.[16])

Overall, events matter, but they matter in two very different ways. First, they matter because other strategic actors have a difficult time properly assigning blame and awarding credit for the manifestation of contingencies. Whose fault is it? Could we have avoided it? Second, they matter because strategic actors will seek to avoid events, realized contingencies, which will be damaging to their interests. In both cases, the best way to understand these dynamics is not to focus on events as they take place, but to consider broadly the implications of uncertainty and potential contingencies for the strategic decisions that shape human political interactions. Taking contingency seriously demands incorporating theories of strategic behavior in the face of future uncertainty into both theoretical and empirical work in political science. The alternative, to ignore uncertainty and strategy, is to overlook one of the basic underpinnings of conflict in all political interactions.

Some Counter-Arguments Addressed

So far, this essay suggests a rethinking of how political scientists should approach the "problem" of contingency in political interactions. By bringing to the fore the idea of anticipatory behavior, it generally suggests a greater focus on the logic of strategic action in anticipation of foreseen contingencies. It particularly advocates for the application of game theoretic models of these complex interactions. Such an approach is not without its limitations, however. Here I briefly explore the confines of this approach by considering three types of objections to the arguments made above.

First, consider the objection that strategic models of interaction require individuals to be supremely rational and selfish utility maximizers. In the example developed above about judicial sentencing behavior, one might object to the characterization of incumbent judges as concerned with retaining office. After all, judges have many motives, including both the desire to "judge" and to be seen positively by other members of their social community. Narrow expressions of judicial preferences as concerned with reelection necessarily understate the true complexity of the "utility functions" judges seek to maximize. Arguments of this sort are not, however, attacks on the idea of modeling anticipatory behavior. Rather, they are criticisms of particular expressions of actors' utility functions and maximization behavior. If strategic actors are other-regarding[17] and concerned about their peers, stating that judges first value reelection may miss the fact that some judges would rather lose than be perceived as punitive. Alternatively, actors may be bad at math, more or less risk averse, or systematically biased in their acquisition and processing of different types of information. Insofar as incorrect formalizations of actors' preferences and decision-making processes are wrong, these are weaknesses with particular models, however, and not the approach of modeling as a whole.[18]

A second and related criticism is that game theoretic models of behavior often overlook the systemic or organizationally induced sources of behavior and outcomes. Bureaucracies, for example, structure decision-making. Therefore, they generate both standard operating procedures and create interests for their participants that are internal to the organizational apparatus.[19] Beyond noting that such organizational incentives are easily incorporated as revisions in actors' preferences, a broad focus on anticipatory behavior suggests stepping back further to recognize the strategic and anticipatory origins of these systems and organizations themselves. (See the above comment on the design of institutions in newly democratizing nations.)

Finally, one might suggest that recognizing contingency means embracing uncertainty about political outcomes above simple deterministic theories of outcomes.[20] Reading this essay as embracing outcome determinacy (even when it originates in strategic behavior) is, however, a mistake. Rather, I am suggesting that acknowledging the uncertainty of outcomes requires us to admit that strategic actors are similarly confounded by uncertainty in making their own choices. Their strategic choices, made in light of uncertainty, in turn affect the outcomes of important political interactions, the realized contingencies that have been the focus of much previous scholarship. Overall, contingencies may be unexplained ex ante, but they are not exogenous. Furthermore, their long shadow shapes important political behavior in anticipation of their occurrence and in ensuring their avoidance.

NOTES

1. I thank Justin Fox, Jacob Hacker, and the reviewers for their helpful comments.

2. For a different categorization of contingencies, see Schedler, this volume. Contingencies of which we are initially unaware are catastrophes in Schedler's typology, although, as I suggest below, many catastrophes are foreseeable. I group Schedler's remaining categories of contingencies together as known contingencies.

3. Huber and Gordon, "Accountability and Coercion."

4. Wielhouwer and Lockerbie, "Party Contacting," p. 216.

5. Hillygus, "Campaign Effects," Figure 1.

6. Gerber and Green, "Effects of Canvassing," p. 658.

7. Gerber, Green, and Kaplan, "Illusion of Learning."

8. See Stokes, this volume.

9. See Londregan, *Legislative Institutions*.

10. Boix and Garicano, *Democracy, Inequality*.

11. Boix and Adsera, *Democratic Stability*.

12. Mayhew, this volume.

13. Holland, CNN, 1998.

14. One could push this line of reasoning even further by arguing that terrorists might have been emboldened to take risky actions precisely because they knew Clinton would have a more difficult time garnering public support to stop their advances during a time of domestic political strife. A purely rational strategic public would have to incorporate this possibility into its evaluation of the likelihood that external events justified the use of force abroad.

15. Canes-Wrone, Herron, and Shotts, "Leadership and Pandering."

16. Ebeid and Rodden, "Economic Geography."

17. See Pettit, this volume.

18. For an extended discussion of the difficulty, and promise, of modeling social and peer effects, see Manski "Economic Analysis."

19. See Jervis, *Effects*; Perrow, *Organizations*.

20. Hacker, "Learning."

BIBLIOGRAPHY

Boix, Carles, and Alicia Adsera. *Democratic Stability and Political Institutions: A Survival Analysis.* Chicago: University of Chicago Press, 2004.

Boix, Carles, and Luis Garicano. *Democracy, Inequality, and Country-Specific Wealth.* Chicago: University of Chicago Press, 2001.

Canes-Wrone, Brandice, Michael C. Herron and Kenneth W. Shotts. "Leadership and Pandering: A Theory of Executive Policymaking." *American Journal of Political Science* 45 (July 2001): 532–50.

Ebeid, Michael, and Jonathan Rodden. "Economic Geography and Economic Voting." *British Journal of Political Science* 36 (July 2006): 527–47.

Gerber, Alan S., and Donald P. Green. "The Effects of Canvassing, Telephone Calls, and Direct Mail on Voter Turnout: A Field Experiment." *The American Political Science Review* 94 (Sept. 2000): 653–63.

Gerber, Alan S., Donald P. Green, and Edward H. Kaplan. "The Illusion of Learning from Observational Research." Institution for Social and Policy Studies Working Paper, Yale University, New Haven, CT, 2002.

Hacker, Jacob. "Learning from Defeat?" *British Journal of Political Science* 31 (Jan. 2001): 61–94.

Hillygus, D. Sunshine. "Campaign Effects and the Dynamics of Turnout Intention in Election 2000." *Journal of Politics* 67 (Feb. 2000): 50–68.

Holland, Keating. CNN. Available at http://www.cnn.com/ALLPOLITICS/1998/08/21/strike.poll/, 1998.

Huber, Gregory A., and Sanford C. Gordon. "Accountability and Coercion: Is Justice Blind When It Runs for Office?" *The American Journal of Political Science* 48 (April 2004): 247–63.

Jervis, Robert. *System Effects.* Princeton: Princeton University Press, 1997.

Londregan, John B. *Legislative Institutions and Ideology in Chile.* Cambridge: Cambridge University Press, 2000.

Manski, Charles F. "Economic Analysis of Social Interactions" *The Journal of Economic Perspectives* 14 (Summer 2000): 115–136.

Perrow, Charles. *Complex Organizations.* New York: McGraw-Hill, 1986.

Wielhouwer, Peter W., and Brad Lockerbie. "Party Contacting and Political Participation, 1952–90." *American Journal of Political Science* 38 (Feb. 1994): 211–29.

Chapter 8

Modeling Contingency

Elisabeth Jean Wood

Men make their own history, but they do not make it just as they please.
— Karl Marx, in *The Eighteenth Brumaire of Louis Bonaparte*

Political assassinations are the quintessential examples of contingent events, events that could well have not occurred yet may have significant causal effects.[1] The assassination of Archduke Franz Ferdinand and the outbreak of World War I is the canonical example. Similarly, many think the Oslo peace process would have gone forward toward a negotiated settlement between the Israelis and Palestinians had Yitzhak Rabin not been assassinated. Wilhelm De Klerk, who as president of South Africa released Nelson Mandela and oversaw the negotiations that culminated in a transition to democracy, believes that had he been assassinated before the referendum of white voters in 1992, the democratization process would not have continued.[2] In contrast, had it occurred after the referendum, he thinks the process would have gone forward. And had the charismatic Chris Hani, the most popular of the African National Congress leadership after Nelson Mandela, not been assassinated in 1993, collective action by leftist youth and trade unionists might have led to different post-election ANC policies; indeed the party might conceivably have split. Thus contingent events such as political assassinations may prevent a transition to a new set of institutions or they may ignite a chain of events with profound institutional consequences.

Contingent events may also spark a transforming mobilization of actors, as in Eastern Europe in the late 1980s. When I investigated patterns of insurgent collective action during El Salvador's civil war, I found to my surprise that those patterns were not well predicted by agrarian structures such as land tenure, poverty, or rural employment. Rather, patterns of mobilization were shaped by much more contingent factors, particularly the trajectory of indiscriminate violence by state actors across the countryside.[3]

Yet despite the transforming consequences of some contingent events, on a closer look some appear less causally effective than others. Given the political rivalry between the European powers at the time, World War I would most probably have occurred had the assassination in Sarajevo not occurred. There may have been a large number of improbable events, any one of which would have triggered the cataclysm; the probability that at least one of these events would occur may have been quite high. In this spirit Friedrich Engels took the view that great political leadership is not necessary for history to take its course:

> That such and such a man and precisely that man arises at that particular time in that given country is of course pure accident. But cut him out and there will be a demand for a substitute, and this substitute will be found, good or bad, but in the long run he will be found. That Napoleon, just that particular Corsican, should have been the military dictator whom the French Republic, exhausted by its own war, had rendered necessary, was an accident; but that, if a Napoleon had been lacking, another would have filled the place . . .[4]

One need not agree with the sweeping scope of Engels' claim to recognize that some leaders to whom exceptional political leadership is popularly attributed happened to have exerted their efforts toward a very probable, if not foreseen, outcome.

In modeling contingency, we should thus like to illuminate why similar contingent events have causal force in some circumstances and not others. We should like to characterize some settings as susceptible to large-scale change (often signaled by rhetorical gestures such as "we are at the brink," or "we are at the crossroads") that could be triggered by a wide range of contingent events, whereas other settings appear immune to any number of such events. We should like to analyze the interaction of contingent events and underlying causes (the social analogues of gravity in physical models), a desiderata identified by David Mayhew.[5] And we should like to account for the frequently observed rapidity of large-scale change followed by long-term persistence of the new, sometimes termed "punctuated equilibria."

In this chapter I present models that may help us formalize our speculative claims about the robustness of some institutions or political processes relative to contingent events, on the one hand, and the vulnerability of others. I identify and present modeling approaches to three types of contingency: stochastic variation of individual behaviors, exogenous shocks to actors' beliefs or to structural parameters (where "exogenous" refers to events outside the existing causal frame of reference; they may of course be explained or explicable in some larger frame), and organized challenges by political actors sparked by contingent events. More *robust* institutions and political processes are those more likely to occur and persist in the possible worlds that might have been given the presence or absence of a multiplicity of contingent events (what Pettit terms *resilience* in his chapter of this volume).

Thus this chapter offers some analytical tools toward addressing the questions: What institutions, alliances, settlements, or processes are robust in the face of contingent events? Which are vulnerable? And we would like to know what types of contingent events are most likely to disrupt particular institutions and processes. Normatively, there are some processes and institutions, such as mobilization against a dictatorship and democratic regimes, that we should like to protect against contingent events that would disrupt them. And there are others whose vulnerability to contingent events we should like to exploit precisely in order to disrupt them, such as genocidal collective action or racial segregation. (Thus this chapter does not assert a normative status quo bias as is sometimes the case in writing about contingent events. For example, Andreas Schedler in his contribution to this volume appears to believe that contingency should be "contained" or "managed," not exploited.)

I begin with a model of institutions as self-enforcing conventions arising from the decentralized interactions of members of two groups. I present a stochastic model of institutional transitions in which they are triggered by the bunching of chance variations in the behavior of group members. Thus in the initial model of contingency, Schedler's dimension of indeterminacy and to a lesser extent the dimension of uncertainty dominate the dimension of conditionality.[6] I argue that while this quintessential model of contingency yields many insights, it does not explain many of the phenomena of interest. I then show how contingent events in the form of exogenous shocks to the costs and rewards of alternative courses of action among strategically interacting actors can trigger institutional transitions, illustrating this process by a model that identifies robust settlements to civil wars. In this second model, all three dimensions of contingency play a role: exogenous shocks are causal but their occurrence and timing are uncertain and thus the course of events is indeterminate. Finally I analyze intentional collective action as the trigger for institutional transitions and explore the role of contingent events in its emergence. In this third model, conditionality plays the major role (transitions are conditional on collective action), but uncertain and indeterminate events may shape the emergence and course of collective action.

Multiple Equilibria and Transitions between Conventions

Si fueris Romae, Romano vivito more.[7]

—Saint Ambrose

Many institutions are well understood as conventions: other institutional arrangements are possible (and perhaps even preferable) but as long as (nearly) everyone else is following the prevailing institution, it is best for each individual to do so as well.[8] A common example is the convention of driving on the right hand side of the road (except in the United Kingdom and some former British colonies, where the opposite convention prevails). There is no inherent advantage in one side or the other, but it is very important that (locally at least) one or the other convention prevail. Much ordinary behavior has this form as well: though I may believe my wage unjust, as long as other workers accept that wage and do not strike, it is best for me to accept it as well. And as long as few other citizens protest a rigged electoral result, it is best for me to acquiesce.

Imagine the interactions underlying a convention occur in the following highly stylized way.[9] The population is divided into group A and group B. In each period randomly selected members of each group interact with each other in pairs made up of a member of each group. Each of the two players proposes one of two contracts, 0 or 1. The proposals are simultaneous. If the proposers agree, that contract is implemented, meaning each gets some positive benefit (not in general equal); if not, neither gets anything. Further assume that group B prefers contract 0 but group A prefers contract 1. Examples of such interactions are drivers heading south and those heading north, workers and employers, lovers considering the terms of a marriage contract, landlords and tenants, buyers and sellers, lenders and borrowers, protestors and police, and so on. We can summarize this generic interaction with the utilities to each player resulting from each pair of offers as follows:

Member of A offers contract	Member of B offers contract	
	1	0
1	a_1, b_1	$0, 0$
0	$0, 0$	a_0, b_0

The first entry of each pair refers to the utility of the A-group member and, correspondingly, the second to that of the B-group member. We assume that the members of A and B prefer different contracts—i.e., we assume $a_0 < a_1$ but $b_0 > b_1$. The two combinations of matching offers are both conventions (Nash equilibria, pairs of strategies that are each the best response to the other and therefore a situation from which neither individual will benefit by unilateral deviation).

If we were to observe a very large number of pairs of groups whose members interact this way, which convention would occur more frequently? Imagine each player knows the structure of the game and chooses to offer the contract that maximizes her expected utility, which depends on which contract she expects her interaction partner to offer. Assume that she bases her expectation on the observation of the prevalence of contracts offered by members of the other group in the previous period (this prevalence is common knowledge among her group). Let the fraction of A players who offered contract 1 in the previous period be t and that of B players be q. Then the expected utility to an A player to offer contract 1 in this period, given her observation that a fraction q of the B-players offer will contract 1 as well, is just the probability of her partner also playing 1 (namely, q) times the utility to her when both play contract 1 plus the probability of her partner not playing 1 ($1-q$) times the utility to her when their offers conflict (namely, zero):

$$P_A^1 = qa_1 + (1-q)0 = qa_1.$$

Similarly, the expected utility to an A player to offering contract 0 is:

$$p_A{}^0 = q0 + (1-q)a_0 = (1-q)a_0.$$

Which expected utility is greater (and thus which contract the A player will offer) depends on q, the fraction of B players that offered contract 1. This can be represented as a tipping graph, shown in figure 8.1. Thus if the A player in the previous period observed a fraction of B players offering contract 1 that was higher than q^*, then all A players will offer contract 1 in this period, their best response. The tipping threshold q^* depends only on the parameters a_0 and a_1.[10] A similar graph exists for members of B and identifies the tipping point t^* (which depends similarly only on b_0 and b_1).

So if $q > q^*$ and $t > t^*$, the resulting convention will be that in which all players offer contract 1, the upper right-hand quadrant in figure 8.2, which represents all possible worlds of this system (the state space). Similarly, if $q < q^*$ and $t < t^*$, the other convention will result and all players will offer contract 0 (the lower left quadrant). In the other two quadrants, a ridge separates initial states that will move toward contract 0 from those that will move toward contract 1. The ridge thus separates the population space into two basins of attraction for the two equilibria. The basin of attraction for an equilibrium is the set of states such that if the system is in a state in

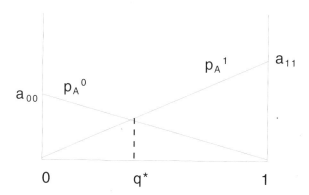

Fig. 8.1. The tipping threshold of members of A, q^*. A's expected utilities to offering contracts 0 and 1 are the lines $p_A{}^0$ and $p_A{}^1$, respectively. The tipping threshold for members of A is q^*—if a member of A observed last period that a fraction of B-group members greater than q^* offered contract 1, then so will she in this period.

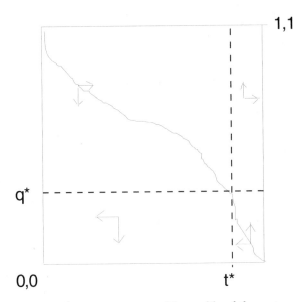

Fig. 8.2. The state space: possible worlds of the system. The tipping thresholds are t^* and q^*. The meandering line from the upper left to the lower right through the saddle point (t^*, q^*) is a ridge separating the basins of attraction for the two conventions. The basin contract 0 is the area below the ridge; that for contract 1 above it.

the set (as an initial condition or as a result of chance variation, see below), the system moves to that equilibrium. Which equilibrium occurs depends on the initial conditions, i.e., the initial distribution of players in each group playing each contract. If the initial states are all equally probable, then the convention with the larger basin of attraction is more likely to be the final state.

As described so far, the outcome is determined: depending on the initial condition (the initial t and q), the system moves to one equilibrium or the other and no transitions between equilibria occur (the equilibria are absorbing states).[11] Extending the model allows us to explore three reasons that transitions may occur: the bunching of chance variation in the behavior of members of a group, exogenous shocks to the payoffs to different pairs of strategies, and intentional collective action by members of a group. I develop each in turn.

Idiosyncratic Play and Stochastically Driven Transitions between Equilibria

History . . . is the natural selection of accidents.

—Leon Trotsky[12]

In contrast to the determined outcome of the preceding model, if we allow that group members sometimes do not follow their best-response strategy and instead occasionally vary their behavior by chance and may as a result offer a contract that is not that of the reigning convention, transitions may occur.[13] Assume that each player makes such an *idiosyncratic play,* by which I mean chooses randomly between her available strategies, with probability e and does so independently of what the other players do. Such idiosyncratic play may occur because players have mistaken perceptions of the last round of play, because they may have values or reasons not captured in this description of the interaction, or because they may simply experiment for reasons outside the model. Whatever the reasons, if sufficiently many idiosyncratically play a strategy distinct from that of the prevailing convention (that is, they do not play their best-response strategy), they will trigger a change to a new equilibrium.

Assume that the existing convention was that of contract o. If sufficiently many of either the As or the Bs (i.e., a fraction more than t^* or q^*) were to offer contract 1 because of the random bunching of idiosyncratic plays, then members of the other group would themselves offer contract 1, their best response. Since all did so, all members of the other group would also switch, and the contract 1 convention would emerge. If we wait long enough, such a random bunching of idiosyncratic plays will occur. And if we wait long enough again, sufficient numbers of one or the other group will happen to offer contract o by "mistake," and the original convention will re-emerge. What fraction of the members of one or the other the group would have to switch to trigger such a transition depends on t^* and q^*. A switch is more likely the smaller the tipping threshold (because the probability of n players making the chance variation independently is e^n.)

A consequence of this idiosyncratic play is that the conventions are no longer absorbing states; chance events will displace the population from the convention and sometimes even usher in a new convention. In the long run, how likely the population is to be in a particular convention is independent of the initial conditions. Can we say anything about the relative persistence of different states? Using the tools of evolutionary sto-chastic game theory, we can predict how likely the system is to be in differ-ent conventions in the very long run. The equilibrium in which the system spends most of the time is termed the *stochastically stable state*.[14] Stochas-tically stable states are *persistent* or *robust:* it takes a large number of con-current idiosyncratic plays to trigger a transition out of the state. Thus, as can be seen from figure 8.1, contract 0 will be persistent if t^* and q^* are large.[15] Such states must also be *accessible:* relatively few idiosyncratic plays are sufficient to trigger a transition *into* the state (so $1-t^*$, and $1-q^*$ must be small). (If there are just two conventions, accessibility implies persis-tence and conversely, but this is not generally the case.)[16]

In this stochastic extension of the initial model, such a bunching of idi-osyncratic play is a quintessentially contingent event, occurring by chance but occasioning significant change. Robert Axtell, Joshua M. Epstein, and H. Peyton Young illustrate the power of this approach in a computer sim-ulation of a model in which *classes emerge endogenously*.[17] In their model, members from a single population are paired randomly in each period, and each offers one of three contracts to share a pie: players making "high" offers demand 70 percent, those making "medium" offers demand 50 percent, and those making "low" offers demand 30 percent. If the offers sum to 100 percent, the contract is implemented; if not, the parties get nothing. The players' expectations about what strategy their partner will play are not formed as above by observing the fractions playing different strategies, but by the fraction playing different strategies *with them* in the past m rounds of play. In other words, they have memories rather than global vision. In addition, agents have "tags" ("blue" or "yellow") and re-member the "tag" of the last m players with whom they played as well as her strategy. The tags are meaningless in that all agents are identical in their strategy set and memory capability; they differ only in their past ex-perience. So in a given round, I might remember that in the last 8 rounds, 4 "blue" opponents played contract 0, 1 "blue" opponent played contract 1, and 3 "yellow" opponents played contract 1. Observing that in this round I am paired with a "yellow" opponent, my expectation is that he will play contract 1 (as all the "yellow" opponents I can remember playing did), so I will play contract 1 as well with a probability of $1-e$ and a randomly cho-sen strategy with probability e (the stochastic element of the model). The authors show that over time the tags may develop social significance as the accumulation of plays reveals that players with certain tags tend to play a certain way. In that case, classes may emerge in the sense that when playing with others who share the same tag, players will make equitable offers, but when playing with someone of the opposite tag, players of one color (say, "blue") will always offer the contract that favors them and the other player will offer the same one. Although the convention in which all players offer all other players the equitable contract is the stochastically stable state, the inequitable states may endure for very long periods.

If such stochastic models well capture an empirical process that occurred independently in various sites across a landscape, one would expect to observe local conformity (a given convention obtains across interacting groups), global diversity (distinct conventions occur), punctuated equilibria (the swift change to a new equilibrium in some localities), and the predominance of the stochastically stable convention.[18] The first two patterns, local conformity and global diversity, are observed in the pattern of sharecropping contracts in India,[19] that of driving conventions in much of Austria and Italy before the adoption of national conventions,[20] and agricultural share contracts in Illinois.[21] Other examples are inheritance rules and marriage contracts.

Such stochastic models capture a particular kind of contingent event —namely, random variation in player strategies—but they have shortcomings in accounting for patterns of observed persistence and change.[22] First, a convention unravels in this model because of the bunching of errors on the part of members of the group *that benefits from that convention,* a pattern unlikely to account for actual transitions.[23] Second, if group size varies between the two groups, the convention that favors the group whose number is greater tends to persist, which contradicts our intuition (due to Mancur Olsen) that coordination is easier among smaller groups. Third, in extensions of the stochastic models where contracts can vary in steps between 0 and 1 (and any $[x, 1-x]$ pair of offers is a Nash equilibrium), transitions tend to occur between extreme values of the contract (between 0 and 1) rather than between adjacent values. Such leap-frogging (for example, between a contract in which workers get everything to one in which employers get everything) is rarely observed. Fourth, an additional concern is that for reasonable population sizes and rates of chance variation, periods between transitions in these models are inordinately long—so long that they are unlikely to capture institutional transition dynamics on the order of observed historical change. However, a range of modifications to the model may well yield reasonable transition times.[24]

Finally and most importantly, such models do not treat cases where rejecting the norm of practices of the prevailing convention is not an error but an intentional act and where bunching of such errors is not a random accident but an instance of intentional collective action (as in the case of the overthrow of apartheid and the Jim Crow legal regime in the U.S. South by the civil rights movement).

Suitably amended with more realistic assumptions about how players make idiosyncratic moves, stochastic evolutionary models address some of these shortcomings.[25] Before analyzing the role of contingent events in collective action, I consider contingent events that take the form of exogenous shocks in triggering transitions between conventions.

Institutional Transitions Triggered by Exogenous Shocks to Beliefs and Payoffs

In the stochastic model, the tipping frequencies (and therefore the basin of attraction of the two equilibria and the stochastically stable state) are determined by the returns to different combinations of strategies. An exogenous shock to any of those payoffs may occasion a transition to the other equilibrium, for a variety of reasons. The simplest reason is that a shock to at least one of the payoffs may render one strategy the dominant strategy (a strategy played irrespective of expectations of which strategy the partner will play) for the members of a group, shrinking the basin of attraction of the other equilibrium to zero (it is no longer an equilibrium). More subtly, a change in the payoffs shifts the tipping points t^* and q^* and, as a result, the basins of attraction of the two equilibria. The net result is to render one of the conventions more susceptible to stochastic variation in the behavior of the players.

An example related to the above model may illustrate these effects. Imagine that neither of the two parties to a civil war believes it will have a decisive military advantage in the foreseeable future and that representatives of the two parties A and B meet and negotiate the terms of a possible settlement.[26] (I assume for the moment that the groups are each unitary actors, neglecting the internal dynamics of the groups.) The settlement terms include the post-war institutions and a division of the resulting goods (power, wealth, etc). Let A's share of the postwar stakes be s and B's $1-s$ (I assume the goods are divisible). A and B each evaluate the expected payoffs to fighting and to conforming to the agreement in light of the value of s and their beliefs about the likely actions of the other party. They then simultaneously implement the strategy that maximizes their expected payoff, given those beliefs. If s lies in the appropriate range (the *bargaining range,* which is determined by the payoffs to combinations of the parties' "fight" and "conform to the agreement" strategies) then mutual peace is a convention, as is mutual fighting. If that is the case, there is no dominant strategy and whether or not a party pursues peace (plays the "conform" strategy) depends on its belief about what the other party will do. If its belief that the other party will play "conform" is sufficiently strong (exceeding some tipping threshold, termed the *critical threshold*), and if that is true of the other party's belief as well, then both parties will implement the "conform" strategy. We can represent this problem exactly as in figure 8.2 but in this case t and q are beliefs about the likelihood of the other party to conform, which may or may not depend only on observed behavior in the last period.

The nub of the distributional challenge to forging an enduring peace is thus that s must be large enough so that A's share makes mutual peace attractive to A under a wide variety of beliefs, yet must not be too large lest B's share be too small and thus unattractive to B.

The distributional parameter s, together with the payoffs to continued mutual fighting, the size of the postwar stakes, and the payoff to one party fighting and the other pursuing peace, define the critical thresholds t^* and q^* and the basin of attraction of the peace equilibrium as indicated in figure 8.3 by the shaded area. The critical thresholds depend on the distributional settlement: It can be shown that as s *decreases*, the A's critical

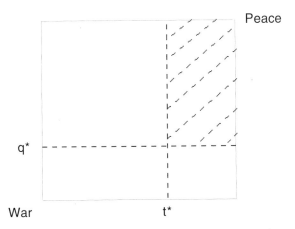

Fig. 8.3. Critical thresholds t^* and q^* and the basin of attraction for the peace equilibrium (the shaded area).

threshold t^* increases but B's threshold q^* *decreases.*[27] If A believes that the likelihood that B will conform is greater than q^*, A will conform to the agreement. If B's corresponding belief is greater than t^*, so will B.

Of course a peace process is not a single interaction; if successful, it requires a series of interactions between the two parties. Consider the case in which both parties initially conformed to the agreement. If we make the assumption that (given the other party's immediate past behavior of conforming) neither side will have reason to lessen its belief that the other party will conform in the next interaction, then both parties continue to conform to the agreement and mutual peace endures. The "system" is in the peace equilibrium.

But peace processes are vulnerable to a variety of disruptive contingent events. One class of such events includes those that undermine the belief of a player that the other player will continue to adhere—that is, a party's beliefs about the other party's next period behavior may be affected by factors other than the opponent's immediate past behavior. (Such variations in player beliefs are formally analogous to the stochastic variations in individual behavior in the preceding model.) Some examples of this are evident if we relax the assumption that the groups are unitary actors. For example, the assassination of a leader of party A by adherents of group B may lessen A's confidence that B intends to continue to conform to the agreement. If doubts become sufficiently strong, A will resume war. Internal political changes (an internal coup, for example) may have the same effect.

The robustness of the peace equilibrium in relation to such "belief shocks" depends on the relative size of the basin of attraction of that equilibrium compared to the "war" equilibrium, which in turn depends on the distributional parameter s (as well as the payoffs to various combinations of the parties' strategies). There exists an *optimal* (from the point of view of a shock-proof peace) choice of s that renders the peace equilibrium *most robust* to such variation in player beliefs[28]—i.e., a choice of s such that the area of the shaded region in figure 8.3 is maximized.

Another class of disruptive contingent events is exogenous shocks to the players' payoffs to various combinations of their strategies, the major focus of this section. Such shocks (if in the wrong direction from the point of view of continued peace) may shrink the basin of attraction of the peace equilibrium with the result that war resumes, as shown in figure 8.4, where $t^{*\prime}$ and $q^{*\prime}$ are the thresholds after the shock and the new basin of

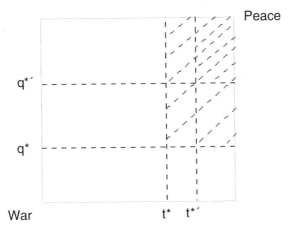

Fig. 8.4. Critical thresholds t^* and q^* and the effect of an exogenous negative shock to the peace dividend. The effect of the shock is to increase the belief thresholds to $t^{*\prime}$ and $a^{*\prime}$ and to shrink the basin of attraction for the peace equilibrium from the singly-shaded area to the doubly-shaded one.

attraction for the peace equilibrium is indicated by the double lines; here, the peace process is more vulnerable to "belief shocks" as described above, and it can unravel should a sufficiently large shock come along. Indeed, sufficiently strong shocks to the payoffs will shrink the basin of attraction to zero.

Such a negative exogenous shock may occur in the size of the postwar stakes. (For example, international prices may shift unexpectedly in a way that lessens postwar income or promised international aid to rebuild the country may fail to materialize.) Such a shock would shift t^* to the right and q^* upward, decreasing the size of the peace basin of attraction. Or an exogenous shock may increase the payoffs to fighting (the discovery by one party of a resource whose income it can control only in wartime, for example), leading to a resumption of war. Exogenous shocks may also occasion consequences through other proximate mechanisms such as intra-party factions. If one party comes under the control of a faction (because of an assassination, for example) that values the negotiated share of the stakes less than the previous controlling faction (perhaps because it believes the stakes of the conflict to be indivisible), conflict is likely to resume.

Thus there may be a large class of institutional transitions triggered by contingent events in the form of exogenous shocks either to the mutual expectations of an institution's stability ("belief shocks") or to the returns to continued adherence to that institution ("payoff shocks"). As discussed by David Mayhew (in this volume), wars are often contingent events in American politics, re-shaping enduring electoral alignments, changing electorates through the extension of suffrage, and creating fundamental policy shifts in taxation, tariffs, unions, and immigration.

Collective Action

However, many institutional transitions are triggered not by such stochastic variation or by exogenous shocks but by intentional collective action by members of a group. Workers in South Africa who rejected apartheid era labor conventions and struck in the 1980s did so in pursuit of new labor relations not governed by racial conventions. African-American residents of Montgomery, Alabama, who walked to work, to shop, and to church for nearly a year did so as part of a campaign to desegregate public buses. In these and similar cases, a crescendo of deviations from the prevailing institution eventually induced members of the dominant group to concede. I first extend the above model to the mobilization process and then consider how contingent events may spark mobilization.

Assume that members of group A in figure 8.5 are workers and those of group B employers. Workers prefer contract 1, under which the workplace is unionized; employers prefer contract 0, in which there is no union. Consider the case in which the system is in the no-union equilibrium. Union organizers try to persuade workers both to desist from playing their best response to the prevailing convention by conforming to a non-unionized workplaceand to demand contract 1 by striking. In the no-union convention, no employer intentionally offers contract 1. So from the no-union convention, intentional organizing by the workers moves the system along the lower edge for $t < t^*$ (as shown in figure 8.5), in contrast to the stochastic case where unintentional idiosyncratic play leads to the occurrence of any state in the state space. If the fraction of workers striking comes to exceed t^*, employers will respond by offering a union contract.

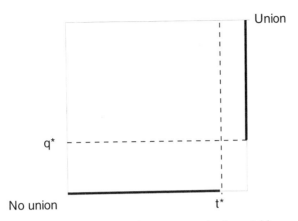

Fig. 8.5. Striking as a non-best response in the neighborhood of the no-union convention. Because of the intentional nature of non-best-response play, the system dynamics are restricted to the two bold lines.

For such a shift to occur, sufficient numbers of workers must be willing to forego present benefits for the chance of long-run gains. The willingness of workers to do so may depend on how many other workers they expect to strike—that is, we need to consider the interaction among the workers as well as that with employers. Consider a tipping model of frequency-dependent mobilization (as pioneered by Thomas Schelling).[29] Each worker evaluates whether or not to participate in a strike whose purpose is to insist on contract 1. Self-interested individuals will not participate if the mobilization takes the form of a pure public good. So we assume that the expected utility to participation increases in the fraction of the group participating, as shown in figure 8.6, because union organizers succeeded in developing selective benefits that increase as the fraction of workers participating does, the pressure of conformism, or a "pleasure in agency" at the prospect of success (which increases in the fraction participating).[30] The worker's choice whether to strike or not thus depends on the frequency of others' participation.

For a given worker, if the fraction she expects to participate exceeds the tipping threshold f^*, she will participate as well. The interaction between workers (figure 8.6) of course has implications for the interaction between workers and employers (figure 8.5). If the employers observe a fraction of

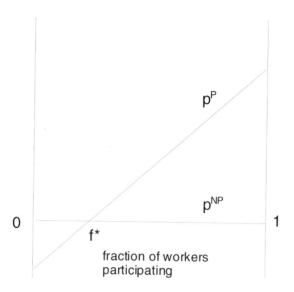

Fig. 8.6. The threshold for participation in collective action. The utility of participation p^P is frequency dependent, increasing in the fraction of workers expected to participate. If that fraction exceeds the threshold f^*, then the worker will join the strike.

workers greater than t^* demanding contract 1, their best response will be to offer contract 1 in the next period, and the system will shift to the unionized equilibrium.

If the threshold f^* is shared by all individuals in the group, none will participate unless at least f^* expect at least f^* to do so. In that case there are two equilibria, none participating and all participating. If expectations depend only on behavior observed in the previous round, no one will mobilize.

More generally, the workers' thresholds will vary within the group, from f_1^* (the lowest) to f_N^* (the highest threshold in the group). The distribution of preference thresholds determines whether or not some initial mobilization tips the group into the mobilization equilibrium.[31] If the thresholds are distributed sufficiently close to zero, even one individual's participating may mean the $n = 2$ individual's threshold is exceeded, so she participates as well, the $n = 3$ individual participates as his threshold is exceeded, and so on. But if the thresholds are too sparsely distributed for low values of f (or indeed for higher values of f), the cascade will not occur as the threshold for some worker (the one next in line) is not exceeded and the strike fails.

In this model, institutional transitions are conditional on sufficient numbers participating in the collective action. Contingent events may contribute to the emergence of sufficient numbers through various mechanisms. For example, such events may provide the necessary fraction of strikers sufficient to occasion the shift to the mobilization equilibrium or they may lower the threshold fraction, leaving the group more likely to mobilize should an initial group do so. A particular mechanism is when such events result in the emergence of a sufficiently large group of workers with strong normative preferences for a unionized workplace. Examples of such contingent events are acts of employers or state violence against striking workers (either on site or in some other locale) that enrage some workers such that they are willing to strike; the successful organization of workplaces in some other locale, which strengthens some workers in their egalitarian preferences; or war, which leaves at least some workers feeling entitled to a larger claim given their wartime sacrifices. For such workers, the p^p line lies above the line for other workers, leading to a lower threshold for the normatively motivated. Indeed, if their norms are strong enough, their threshold will be zero, and they will strike unconditionally, as when egregious state violence against a non-violent social movement in the late 1970s in El Salvador resulted in the emergence of individuals willing unconditionally to defy the regime.[32] If they are sufficiently numerous, the participation threshold for other workers is exceeded and all strike.

In an extension of the model with tags discussed above, Robert Axtell and Shubha Chakravarty show how the presence of agents with normative preferences who unconditionally pursue those preferences greatly alters the dynamics of stochastic models.[33] They simulate the consequences of the presence of radical agents who always play the egalitarian strategy, revolutionary agents who want to invert unegalitarian social orders and thus always play "high" when the best response would be "low," and reactionary agents who always play the status quo strategy. They find that small numbers of radical or revolutionary players can quickly induce a transition to a more equitable convention with high probability. The authors note:

> However, while such radical and revolutionary agents are crucial in social change, whether or not they will ultimately be effective is often very uncertain right up to the moment of (sudden) transition, when society 'tips' from

one configuration to another. That is, the history of nearly any successful social revolution is a long series of starts and stops, effective and ineffective protests, high expectations confronting harsh reality, incendiary yet ineffective manifestos, and still-born policy demands.[34]

Their simulations demonstrate how the unraveling of conventions can be both unexpected and rapid.

A second mechanism whereby contingent events may occasion collective action is the exogenous decrease in the expected costs of participation for at least some workers, which lowers their participation threshold, shifting the distribution of thresholds to the left. Such a shock may take the form of a change in policy of a powerful outside actor, as when some Eastern Europeans came to believe that the Soviet Union under Gorbachev would no longer act against mobilization demanding change in their countries. A closely related mechanism occurs when group members observe similarly situated people elsewhere mobilizing without suffering the expected costs; such an "informational cascade" may lead to the deepening and/or spread of collective action, as in Leipzig and then other East German cities in 1989.[35] Such demonstration effects may also include the revelation of unanticipated benefits as well. When a few insurgent-allied cooperatives formally occupied land they already farmed in the province of Usulután during El Salvador's civil war, their "pleasure in agency" led to the spread of further occupation across neighboring areas.[36] These mechanisms take the general form of contingent events disrupting the dependence of the future on expectations based on local past history.

The model also illuminates why a given contingent event in one setting leads to mobilization but the same or similar event does not in another, apparently identical, setting. Imagine two populations that are quiescent but the underlying distributions of private preferences for participation, that is their critical thresholds, are different, with the distribution closely packed toward zero in the first but not the second.[37] The same contingent event may lead to a cascade of participation in the first case but not in the second.

A third and related mechanism whereby contingent events may influence collective action (by suppressing it) is when some contingent event happens to remove (or render ineffective) an individual whose mobilization is key to triggering that of the rest because of her threshold's position in the overall distribution of thresholds.

Conclusion

A Thing to which people attach many labels with subtly or grossly different meanings . . . is probably not a Thing at all but many Things.

—Robert Dahl[38]

As is evident in this volume, "contingency" may be the sort of "Thing" that Dahl had in mind in speaking about power. In this chapter, contingent events are modeled in three ways, as stochastic variation in individual behavior, as shocks to the beliefs or payoffs of strategically engaged political actors, and as intentional non-best responses to a prevailing convention to force a transition to a more favored convention. The causal force of contingent events is modeled as occasioning transitions between equilibria, thus capturing the interaction between such events and underlying causes. Robust institutions are those less vulnerable to such events because their basin of attraction is large.

Among the desiderata listed in the introduction was to understand why similar contingent events have causal force in some circumstances and not in others, and why some settings appear susceptible to a wide variety of contingent triggers, any one of which would leave profound political change in its wake. The models developed here explain such contrasts in terms of the relative size of the basin of attraction of the prevailing institutional equilibrium. Where that basin is small, a contingent event may have profound causal force, leaving transformed institutions in its wake. But if the basin is large, even quite dramatic events will have no lasting effect. The understanding of institutions as conventions, which prevail through the decentralized interaction of members of a population because it is in the interest of all to adhere to them as long as most others do, helps account for the rapidity of large-scale change, another desiderata in modeling contingency. Once sufficient numbers expect that sufficiently many others will no longer adhere to the convention (for whatever reason), those individuals will switch strategies—observing which, many others will quickly switch as well, with the result that the old convention unravels and a new convention emerges.

In particular, I suggested ways in which contingent events can be incorporated into models of civil war settlement and collective action. I identified in these cases the factors on which the robustness of particular equilibria depend—namely, the distributional settlement in the case of negotiations to end civil wars and the distribution of participation thresholds for that of collective action. Throughout I explored what we might term "contingency from below," the shift toward institutions more favorable to the less well off either through chance or their collective action, and the contingent events that impel such transitions.

NOTES

1. I would like to thank Robert Axtell, Samuel Bowles, Duncan Foley, David Mayhew, Suresh Naidu, and H. Peyton Young for discussion and comment, and Yale University and the Santa Fe Institute for research support.

2. Interview with Ian Shapiro, cited in Jung, Lust-Okar, and Shapiro, "Problems and Prospects for Democratic Settlements," p. 317.

3. Wood, *Insurgent.*

4. Engels, "Letter to W. Borgius," p. 704–705. Engels went on to say, consistent with this view, that this was true of Marx himself: "While Marx discovered the materialist conception of history, Thierry, Mignet, Guizot, and all the English historians up to 1850 are the proof that it was being striven for, and the discovery of the same conception by Morgan proves that the time was ripe for it and that indeed it had to be discovered."

5. See his chapter in this volume.

6. See his chapter in this volume.

7. When in Rome live as the Romans do. From Titelman, *Random House,* p. 366.

8. Young, "Evolution."

9. From Bowles, *Microeconomics,* pp. 406–11.

10. It is easy to show that $q^* = a_0 / (a_0 + a_1)$.

11. However, if the initial condition is some point on the ridge, the outcome is the saddle point (t^*, q^*), an unstable equilibrium.

12. Trotsky, *My Life,* pp. 494–95.

13. Here I draw on recent work in stochastic evolutionary game theory, principally that of H. Peyton Young (see Young "Evolution"; Young, "Economics"; Young, *Individual Strategy*; Young, "Conventional Contracts"; Young, "Bargaining"). The results I summarize depend on some further (innocuous) technical assumptions, not developed here. See Young , "Economics," for an introduction to this field.

14. Foster and Young, "Game Dynamics."

15. More precisely, the smaller of t^* and q^* should be larger than the smaller of $1-t^*$ and $1-q^*$.

16. Young shows that, as our intuition would suggest, the contract-o conven-

tion will be stochastically stable if $t^*q^* > (1-t^*)(1-q^*)$. See Young, *Individual Strategy,* pp. 66–70.

17. Axtell, Epstein, and Young, "Emergence of Class."

18. Young, *Individual Strategy,* final chapter.

19. Bardhan, *Land, Labor.*

20. Young, "Economics."

21. Young and Burke, "Competition and Custom."

22. Bowles, *Microeconomics,* pp, 432–35; see also Naidu and Bowles, "Equilibrium Selection."

23. Which is not to say that gross political errors by those who stand to lose do not contribute to transitions, as did the overconfidence of the Polish Communist party before the parliamentary elections of 1989 (Kaminski, "Communism"). But we would like to account for the various types of transitions triggered solely by the collective action of those who believe institutional change is in their interest. This the model fails to do.

24. Bowles, *Microeconomics,* pp. 434–35.

25. For example, Naidu and Bowles develop a model of intentional collective action in which the mistakes made by group members are not random but occur only in the direction that favors their interests. See Naidu and Bowles, "Equilibrium Selection."

26. Technical details of this model are developed in Wood, "Robust Settlements."

27. Wood, "Robust Settlements."

28. Ibid.

29. Schelling, *Micromotives.*

30. Wood, *Insurgent.*

31. Kuran, "Now out of Never."

32. Wood, *Insurgent,* pp. 238–39 and 270.

33. Axtell and Chakravarty, "Radicals."

34. Ibid., p. 17.

35. Lohmann, "Dynamics."

36. Wood, *Insurgent,* pp. 160–92 and 234–37.

37. Kuran, "Now out of Never."

38. Dahl, "Concept of Power," pp. 202–203.

BIBLIOGRAPHY

Axtell, Robert, Joshua M. Epstein, and H. Peyton Young. "The Emergence of Classes in a Multi-Agent Bargaining Model," In *Social Dynamics,* edited by Stephen Durlauf and H. Peyton Young, pp. 191–222. Cambridge: MIT Press, 2000.

Axtell, Robert L., and Shubha Chakravarty. "Radicals, Revolutionaries and Reactionaries in a Multi-Agent Model of Class Norms. Center on Social and Economic Dynamics," unpublished paper. The Brookings Institution, Washington, DC, 2005.

Bardhan, Pranab. *Land, Labor, and Rural Poverty: Essays in Development Economics.* New York: Columbia University Press, 1984.

Bowles, Samuel. *Microeconomics: Behavior, Institutions and Evolution.* Princeton, NJ: Princeton University Press, 2004.

Dahl, Robert. "The Concept of Power." *Behavioral Science,* 2 (1957): 201–15.

Engels, Friedrich. Letter to W. Borgius, January 25, 1894. In Karl Marx and Friedrich Engels, *Selected Works,* pp. 704–705. Moscow: Progress Publishers, 1968.

Foster, Dean, and H. Peyton Young. "Stochastic Evolutionary Game Dynamics." *Theoretical Population Biology,* 38, No. 2 (October 1990): 219–32.

Jung, Courtney, Ellen Lust-Okar, and Ian Shapiro. "Problems and Prospects for Democratic Settlements: South Africa as a Model for the Middle East and Northern Ireland?" *Politics and Society,* 33, No. 2 (June 2005): 277–326.

Kaminski, Marek. "How communism could have been saved: Formal analysis of electoral bargaining in Poland in 1989." *Public Choice* 98 (1999): 83–109.

Kuran, Timur. "Now out of Never: The Element of Surprise in the East European Revolution of 1989." *World Politics* 44, No. 1 (1991): 7–48.

Lohmann, Susanne. "The Dynamics of Informational Cascades: The Monday Demonstrations in Leipzig." *World Politics* 47, No. 1 (1994): 42–101.

Naidu, Suresh, and Samuel Bowles. "Equilibrium Selection by Intentional Idiosyncratic Play," unpublished manuscript. Berkeley, CA: Department of Economics, UC Berkeley, 2005.

Schelling, Thomas C. *Micromotives and Macrobehavior.* New York: W. W. Norton & Co., 1960.

Titelman, Gregory Y. *Random House Dictionary of Popular Proverbs and Sayings.* New York: Random House, 1996.

Trotsky, Leon. *My Life, An Attempt at an Autobiography.* New York: Pathfinder Press, 1970.

Wood, Elisabeth Jean. *Insurgent Collective Action and Civil War in El Salvador.* Cambridge, UK, New York: Cambridge University Press, 2003.

Wood, Elisabeth Jean. "Robust Settlements to Civil War: Distributional Compromises and Indivisible Stakes." Under revision for re-submission to *Journal of Peace Research,* 2005.

Young, H. Peyton. "Conventional Contracts." *Review of Economic Studies,* 65, No. 4 (1998): 773–92.

Young, H. Peyton. "The Economics of Conventions." *Journal of Economic Perspectives,* 10, No. 2 (1996): 105–22.

Young, H. Peyton. "An Evolutionary Model of Bargaining." *Journal of Economic Theory,* 59, No. 1 (1993): 145–68.

Young, H. Peyton. "The Evolution of Conventions." *Econometrica*, 61, No. 1 (1993): 57–84.

Young, H. Peyton. *Individual Strategy and Social Structure: An Evolutionary Theory of Institutions*. Princeton, NJ: Princeton University Press, 1998.

Young, H. Peyton, and Mary A. Burke. "Competition and Custom in Economic Contracts: A Case Study of Illinois Agriculture." *American Economic Review*, 91, No. 3 (2001): 559–73.

Chapter 9

When Democracy Complicates Peace
How Democratic Contingencies Affect Negotiated Settlements

Courtney Jung

In the 1970s, the political conflicts in South Africa, Northern Ireland, and the Middle East were widely viewed as among the world's most intractable.[1] Based on profound racial, ethnic, or religious animosities, they were reinforced by cultural and economic differences and solidified by decades of more-or-less violent confrontation. They were often held out as paradigms of "divided" societies, and there seemed little chance of a transition to democratic arrangements in any of them. Whether one focused on the players contending for power, the histories of the conflicts, or the capacities of outsiders to influence events, the prospects for negotiated settlements seemed dim.

During the 1990s, however, the paths of these three conflicts diverged quite dramatically. South Africa moved through a comparatively peaceful four-year transition to majority rule in a unitary state. Democratic elections in 1994, 1999, and 2004 put the African National Congress securely in power without civil war, economic collapse, or catastrophic white exodus. The continuing economic and social challenges are enormous, with a third of the population unemployed and one in nine infected by the HIV virus. But by most measures South Africa has weathered the transition well. Democracy may not yet be entrenched, but it seems at least to have a fighting chance.

Northern Ireland has also made important advances since real negotiations began in 1996. Both Republicans and Loyalists committed to cease fires that have held, and most serious violence has abated sufficiently so that people have started to think peace a realistic possibility. In 1998 the two sides signed an agreement that majorities of both Catholics and Protestants supported. Yet the future of the Good Friday Agreement remains precarious. The power-sharing government was repeatedly suspended by Westminster, leading to the re-imposition of direct rule in October 2002. Whether the paramilitary groups will disband and the Executive and Assembly will be revived was still an open question in 2005.

Establishing peace between the Palestinians and Israelis has been even more elusive. There have been some major turning points in the Arab-Israeli conflict, and periods of great optimism, most notably following the negotiation of the Camp David Accords, the Israeli-Egyptian peace treaty in 1979, and the Palestinian-Israeli negotiation of the Oslo Accords in 1993 and 1995. These opened windows of opportunity. However, the principals have often been either unable or unwilling to seize the opportunities that emerged when one side made concessions. In 1998, Netanyahu rendered Arafat's concessions in the Wye Accord useless when he unilaterally suspended implementation of the agreement. Arafat refused Ehud Barak's concessions at Camp David II in 2000. Backtracking and disappointing failure have been so frequent that the Israeli peace process often seems ritualistic and pointless. It continues to vindicate the 1970s diagnosis by going nowhere—if often by Byzantine routes at enormous human and economic cost.

How can we explain these divergent outcomes? Why were some violent conflicts more amenable to solution than others? Why did three situations that seemed similarly resistant to transformation take such different paths during the 1990s?

This chapter focuses attention on the ways in which settlements in South Africa, Israel, and Northern Ireland have been both facilitated and constrained by the contingencies inherent in the flawed democratic settings that have structured these peace processes. Over the course of the 1990s, opposition groups re-framed their struggles as demands for democratic government, parties were able to remain in negotiations only so long as they could maintain popular support, and settlements came to depend more on installing "democracy" than on merely achieving "peace."[2]

Democracy however, is neither a neutral bargaining context, nor a neutral goal. The pseudo-democratic contexts in which contemporary peace processes take place offer opportunities and constraints that do not exist in other bargaining situations, and are likely to be important to a number of contemporary and future negotiation processes.

Specifically, pseudo-democratic settings have distinct implications, and operate in distinct ways, in each of the three phases of the peace process: initiation, negotiation, and implementation. Such settings may make initiation easier, I argue, but they tip the scales during negotiations, and they make implementation harder. In Section 1, I examine the need for democratic legitimacy in the initiation phase. The regime in power is heavily dependent on democratic principles of legitimation, which it nevertheless routinely violates. This imperfect democratic setting delegitimates the government and plays a role in pushing it into negotiations. In Section 2, I argue that democratic imperatives can offer a solution to the commitment problem during the negotiation phase, but may also tip the balance of power in favor of the government. In Section 3, I examine the effects of democratic elections on implementation. When settlements are built around democratic principles of electoral support, implementation is persistently vulnerable to the danger that the moderate coalition that agreed to the settlement will be voted out of office. It is specifically in the implementation phase that the peace processes in the Middle East and Northern Ireland have been mired, in Israel for over a decade, and in Northern Ireland since 1998. Unless elections return a clear majority in favor of an agreement, as in South Africa, implementation remains vulnerable to resistance from radical flank parties with a voice at the polls.

Over the course of negotiations, democracy acts variously as a normative commitment, an institutional setting, and a decision-making mechanism. It is partly the need for democratic legitimation that drove so many long-standing conflicts into peace processes during the 1990s. Once there however, democratic institutions and decision mechanisms introduced contingencies that made agreements easier to reach but harder to implement. Democratic settings and goals affect the power and negotiating leverage of each player, dependent as they are on unstable constituencies. Each side attempts to use democracy to their advantage, but it is rarely clear whether they will succeed in building support for a settlement, or how long they will manage to sustain it. Democratic norms focus attention on the relationship between players and their constituencies, and introduce contingencies that both support and challenge peace processes by making all players perpetually vulnerable.

Democracy introduces all three of the conceptual pillars that Andreas Schedler[3] identifies as constitutive of contingency: indeterminacy (y could be otherwise), uncertainty (y may change in future), and conditionality (y depends on x). These affect the legitimacy of the players, the strength of the players, the capacity of the players to make commitments, and the ability of the players to convince the other side that they can keep commitments. Everyone knows that the relevant parties to negotiations could be otherwise, could change, and depend on popular consent. This, I argue, has had different implications in different phases of these three peace processes.

Initiation

Initiation is when two warring sides in a conflict, A and B, recognize one another and agree to enter into talks that are ostensibly aimed at reaching an accommodation. This phase is tentative and normally includes a great deal of posturing as each side tries to gauge the strength and real position of the other. Initiation may happen for various reasons such as military defeat, external pressure, or economic crisis.

In these cases however, the governments were not under decisive military, foreign, or economic pressure to enter negotiations. None of them ever came close to military defeat, all of them were under external pressure that they nevertheless could have withstood, and only one, South Africa, was under serious economic pressure. The status quo was not unsustainable in any of the three cases.

The South African, Israeli, and British governments did rely heavily, however, on appeals to democratic legitimacy. Their conspicuous failure to live up to these standards brought them under particular pressure after the fall of the Soviet Union, when democracy emerged as the only game in town. Although there are countless reasons that each government independently calculated that it should enter negotiations, together the governments had in common democratic reference points that help to account for the fact that all three powers were engaged in peace talks during much of the 1990s.

In the initiation phase, it is mainly in the breach that democracy affects the peace process. How, precisely, were these governments imperfectly democratic?

The National Party government in South Africa was first elected in 1948 on a platform of "separate development" that limited full political representation to white South Africans. The mal-distribution of land and other resources at the center of this plan, as well as the forced removals of tens of thousands of people from their homes, meant that the government was always hopelessly illegitimate in the eyes of non-white South Africans, and much of the rest of the world. Efforts to reform the government through the Tri-cameral Parliament in the 1980s merely highlighted the racist discrimination at the core of the system.

Israel, too, was conceived as a democratic state from the beginning. If the treatment of Israeli Arabs as second-class citizens made this problematic, this issue was nothing compared with the legitimacy problems that would pile up in the decades after the occupation of the West Bank and Gaza in 1967. Moreover, Israel's identity as a Jewish state puts it into some jeopardy from the standpoint of democracy, and the tension between democracy and Jewish identity has only been exacerbated by Israel's expansion beyond its 1967 borders. As in South Africa, the introduction of partial democratic reforms has failed to remove the stain of exclusion.

The democratic legitimacy of Northern Ireland was also undermined by the gerrymandered origins of the state. From the beginning, Catholics rejected British rule as imperialism. The great majority of them saw the partition in 1921 as a cynical ploy to create an artificial Protestant majority, and resisted separation from the rest of Ireland, which they explicitly perceived as undemocratic. As a result, the partition could be sustained only through repression. The British resorted repeatedly to special powers legislation and proscription, both of which suspended individual rights in ways that were strikingly similar to the emergency regulations that became semi-permanent features of Apartheid South Africa and Israel's Occupied Territories.[4]

In all three cases the governments faced an inescapable tension between their ostensible democratic commitments on the one hand, and their undemocratic practices on the other. By the late 1980s and early 1990s, in the context of the height of the third wave of democratic transitions, the African National Congress, the Irish Republican Army, and the Palestine Liberation Organization were accusing the governments of South Africa, Britain, and Israel, respectively, of being undemocratic, and they had good evidence to substantiate their allegations. Demands for democracy gave these opposition groups greater international legitimacy and credibility —that is, greater credibility as "democrats" than they had been able to muster as "terrorists." The inability of these regimes to defend themselves against the charge that their rule violated basic democratic principles was partly responsible for driving each government to acknowledge its internal opposition. Though it is by no means the only thing that prompted the beginning of peace talks, the international currency of democratic discourse helps to explain why all three of these long simmering conflicts entered into a negotiation phase during the 1990s. Flawed democracy played a role in pushing negotiators to the table.

Negotiations

By entering negotiations, reformers acknowledge, however implicitly, this democratic deficit in their system. This means that they are usually on the defensive—arguing about the terms and pace of change rather than its necessity. The need for democratic legitimation greatly complicates negotiations, defying attempts to reduce them to stylized elite games, and highlighting the need to focus attention on the larger political contexts within which they occur. An interactive view of negotiations focuses as much attention on negotiators and their constituencies as it does on the link between negotiators. Negotiators are constrained by popular opinion, but to succeed, elites must make the right choices at critical junctures—including choices about how to respond to popular opinion and when to try to shape it. The logic of this argument is familiar from Putnam's theory of two level games.[5]

The central question in all bargaining situations is: can the reformers and moderates agree on a settlement and successfully face down the hardliners and radicals on their flanks? During the negotiations phase of the peace process, the democratic imperatives that hang over these negotiations can help to solve the classic commitment problem described by Thomas Schelling: if each side knows that the other might subsequently defect, why should either agree?[6]

In theory, commitment problems are ubiquitous in democratic politics, given the lack of third-party enforcement. Nevertheless, there are reasons to expect commitment problems surrounding peace processes to be particularly acute. Following decades of sometimes-violent conflict, these are marriages of convenience among parties with little reason for mutual trust. As Rabin put it in 1993: "Peace is not made with friends. Peace is made with enemies, some of whom I loathe very much."[7] Even if reformers and moderates are willing to move toward agreement, they will be skeptical of one another's good faith.

This problem is further complicated in the quasi-democratic settings characteristic of these cases, because the negotiating partners must be responsive to their support bases. It is possible for opponents of negotiations to use public opinion to undermine reformers or even to remove them from power. Unless the reformers and moderates build support for the idea of an agreement among the grass-roots constituencies they depend on, the rug will be pulled out from under them.

By the same token negotiators can also employ the constraints of democratic legitimation to signal their commitment to a settlement. By making concessions public, political elites bind themselves to positions they will not easily be able to abandon without damaging their political careers. They cut ties to existing sources of legitimation, and are forced to look for new sources of support. In this sense the democratic imperative that shadows these negotiations—the fact that each side can remain at the table only so long as it can maintain a constituency for doing so—may offer possibilities for dealing with commitment problems that are not available in other settings. This side of contingency, which Schedler identifies as its conditional aspect (y depends on x), may counter-intuitively increase the credibility of negotiators by tying their hands.[8]

Both sides must be concerned not only with an adversary's political will to reach an agreement, but also with its capacity to deliver. As a result, the credibility of negotiating commitments is dependent on how successful reformers and moderates are at co-opting or marginalizing flank attacks. You have little reason to trust even an adversary you believe to be sincere if you think that the ground may be cut out from under him. This concern can be forestalled in various ways. One is to actually be the flanking force. This Nixon-to-China logic suggests that the closer negotiators are to the ideological extremes in their parties, the more credible their commitments will be. The alternative is to face down the flanking opposition at critical junctures.

Decisions made by Mandela and De Klerk early in the negotiations helped diminish their commitment problems. De Klerk's bold steps in 1992 showed how bridge-burning enhances credibility and how even flawed democracy can be used to move negotiations forward. In 1990 and 1991 he lost a series of by-elections to the Conservative Party while he was negotiating with the ANC. The white right used these election results to insist that De Klerk had no mandate to negotiate. He called their bluff by calling a snap referendum, on his birthday in March 1992, which he won with a two-thirds majority among the white electorate in every region of the country. Once De Klerk had made his move, the ANC helped him satisfice by compromising on the power-sharing issue in the interim constitution. This was essential for him to retain his grass-roots support.

Although the ANC had no similar electoral constraint, Mandela also faced challenges to his leadership from a radical flank within the ANC which included Winnie Mandela, Chris Hani, and Peter Mokaba. This trio held massive rallies of ANC Youth, in which they openly opposed negotiations and accused Mandela of being a sell-out. Talks did not advance far until this opposition was neutralized.

Though in some ways more challenging, the commitment problems facing the principals in the Middle East in the early 1990s were not insuperable. Like Mandela and De Klerk, Rabin and Arafat were well placed to manage hostile flanks. Israelis viewed Rabin as a war hero dedicated to Israeli security, and Arafat also had the clout of being a long-time Fateh leader-in-exile.

Yet the Middle East negotiations differed from those in South Africa from the perspectives of both sides. The Oslo formulation was widely seen as Arafat's attempt to shore up his personal power, and it was far from clear that he could sell the agreement to a majority of Palestinians. Nor was the Israeli side propelled by an imperative to consummate an agreement. Israel's decision to enter negotiations was based, in part, on the perception that a weakened Arafat would be easy to bargain with.

This reality generated commitment problems that Arafat and Rabin both dealt with by cutting ties to their flanks. Arafat accepted a partial agreement that postponed deciding the most important issues, including control over Jerusalem, full establishment of a state, the return of refugees, and water rights.[9] He also stepped decisively into the Rubicon by recognizing Israel's right to exist, and committing himself to policing the West Bank to provide Israel security from Palestinian attacks. In November 1994 Palestinian police faced down several thousand Hamas supporters demonstrating outside the largest mosque in Gaza.

Rabin also faced down hard-line opponents. Labour dominance in the Knesset allowed him to move forward in negotiations, but as he converged on the peace settlement and signed Oslo II in September 1995, an increasingly vitriolic opposition attacked his cooperation with Arafat, shouting "Death to Arafat" and portraying Rabin wearing Arafat's trademark kaffiyeh.[10]

Had they been able to keep going, Arafat and Rabin might well have consummated an agreement whose benefits would have replenished their political capital as in the South African model, but Rabin's murder in November 1995 eliminated that possibility. It was not the removal of Rabin from office through undemocratic methods that suspended the peace process, however. It was Peres' inability to take advantage of the opportunities that negotiating in a flawed democracy can afford. His failure to call a snap election as soon as he replaced the fallen Rabin was one the most consequential missed opportunities in the history of Israeli politics.[11]

Negotiations in Northern Ireland proceeded in fits and starts from the 1995 signing of the Frameworks Document until a Labour landslide put Tony Blair into office in London in June 1997. John Major's room to move the peace process had been constrained by the fact that his government relied on Ulster Unionist parliamentary partners. Blair had no electoral debts to the Unionists, and immediately expressed his commitment to "solving" the Northern Ireland crisis. His first trip was to Northern Ireland, where he warned Sinn Fein, "the settlement train is leaving. I want you on that train. But it is leaving anyway and I will not allow it to wait for you. You cannot hold the process to ransom any longer."[12] In June and July the British government worked hard to bring Sinn Fein into talks, to the growing distress of Unionists who feared Britain would sell them out to achieve peace. The British and Irish governments recognized that no settlement would be enforceable without Sinn Fein's participation, and they made a key decision to include all potential spoilers to the agreement.

Bringing Sinn Fein into talks nevertheless jeopardized the political strength and negotiating position of Trimble's Ulster Unionist Party, the UUP. If Unionist support for negotiations crumbled, Trimble would be forced to leave the table, and the peace process would disintegrate. Moderators and guarantors were therefore careful to shore up the Unionist side, to protect it from its own right wing.[13] George Mitchell catered to the Unionist demand for IRA arms decommissioning, for example, by giving the issue prominence at the start of the talks.[14]

The IRA responded by announcing a second ceasefire, but refused to decommission in anticipation of negotiations. Since the Unionists had made decommissioning a precondition of the talks, Trimble took a risk when he decided to enter talks that could have gutted his support base. In July 1997 the debate over whether Sinn Fein should be admitted to talks without prior decommissioning came to a head in a vote. The Unionist parties all voted against it, with the result that when talks reconvened in September, Sinn Fein was at the table but the Unionist parties were gone.[15]

The Loyalists had left for good, and they tried to force the Unionists to walk out by accusing them of betrayal. Opinion polls showed that the UUP had a slim popular mandate for remaining in the talks, but party leaders were under extreme pressure from politicians within their own ranks.[16] The UUP was operating on a narrow margin when it finally entered negotiations under Trimble's leadership in October 1997. Talks concluded in April 1998 with the Good Friday Agreement committing all parties to share power in government. A clear majority in both Ireland and Northern Ireland supported the agreement, although Unionist support for the agreement never stood above 55%.[17]

During negotiations in pseudo-democratic settings, negotiating principals can remain at the table only so long as they maintain a constituency for peace. In this phase the governing power is subject to actual elections, while the level of support for the other side, though it is still important, is never actually put formally to the test. This lends negotiations an asymmetry. Mandela, Adams, and Arafat were never as vulnerable—*in this sense*—as De Klerk, Trimble, and those Israeli leaders who were intent on reaching a settlement: Rabin, Peres, and Barak.

The logic of negotiations implies that the government, whose constraints are so evident and whose win set is so narrow, would be strengthened by this asymmetry. This is the flip side of the solution democracy offers to the commitment problem. Bargaining theories show how negotiators can use the limits of their own room to maneuver to force their negotiating partners into agreements that come closer to their preferred outcome. At different times, these astute politicians have all been able to capitalize on their own vulnerability. Trimble forced a last minute renegotiation of the North-South Agreement because he insisted he could never sell the existing solution to his party; De Klerk forced the ANC to agree to power-sharing for the same reason; and Rabin got Arafat to agree to a settlement that left almost everything that mattered to him off the table. The latitude implied by the fact that opposition leaders did not have to win elections actually weakened their bargaining position. Other things being equal, the need for electoral approval alone would appear to favor the party in government. Democracy is not a neutral bargaining context.

Implementation

This asymmetry may change in the implementation stage. In the post–Cold War period in particular, negotiations have been tied not just to achieving peace, but to installing democracy. Elections follow quickly on the heels of agreements. As they get down to implementing the settlement, both sides are subject to formal electoral approval. Here, the asymmetry that favored the regime in the bargaining phase of the peace process no longer exists.

The fact that implementation depends on election results generates its own pathologies, though, and these are different depending on what the election results actually are. It is here in the implementation stage that South Africa diverges most significantly from the other two cases.

In South Africa, the democratic character of the settlement facilitated implementation of the agreement. Once elections were held and the ANC won over 60% of the vote, the party simply implemented the accord. Along the way, they revised the constitution to eliminate the interim power-sharing clause they had agreed to in order to achieve a settlement. Democratic elections returned a majority in favor of the settlement, giving South Africa an enforcement mechanism that has been lacking in both Israel/Palestine and Northern Ireland. When democratic elections yield a clear majority in support of transition, an agreement can lead directly to implementation.

More often, the democracy solution leaves each negotiating partner permanently vulnerable at the polls, in perpetual danger of losing elections to its radical flank. Implementation depends on all parties living by the terms of the accord for a long period of time, and it depends on reaching consensus on the many issues that were left outstanding in the settlement itself. Any misstep can provoke a backlash; a change in government can scuttle the whole process. In several desperate attempts to forestall such an outcome, Tony Blair repeatedly suspended democratic government in Northern Ireland. There is no external force capable of doing that in Israel or the Palestinian territories.

In Israel, the Oslo Accord has defied implementation for over a decade. Following Rabin's assassination, Shimon Peres missed an important opportunity to begin implementation of the agreement by failing to call an election that would have capitalized on a strong wave of sympathy for the martyred Rabin. Instead, Peres waited, and tacked to the right. He permitted the assassination of Yahya Ayyash in January 1996, and responded to attacks from Southern Lebanon by bombing Lebanese refugee camps in Operation Grapes of Wrath. A wave of suicide bombings in the spring of 1996[18] led Israelis to seek a "firmer stance" in negotiations.[19] Likud was able to regroup while Peres alienated himself from Israeli supporters of the negotiations, particularly Israeli Palestinians. Palestinian radicals thus helped secure the victory of the Israeli right, and when elections were held in May 1996, Peres lost the race to be Israel's first directly elected prime minister by 29,000 votes.

Facing defeated partners in peace left Arafat massively weakened. Initially, he responded by attempting to push the peace process forward, courting Netanyahu in an attempt to gain recognition as a legitimate negotiating partner. Netanyahu, facing U.S. pressure and an Israeli constituency pressing for a "secure peace," finally agreed to sign the Hebron Accord and the Wye Accord. Arafat responded with increased concessions, but it was clear that Netanyahu was neither a willing nor a committed partner in the peace process. Facing competing constituencies at home, he refused to implement the agreement and continued expanding settlements in the Occupied Territories.

As Israel continued to fail to comply with Oslo, popular support for the Palestinian Authority declined, with the majority of Palestinians coming to see it as corrupt and powerless.[20] The costs of selling any agreement with compromises thus rose dramatically for Arafat as Netanyahu piled up violations against the agreements. Seventy percent of Palestinians polled in June 1999 continued to support the peace process, but did not trust Israel to comply with an agreement.[21] Arafat faced opposition not only from Hamas and Islamic Jihad, but from his own rank and file.

By the time Barak went to Camp David in 2000, intending to make major concessions, Arafat could no longer meet him half way.[22] Barak came into office on a wave of anti-Netanyahu sentiment, and knew his landslide victory in May 1999 was a mandate to make an agreement.[23] As a directly elected prime minister, he enjoyed a degree of independent legitimacy, and the possibility of holding a referendum on an agreement even in the face of a hostile Knesset.

By then however, Arafat was too weak to make concessions on such key issues as Jerusalem and the Palestinian "right of return."[24] His only hope of maintaining Fateh dominance was by responding to Palestinian popular opinion.[25] As *The Economist* reported that month, "the more he withstands the heat, the higher his stock will rise."[26]

The United States and Israel ignored the imperative for democratic legitimacy when they decided they would no longer deal with Arafat and forced the PA to appoint Mahmoud Abbas as prime minister in 2003. Abbas had no domestic popular support, which rendered the PA impotent to rein in the violence that followed the Aqaba summit.[27] The more Abbas was praised as "reasonable" in Jerusalem and Washington, the weaker he was bound to become in Ramallah. Parties cannot choose their own negotiating partners, but they can stall implementation by sidelining those leaders who could actually guarantee a settlement.[28]

On the Israeli side, Ariel Sharon came under serious pressure in the fall of 2004 when he tried to get Israeli withdrawal from Gaza and parts of the West Bank through the Knesset. In the run-up to the October election, members of his own party threatened to defect and leave him without a majority.[29] In the end, 17 members of Likud did in fact vote against withdrawal. At the time, many people feared that Sharon's government would collapse, which would have required him to call early elections and halted execution of the withdrawal plan. In the end, Sharon won by 67 to 45 votes, and he subsequently shored up his position by entering a coalition with Labour in January 2005. His position remained sufficiently vulnerable, however, that his advisors thought it wise to forestall his critics by letting it be known that his reason for withdrawing from Gaza was to stall, not advance, the peace process.[30]

Western prognosticators rushed to hail Arafat's death in November 2004 as an opportunity for peace. In December 2004, municipal elections were held in 26 districts in the West Bank for the first time since 1976. This election was the first contested by Hamas, which won 9 councils to Fateh's 16.[31] Neither Hamas nor the popular Marwan Bargouti participated in the January election for president of the Palestinian Authority, however, which Mahmoud Abbas won handily with over 60% of the vote. Experts nevertheless worried that support for Abbas was dangerously weak, affording him little room to maneuver.

In late 2005, Ariel Sharon led an influential contingent out of Likud to form a new party, Kadima, dedicated to fulfilling his vision for withdrawal from Gaza and the West Bank. His subsequent stroke left Israeli politics in disarray, but was instrumental in securing a victory for Kadima in March 2006. The party made an alliance with Labor to form a government, suggesting that Israel could pursue Sharon's policy of unilateral withdrawal without negotiations. Since Oslo, however, labor has lost one third of its electoral support, and many observers agree that the Israeli electorate is moving to the right.[32] The Israeli left has been decimated by the failure to implement an agreement.

In the meantime, Hamas won a majority in the Palestinian Legislative Council in early 2006. Although Hamas was expected to do well in elections, nobody anticipated that disaffection with Fateh was sufficient to produce a victory for Hamas. Washington and Tel Aviv immediately denounced the election results, cutting off aid and scheduled payments to the Palestinian Authority, insisting that Hamas could not form a government without first recognizing Israel, and finally arresting a third of the Palestinian cabinet in retaliation for the kidnapping of an Israeli soldier. As of mid-2006, the Israel-Palestine peace process was paralyzed, in no small part because of election results that had gutted the moderate center on each side.

As with the Oslo Accord, but unlike the ANC–NP settlement, the Belfast Agreement did not mark the end of negotiations and the beginning of implementation. For almost two years, London continued to govern Northern Ireland as implementation snagged on the controversial issues that had been left outstanding in the Good Friday Accord. It seems clear that part of the obstacle to implementing the Belfast Agreement was that a substantial portion of Unionists never believed that the status quo was unsustainable. Achieving a settlement might require that their government force them to accept it.

But this is easier said than done under democratic constraints. Trimble and his pro-agreement allies were unable to face down the right wing that opposes the Good Friday Accord. From the outset, moderate Unionists had only a narrow margin of support for the settlement. Exit polls from the May 1998 referendum showed Protestants almost evenly divided between support and opposition. The Protestant middle class appeared ready to defect from the settlement over the early release of prisoners.[33]

Elections for the Northern Ireland Assembly were held in June 1998. The Ulster Unionist Party won 28 seats, and the Catholic Social Democratic and Labour Party won 24. But the UUP was comparatively vulnerable as the anti-agreement camp also won, between them, 28 seats. Analysts predicted before the election that the UUP would need to win at least 30 seats to avoid deadlock in the Assembly and to make the North-South council work.[34]

The election campaign also laid bare differences within the UUP over the settlement. Jeffrey Donaldson, a UUP Member of Parliament at Westminster, emerged as the most important opposition figure within the party, but almost half of the leadership of the UUP openly opposed the accord. Some of them took seats in the Assembly, but did not vote the party line, further diluting the pro-agreement bloc.[35] Trimble barely squeaked by in elections for party leadership after 1998, as he faced powerful opposition to implementing the accord.

Finally, in November 1999, a slim majority of 58% of UUP delegates approved entry into a joint government, and Britain and Ireland transferred power from London to Belfast within days. Under a power-sharing formula, Trimble became First Minister, and Seamus Mallon, leader of the Nationalist Social Democratic and Labour Party (SDLP), the co-equal Deputy First Minister. Ten other cabinet seats were divided proportionally among Ulster Unionists, the SDLP, Sinn Fein, and the Democratic Unionist Party (DUP). The UUP was left deeply divided by the split vote, and the terms of entry included a clause committing the party council to reconvene in February to review the decision.

When the IRA refused to move on decommissioning, London responded by suspending the Assembly in February 2000 to protect Trimble from another divisive UUP vote that threatened to sink his leadership. Westminster suspended devolution three more times over the next three years in order to protect the coalition that supported the agreement from losing power through elections. The government at Stormont has remained in suspension since 2002. Blair has repeatedly stepped in to halt or postpone democratic elections in Northern Ireland in order to keep the Good Friday Agreement alive. As it turns out, he may have had good reasons for doing so. When elections were held for the Northern Ireland Legislature in November 2003, the UUP and the SDLP both lost to the DUP and Sinn Fein. The centrist parties that reached agreement in the Good Friday Accords have lost power to the radical flank parties who opposed the peace process from the start.

Conclusion

The democratic imperative that hangs over contemporary peace processes generates contingencies that provide both opportunities and constraints for settlements.

Focusing attention on elections, mandates, and the need for democratic legitimacy highlights the ways in which peace processes proceed, or fail to proceed, in the exchange between elites and their constituencies. Democracy can spur talks, but it can also obstruct implementation, and its effect depends significantly on how it is used and managed. It may be in this setting that it is most evident that democracy is a system of institutionalized uncertainty.

Peace processes—or attempts to pursue them—also make clear that democratic institutions can distort the relationship between constituents and their elected leaders. In both Israel and Northern Ireland, popular support for a settlement has more than once been subverted by hard-line politicians who refused to deal. In the fall of 2004, polls showed that a majority of Israelis favored withdrawal from Gaza, even as Sharon faced serious opposition within the Knesset to his plan.[36] A majority of people in Northern Ireland believes that such issues as unemployment and road safety are more important than the sectarian divide.[37] This reality suggests that referenda, in which support for negotiations is put directly to the public as it was in South Africa in 1992, might advance talks and implementation at key moments by circumventing recalcitrant players in government. Peace processes may be advanced by using direct democracy to sideline elected politicians.

At other times, it might be wise to use political institutions to limit democracy and to insulate negotiating moderates from their flank parties. A presidential government with a strong party whip system and fixed terms in office may allow negotiators to implement peace plans in the period of time they know they have. Directly elected presidents with their own mandates and fixed terms will, other things being equal, have more room to push through reforms during their time in office. Parliamentary systems, in which leaders are constantly vulnerable to votes of no confidence and to losing their majority, do the worst job of insulating politicians intent on reaching peace agreements. Implementing agreements may sometimes depend on limiting democracy.

Whether one focuses attention on using direct democracy or on limiting democracy, on using more democracy or less democracy to advance the peace process, it should be clear that democracy does not offer a neutral bargaining context, and it is not a neutral goal. Since 1990 in particular, conflict resolution theorists and practitioners—the people who study conflicts and the people who mediate resolutions—have been especially sympathetic to the needs of elected governments to stay in power long enough to reach an agreement. This is important, of course, but it should not blind us to the way that such genuine concerns tip the balance of power in favor of the party in power.

Perhaps even more importantly, theorists and practitioners have uncritically embraced democratic solutions to protracted conflicts. This will have an effect on implementation. In the South African case the effect was salutary; in the other two cases it has not been. This is a cautionary tale, a warning that what appears to be a straightforward and obvious solution to violence—democracy—may have its own pathologies.

NOTES

1. While this chapter is drawn from Courtney Jung, Ellen Lust-Okar, and Ian Shapiro, "Problems and Prospects for Democratic Settlements: South Africa as a Model for the Middle East and Northern Ireland?" it makes a substantially different argument. I thank Ian Shapiro and Ellen Lust-Okar for permission to revise our article, Noreen O'Sullivan for research assistance, and Patrick Macklem and two anonymous reviewers for helpful comments.

2. As a result, it is useful to consider these peace processes in light of the literature on democratic transitions such as Huntington, *Third Wave*, O'Donnell and Schmitter, *Authoritarian Rule*, and Przeworski, *Democracy*.

3. Schedler, this volume.

4. Under the Special Powers Act (1922) the Minister for Home Affairs could, among other things, "arrest without charge or warrant, intern without trial, prohibit the holding of coroners' inquests, flog, execute, use depositions of witnesses as 'evidence' without requiring them to be present for cross-examination or rebuttal, destroy buildings, requisition land or property, ban any organization, be it political, social, or trade; prohibit meetings, publications, and even gramophone records." McGuffin, *Internment!*, p. 22. Proscription is the power to outlaw organizations, enshrined in the 1887 Criminal Law and Proceedings (Ireland) Act. "Proscription in its contemporary guise is located in Section 21 of the Northern Ireland (Emergency Provisions) Act 1978." "A person is guilty of an offense if he belongs or professes to belong to a proscribed organization." Walker, "Political Violence," p. 612.

5. Putnam showed that negotiations operate simultaneously on two levels—in his case both within countries and between countries. What happens within countries affects the leverage of each side as they negotiate at the second level between countries. Democratic settings make all negotiations into two level games. Putnam, "Diplomacy."

6. Schelling, *Strategy*.

7. "From Setbacks to Living Together," *The New York Times*, September 5, 1993.

8. Schedler, this volume.

9. According to Edward Said, as early as 1992 Arafat seemed to be "staking his entire future on Rabin's electoral win." "Interview with Edward Said by al-Sinnawi," *al-'Arabi*, p. 179.

10. On opposition in the Settlements, see Friedman, "Report from the West Bank," pp. 54–56; Ehud Sprinzak, *Brother vs. Brother*; "Rabin Decides to Close

Gazan Roads near Settlements, Arafat Condemns Attacks," *New York Times,* October 4, 1995; "Five Killed in Suicide Bombing of Bus 26 in Jerusalem," *New York Times,* August 21, 1995.

11. Fifteen out of the top business executives we surveyed in 2003 thought this had been a strategic mistake by Peres. Nine of them thought his hard-line strategy in the run-up to the 1996 election harmed the prospects for peace.

12. Mitchell, *Peace,* p. 101.

13. *Ibid.,* p. 104.

14. No agreement was in fact reached over decommissioning, however, which continued to act as a stumbling block to implementation as late as 2005.

15. Mitchell, *Peace,* p. 109.

16. *Ibid.,* pp. 111, 117.

17. Elliot and Flackes, *Conflict,* p. 125.

18. By March 1996, Israelis had experienced 12 suicide bombings during the Oslo process. Four of these came in February and March 1996 alone, killing 59 Israelis. Aish HaTorah, "Myths and Facts," http://www.aish.com/Israel/articles/Suicide_Bombings.asp (6/25/03).

19. A June 1996 poll by the Tami Steinmetz Center for Peace Research (TSC) found that 70.7% of Israeli Jews supported a firmer stance towards the Palestinians. TSC, "Peace Index June 1996," spirit.tau.ac.il/socant/peace/peaceindex/1996/files/JUNE96e.pdf (6/25/03).

20. A poll conducted by the Center for Palestine Research and Studies (CPRS) from June 3–5, 1999, found that 71% of Palestinians believed the PA was corrupt, and that 66% believed that the level of corruption would remain the same or increase in the future. CPRS, "Public opinion poll #41," www.pcpsr.org/survey/cprspolls/99/p01141a.html (6/17/03).

21. The CPRS poll conducted from June 3–5, 1999, found that 70% of Palestinians surveyed supported the peace process, while 27% opposed it. At the same time, however, 66% of the respondents did not trust the peaceful intentions of the Barak government, in contrast to the 23% who expressed trust in the newly elected Israeli government. Similarly, 55% did not believe that final status negotiations would lead successfully to a permanent settlement, and 45% supported the continuation of armed attacks against Israel. *Ibid.*

22. The extent to which concessions offered at Camp David were "major" and intended to meet Arafat half way remains controversial. However, it appears clear that these concessions went beyond previous Israeli offers (much to many Israelis' dismay), and indeed exceeded offers that Arafat had previously found more acceptable.

23. Barak won the 1999 elections for prime minister with 56.08% of the popular vote, vs. 43.92% for Netanyahu. See "Election Results 1999," *Jerusalem Post,* http://info.jpost.com/1999/Supplements/Elections99/final.html (6/22/03).

24. When Palestinians were asked, "Are you confident or not confident in the

Palestinian negotiating delegation in Camp David?" 34.7% lacked confidence and 7.8% "did not know." Jerusalem Media and Communications Centre (JMCC), "JMCC public opinion poll no. 38 on Palestinian attitudes towards the Camp David Summit, July 2000," www.jmcc.org/publicpoll/results/2000/n038.html (6/17/03).

25. According to a Palestinian Center for Policy and Survey Research (PCPSR) poll, 68% of Palestinians believed Arafat's overall position at Camp David was "just right," while 15% believed he had compromised too much. PCPSR, "Public opinion poll #1," July 27–29, 2000, www.pcpsr.org/survey/polls/2000/pla.html (6/17/03).

26. "The Ballad of Camp David," *The Economist,* July 2, 2000.

27. The Oslo process weakened Fateh and the PA vis-à-vis Hamas, which provided critical social services to an increasingly impoverished Palestinian people. See Ian Fisher, "Defining Hamas: Roots in Charity and Branches of Violence," *New York Times,* June 16, 2003. In December 1996, support for Fateh was 35.2% and for Hamas 10.3%. Similarly, 41.2% of Palestinians most trusted Yasser Arafat, and 4.8% trusted Sheikh Yassin. Only 19.5% of Palestinians did not trust anyone. By December 2001, support for Fateh dropped to 26.1%, while that for Hamas rose to 21.3%. Similarly, trust in Arafat declined to 24.5% and that in Yassin rose to 12.8%. By April 2003, Fateh remained the single most-trusted faction in Palestinian politics, with 22.6%, although overall support for Fateh trailed the combined support for Hamas and leftist factions (22.0%), Islamic Jihad (6.3%), Popular Front for the Liberation of Palestine (2.0%), and other factions (3.1%). However, more 34.3% responded that they "don't trust anyone." JMCC, "Public Opinion Poll #43," http://www.jmcc.org/publicpoll/results/2001/n043.htm (6/25/03); JMCC, "Public Opinion Poll #18," http://www.jmcc.org/publicpoll/results/1996/n018.htm (6/25/03).

28. Whether Arafat could actually have guaranteed a settlement at that late date is an open question. He had lost a great deal of credibility among his supposed constituents. Nevertheless, as an elderly statesman with strong "struggle credentials," Arafat was better placed to rally support for a settlement than Abbas.

29. Aluf Benn, "Facing Myriad Obstacles, Sharon Sees His Magic Evaporate," *Daily Star,* October 21, 2004.

30. "Sharon Savors Victory over Gaza Pullout but Coalition in Ruins," *Daily Star,* October 28, 2004.

31. David Dreilinger, "Coming in from the Cold? Hamas Enters Political Realm," *Daily Star,* February 9, 2005.

32. Ian Fisher, "Israel's Defense Minister is Faulted by Left and Right," *New York Times,* June 26, 2006.

33. *Ibid.*; Frank Millar, "London Is Relieved but Difficulties Lie Ahead," http://www.ireland.com/special/peace/results/road/ahead3.htm (5/25/2000).

34. Gerry Moriarty, "How the Parties Could Share Out Seats," *The Path to Peace,* website, http://www.ireland.com/special/peace/results/road/ahead4.htm (5/25/2000).

35. Paul Bew, "Initiative to Trimble but His Edge over Opponents Is Thin," *The*

Path to Peace, website, April 1998, http://www.ireland.om/special/peace/results/ analysis/analysis10.htm (5/25/2000).

36. "The Politics of Gaza Withdrawal and the Israeli Palestinian Peace Process," October 25, 2004, www.newsinformant.com/articles/2004_10_25/000853.php

37. In the 1999–2000 Northern Ireland Life and Times survey, respondents were asked to identify the most important priorities for the new assembly. Forty percent chose improving health services and 37% cited employment. www.qub.ac .uk/ss/csr/nilt (6/5/2003).

BIBLIOGRAPHY

al-Sinnawi, Abdullah. *al-'Arabi,* Cairo (January 30, 1995), trans. Joseph Massad in Edward Said, *Peace and its Discontents.* London: Random House, 1995.

Elliot, Sydney, and W. D. Flackes. *Conflict in Northern Ireland: An Encyclopedia.* Belfast: Blackstaff Press, 1999.

Friedman, Robert. "Report from the West Bank: An Unholy Rage," *The New Yorker,* March 7, 1994: 54–56.

Huntington, Samuel. *The Third Wave.* Oklahoma: University of Oklahoma Press, 1991.

Jung, Courtney, Ellen Lust-Okar, and Ian Shapiro, "Problems and Prospects for Democratic Settlements: South Africa as a Model for the Middle East and Northern Ireland?" *Politics and Society* (Summer 2005).

McGuffin, John. *Internment!* Tralee, Ireland: Anvil Books, 1973.

Mitchell, George J. *Making Peace.* New York: Alfred Knopf, 1999.

O'Donnell, Guillermo, and Philippe Schmitter. *Transitions from Authoritarian Rule: Comparative Perspectives.* Baltimore: Johns Hopkins University Press, 1986.

Przeworski, Adam. *Democracy and the Market.* New York: Cambridge University Press, 1991.

Putnam, Robert. "Diplomacy and Domestic Policy: The Logic of Two-Level Games," *International Organization* 42 (Summer 1988).

Schelling, Thomas C. *The Strategy of Conflict.* Cambridge: Harvard University Press, 1960.

Walker, Clive. "Political Violence and Democracy in Northern Ireland," *The Modern Law Review,* Vol. 51, No. 5 (September, 1988).

Chapter 10

Contingency in Biophysical Research

Robert G. Shulman and Mark R. Shulman

The 2002 meeting in this series asked whether social scientists should select questions that their most reliable methods can answer or should they address the most important questions, sacrificing reliability. Should they focus on methods or problems? The disrupting consequences of contingency that undermine the ability to find causal relations are common to both directions. Often social scientists look up to "hard" science as a methodology that has satisfactorily handled the uncertainties raised by contingency. The extent to which such science has successfully replaced uncertainty and contingency with reliable relations or laws is best illustrated by physics and its applications. The hope that physical science can help to eliminate contingency suggests that a somewhat detailed examination of the varying roles contingency plays in physical science might reveal insights that advance the goals of the present volume.

In physical science many laws have been so thoroughly tested that they are generally accepted as true, although it is well known that no generalization is ever proven regardless of the many times it fits the data or predicts the outcome. Newton's laws of motion held for more than two centuries of intense examination until Einstein was able to show that their application was valid only in a limited range of velocities. Notwithstanding their limited validity, and the fact that no induction is ever absolutely true, still we bet our lives and everything dear to us on the expectation that the laws of classical mechanics will hold in our everyday life when we drive a car or cradle a baby. This reliance upon the causal relationships embodied in these laws is what we mean when we allow ourselves to think that causality has been established in physical science and contingency has been banished. However, when physical science is applied to the study of organic life, to the biology or social behaviors of individuals or social groups, even the believers in an absolutely true physics will acknowledge that the confidence introduced by reliable laws is eroded. In these applications contingency emerges as a factor that must be considered similar but not identical to its role in the social sciences. My argument is that physics is trustworthy within the inorganic world, but when its methods are applied to the biological world, reliability suffers, although, as we shall see, it does not disappear. The reliability of physical understanding then depends upon the methods and assumptions in use, and thereby varies considerably, ranging from the near certainty of physical laws to the levels of uncertainty that haunt many efforts in the social sciences. In the biophysical world, all studies are, like George Orwell's pigs, equally contingent but some are more equal than others: equally contingent because they are all human creations, not absolutes dictated by nature; more equal because some are based upon sound physical mechanisms and laws that limit the uncertainty of our human interpretations.

To distinguish the different applications of contingency requires a thumbnail sketch of the levels referred to above. The absolute, inescapable level of contingency is that proposed by Richard Rorty, among others, when he says that all understanding of the world is contingent because it is created by humans and expressed in language. Our concepts are not discovered in nature, writ in stone, but are proposed by humans and should be valued only by their usefulness. Although many prominent scientists disagree with this description, I find it valuable and will accept it in this essay. The next level contains the highly reliable, well-tested laws and methods developed for physical science, which, while still contingent, are human creations that only resemble absolute truths in the ways they are useful for understanding and controlling the world. Finally, in the third level lie all the remaining human efforts to understand the world and to navigate through life, where innumerable factors exist beyond our understanding and control. At this level the contingent nature of human efforts are most evident. It is this third kind of contingency that I assume social scientists are interested in minimizing and for which they sometimes turn to the physical sciences for guidance. In this chapter we illustrate two different ways that physical science can be used to limit contingency in studies of humans, taken from long-term research projects my colleagues and I have conducted.

In biophysical chemistry we study the place that biochemical reactions occupy in the overall functions of complex organisms with an eye toward a better understanding of life. These studies are considered physical science because their explanations are acceptable only to the extent they can be expressed in terms of the laws of physics. We study biochemical pathways *in vivo* in bacteria, animals, and humans with highly technical methods and machines that have been developed in the past thirty years. The research designs and the interpretation of the results depend upon the century old physics of quantum mechanics, spectroscopy, and thermodynamics. Historically, thermodynamics has supported many important applications of physical laws to biological questions, and its well-established laws have provided valuable guidance for studying and interpreting normal and abnormal human physiology. Before considering different examples, I would again emphasize that reliance upon physical laws, with their quite dependable causal interpretations, is itself a starting point dedicated to minimizing contingency. Relying upon the methodology of thermodynamics in biophysical research limits the biological questions that can be addressed but improves the reliability of the answers. The use of thermodynamics depends upon the ability to make quantitative measurements of work, energy, and rates of well-delineated chemical systems. Very few biological systems and even fewer experimental methodologies can provide such information, so that choosing subjects because of their suitability for this kind of study places our research in the methodological camp. The strengths of physics that have guided our method-driven studies can minimize contingency; they do not eliminate it, but they can localize it and limit its consequences. This criterion for choosing subjects differs from the majority of biophysical or biochemical studies in which the problems are selected by their worldly significance and the standard methodological rigor of physical science is sacrificed. A well-publicized example of the approach we have not taken is offered by genomics in which the DNA sequence is confidently predicted to explain important biological functions —e.g., inheritable traits, behavior, and disease. However, answers to these questions are still unavailable since they await resolution of the thorny methodology required by genetic determinism.

To illustrate how physical science encounters contingency in the complexity of humans as subjects of investigation, or as investigators of the subject, in this chapter we present two cases illustrating how biophysical research proceeds until it runs head long into unyielding contingencies.

Diabetes and the Management of Contingency

The first example, a study of diabetes, illustrates the management of contingency in a well-defined biomedical question. In Non Insulin Dependent Diabetes (NIDD), the pancreas secretes insulin but the body does not use it effectively to remove glucose from the blood. NIDD has a genetic component, as evidenced by high correlation to family history and by its high concordance in identical twins. Certain life-style practices play important roles since a controlled diet and active exercise can contribute to delaying or ultimately avoiding the high blood glucose and its harmful consequences. Absent these preventative lifestyle changes—and sometimes in spite of them—the disease follows a fairly predictive course. In early life the pancreas over-produces insulin which compensates for its ineffectiveness, so that blood glucose concentrations are maintained in the normal range. However, in later life the over-production may cease, creating high concentrations of blood glucose that subsequently damage muscle, eyes, or other organs with devastating consequences for the quality and duration of life. Based upon these properties and the definition of the disease developed over the centuries by medical science, as well as being armed by earlier biochemical studies, my colleagues and I studied this disease in humans by the use of thermodynamic methods we had developed to follow metabolic fluxes by Nuclear Magnetic Resonance Spectroscopy. Similar to the more familiar Magnetic Resonance Imaging (MRI), which follows water non-invasively in the body, Nuclear Magnetic Resonance Spectroscopy (MRS) can measure the flow of biochemicals such as glucose non-invasively in humans. MRS has enabled us to locate the particular chemical step in diabetic patients responsible for the slower clearance of glucose under insulin stimulation. Further, we showed how the well-known protocols of diet and exercise can restore normal glucose storage rates by normalizing this particular step.

It was at this point, however, that we were forced to confront the limitations of biophysical science with its powerful tools for explaining causality. In some patients genetically predisposed to the disease, the pancreas continues to overproduce insulin even later in life, and the glucose levels remain at tolerable levels, so the patient stays healthy. We do not know why some fare better than others. Despite the odds, some sedentary, obese subjects remain healthy while some vigorous, lean subjects fall ill. In both groups factors beyond our ken, arising from the individuals' contingent histories, have an effect on their fate. We face two distinct limitations on our ability to help patients. The first comes from failing to understand the mechanism of pancreatic failure. Fortunately, we can reasonably expect that this complex and seemingly contingent event will soon be understood by additional research. But the second factor that determines who gets the disease, is life-style: some subjects simply cannot stick to a healthy regimen of diet and exercise, a fact that reflects the contingencies of the human mind, and such mechanisms are presently not explainable by spectroscopy.

Our research on diabetes has built upon the cumulative advances in medicine, chemistry, and physics over the centuries. Diabetes has long been recognized, and the anomalously high blood glucose has been identified as a pathology whose resolution would be beneficial. Reliable advances in understanding and control of the questions identified in this disease have been made by our modern Magnetic Resonance methods. This progress has assuaged the need for questioning the methods of science. Some uncertainties such as pancreatic failure remain as challenges, practical contingencies which further study will probably explain. Disagreements about how to proceed abound, but presumably many such questions can be resolved by experiment and theory. The study of diabetes illustrates the successful results of a scientific research program: there is a well-identified question, and we are learning more about how to answer it. This is precisely the sort of technical problem our methods are best suited to explain. However, the limitations that arise from a patient's inability to follow treatment reflect an individual's mind which, in the context of diabetes, is a contingency. Contingency, I propose, is an uncontrolled complex phenomenon that affects a study; if such a phenomenon could be understood, doing so appears to require an effort in a different direction from that of the original study.

Achieving such as optimistic posture of scientific progress may seem a laudable goal for political science also. During times of normal science, Thomas Kuhn claimed, puzzles are solved which are the strengths of science. To reach the felicitous advances in understanding diabetes celebrated above, advances in many sub-fields had to be brought to bear upon this disease. Genetics and population analysis had to be developed sufficiently so as to identify the inheritable component of NIDD. Likewise, comprehensive biochemistry and highly technical magnetic resonance methods had to be developed to enable us to undertake the *in vivo* studies. These advances were made during a period of "normal" science during which biophysical research managed to reduce, but not completely eliminate, the prevailing contingency. These findings are now being exploited to develop drugs and other treatments that would increase our control of the disease by going around the non-treatable contingent resistances to medical advice. Scientific advances sometimes follow military strategies and fortified, resistant positions are overcome not by direct attack but by circumventing them. The NIDD research is an example of the second level of investigations, described above, in which studies are based upon defined physical parameters like the mass of glycogen and the rates of its formation and are explained by physical laws like the conservation of mass—e.g., the mass of glucose stays constant as it flows into glycogen. These results show how reliance upon physical research allows progress to be made by avoiding a confrontation with inexplicable contingencies.

Contingency and Brain/Mind Research

My second example of recent biophysical research is found in studies of Brain/Mind—a field roiling in the throes of changing scientific directions, a field in which novel methods and vast accumulations of data have encouraged scientists to ask previously unanswerable questions about the material nature of mental activity. However, I hope to make clear that when scientists plan to study mental activity, they leave behind the hard won strengths of physics and chemistry which have no definition of mental activity. To study mental activities, or Mind, scientists have been describing Mind as the function of Brain. Although this starting point has a long history, the present scientific usage owes much to the computer scientist David Marr, who, in 1972, declared we must know the brain's function before studying how it serves that function, and who thereupon claimed that the brain's function was to handle intelligence, or to compute.[1] This assumption, although understandably appealing to a computer scientist, has been transformed into other fields so that, for example, psychologists study the computer-like brain by cognitive psychology and economists by rational-choice or game theory. In fact, once one is allowed to assume a function for Brain there are no limits; any experimenter can assume anything about brain function and test the assumption a by highly technical scientific measurements. And as we shall see, this is the present state of the field.

The structure of this procedure for study resembles Descartes' early formulation of scientific method when he proposed that to understand the whole it should be broken into parts. The parts then were to be studied and the understanding so gained would reflect back upon the original whole. For Descartes the starting point, the whole that was chosen, was in his opinion indubitable. This was the importance of his claims for the statement "I think therefore I am." The remaining years of the seventeenth century century, culminating in Newton's studies, created modern physical science by relinquishing the absolute certainty accorded by Descartes to his starting assumption and instead starting with hypotheses that were to be evaluated by experimentation. I propose that a large fraction of Brain/Mind studies are making Cartesian-like assumptions about brain functions which are then supported rather than tested by experiments. In such a tumultuous stage of research, scientists can find practical insight and support in the views of such modern philosophers as Richard Rorty, who emphasizes the contingent nature of all assumptions about the world. We do not find scientific laws, says Rorty, we create them—we do not find scientific problems, we formulate them. Assumptions are completely contingent, depending upon the who, what, when, and where of their formulation and are to be judged not by any absolute standards but merely by their usefulness. Scientific problems are man-made constructs that are created as we seek to master "nature" or our environment. This philosophy emphasizes that scientific discovery depends upon contingent happenings similar to all creative acts. Likewise, "science" is a human activity not an abstract law waiting to be revealed. Where science differs from other creative acts is that well-established methods of experimentation and reasoning have provided support for the usefulness of the hypothesis, as in our example of thermodynamics. Apples always fall from trees and never rise to them.

In the unsettled Brain/Mind field, however, when assumptions about mental activities stimulate research, the degree of contingency is very high. The scientist no longer starts with the very well-tested, but still intrinsically contingent, hypotheses of physical science, but rather with a view of mental activity from some different perspective. Biophysical research in this field is met by a fundamental contingency at the onset, not after substantial progress towards understanding a goal. In studying the pathological state of Non Insulin Dependent Diabetes, the goal was well defined—to understand in biophysical terms the origins and mechanisms of glucose disposal in this diseased state. We were seeking there to correct one of the most readily observed and agreed upon pathologies. But how can we study the origins and mechanisms of Mind when the chemical nature of Mind is an unsettled assumption, and where the definition of Mind is itself the question?

Because of the human complexities involved in Mind/Brain studies, where forces such as intent, will, or the passions are not at home in physical science, the starting assumptions and the goals in brain studies vary greatly. There is little commonality even in sub-fields of biophysics where varied standards make it difficult to identify a biophysical formulation of Brain/Mind beyond the common assumption that something like Mind is created by some activity of Brain.

A most active contemporary methodology, responsible for much of the optimistic expectations of understanding Mind is Functional Magnetic Resonance Imaging (fMRI). When I first did fMRI experiments of the brain my wish, as a naïve biophysicist, was to find a collaborator who knew how the Mind worked, who could describe the functions of Brain which these novel experiments could localize and identify as the Brain correlates of Mind. This wish flowed from the Cartesian philosophy that is the foundation of physical science—identify the whole and break it into parts that can be studied. Previous studies of other organs had built comfortably on the knowledge that kidneys, liver, and muscle had specific chemical functions, and the research had revealed how these functions were fulfilled by molecular mechanisms. This conventional methodology, so successful in physical science, has been replaced in the usual formulation and interpretation of Brain/Mind experiments by psychology. Qualities that are assumed in functional imaging experiments to constitute Mind are now almost universally derived from a particular top-down form of psychology. A psychology that has broadly accepted a Computer Theory of Mind (CTM) is cognitive psychology. In this theory, concepts such as memory, attention, or awareness are assumed to exist as representations which are operated on by a computer-like brain. Computational Theories of Mind identify such components of Mind and embody them—for example, memory in a task—which subjects are requested to perform while their brain responses are imaged. For comparison, the brain is imaged with the subject in a "control state" where memory, the brain component being studies, is presumably not being exercised. Subtracting one image from another, increments are found in several regions, and investigators claim that these incremental activities identify and localize the activity, in this case of memory. These localized responses have generated excitement based on their claims that, in contrast to all previous brain studies, brain activity relating inputs and outputs is actually measured, and is now finally and objectively identified. The brain, it is claimed, is merely a complex machine in which specific stimuli will be supported by identifiable regional activity.

However, the results of these efforts do not support the model of a rational brain operating by fixed computer-like rules to evaluate qualities of Mind as defined in cognitive psychology. Although many interesting correlations have been found, particularly in sensory responses, confounding factors that are inconsistent with a Computer Theory of Mind are clearly at work. In such a model of Brain, a representation of a particular mental activity—i.e., memory—when performed by a logical, computer-like brain would activate a specific brain region, and that region, being the source of memory, would not be activated by any other mental activity. From the very first experiments on cognitive concepts, it was seen that this is not what happens. No matter how tightly the mental representation is defined, no matter how it is broken down into possible components, non-reproducible, different brain regions are activated by the same concept when embodied in different tasks. In other words, the context in which the proposed mental activity is embedded, as well as the modality of its presentation—e.g., visual, aural, or sensory—are just some of the factors that differ from the expectations of a logical, computer-like brain. In the early days of CTM these departures from the predictions of this model were designated "parallel processing." More recently they are called "context," and responses are acknowledged to be "context dependent." These factors are not small perturbations of otherwise perfectly rational brain activity; they are very significant in magnitude. Considerable efforts have been made to patch up the model so as to retain the mantle of rationality. But careful philosophical analysis, such as that conducted by Jerry Fodor,[2] showed that once the rational model requires consideration of context, it has failed and cannot be fixed. Any attempt to explain "context" requires recourse to empiricism, and empirical inputs explaining contextual contributions undermine the claim that a system is purely rational.

Attempts to control context are limited by the very uncertainties of the concepts that are in play. For example, considering "simplicity" as a concept, Fodor notes it has entirely different meanings depending what is being simplified. To simplify some texts, for example, would require more explanation, in others less, so that the activities directed by "simplicity" can be opposites in different contexts. Similarly "memory" and other such concepts float with their context. The attempt to identify absolute concepts of mental activity, entirely independent of their contingent context, fails because theories of a rational mind are undermined by the contingent nature of the presumed activities of Mind. Assuming there are pure concepts, as cognitive psychology does, always fails because as is said in the title of Fodor's small book, "the mind doesn't work that way." Most imaging scientists cling to the validity of their view of Mind by interpreting their rich imaging data sets so as to support their assumptions. The alternative, of using the data to refine assumptions about the nature of mental activites, while formally more in accord with scientific methods, has not been much followed.

In addition to the contingencies implicit in specifying mental concepts, the response of an individual to a task depends upon the individual's intrinsically contingent history—a history dominated by chance events that can be traced back at least as far as the particular antecedent sperm and egg. A specified task does not mean the same to different individuals. Responses are affected by subjectivity, and individual subjective responses differ. The result of these uncontrolled responses to the task further negate the model of a rational Mind whose relations to Brain are presumed to be uniquely determined in the imaging experiment. The attempts of CTM to ignore or eliminate contingency from scientific studies of the Brain, while to many representing progress, in my opinion, leads science down paths with dead ends.

But if we regard all understanding of the larger subjects like Mind to be not an absolute description, found in nature, but a contingent description discovered and proposed by humans, how can we begin to explain Mind in terms of Brain activity? How can we bootstrap ourselves into an understanding of higher order functions? How can we take advantage of the validity of physical science to study properties that we cannot identify?

The answer is near at hand if we examine what biological scientists actually do. They are, in fact, quite opportunistic, using whatever tools or methods are available. They adopt neither a top-down approach that starts from a fixed view of Mind nor a bottom-up view in which molecular features would be studied regardless of their possible relevance to brain function. In analyzing scientific methodology, Robert Brandon rejects the either-or alternatives of reductionism and holism.[3] Brandon claims that biology follows neither approach. Nor, he argues, should it. Instead, he says, biologists are indifferent to this distinction and move freely in both directions. Their goal is to find a causal mechanism, and such an understanding can only be achieved, he suggests, by considering parts and whole together. The piston can only be understood as part of an engine.

In this way, mechanisms of cerebral neuronal activity, the work of the brain, can be studied by physical scientists. The distinction between method and importance becomes, for the physical scientist, a straw man. Out of this integration of approaches searching for mechanisms relating Mind and Brain, a clearer understanding of function can emerge. The reliable physical understanding produced by thermodynamic research of brain energy and work provides a basis for redefining Mind in terms of physically defined causalities. Concepts of Mind derived from psychology or everyday experiences, which incorporate large common assumptions about Mind, may or may not provide a suitable basis for biophysical studies. In my opinion, attributes of Mind based securely upon physical results have a better chance of allowing a reformulation of Mind that would facilitate future study. The advantage of a reliable basis, or methodology, is that it can support such a conceptual structure, in contrast to less certain direct studies of the larger questions of Mind.

Relevance for Political Science

The diabetes study allows us to make the point that a "hard science" such as biophysical chemistry can navigate in seas of contingency. The molecular findings in the diabetes studies have moved forward until they reached the contingencies of human mind, and could still advance around those uncertainties when necessary. The descriptions of how biophysical science struggles for explanations while reckoning with the coexistence of contingency and scientific mechanisms might provide political scientists, engaged in a similar struggle, with examples of a reliable methodology.

To a great extent the method in political science that Ian Shapiro calls scientific realism closely resembles the scientific methodology we used in the diabetes research.[4] In the core methodology of physical science, general laws are recognized to be hypotheses capable of being disproved, while in some fields like physics, they have been refined to be of wide applicability. However, his definition of scientific realism —"I take the core commitment of scientific realism to consist in the twofold conviction that the world consists of causal mechanisms that exist independently of our study—or even awareness—of them, and that the methods of science hold the best possibility of grasping their true character"—soon raises some differences of emphasis about the scientific method. In contrast to his goal of finding truth, I have emphasized the contingent nature of all hypotheses, including scientific generalities, when describing the scientific method. Following Rorty, I have proposed that scientific hypotheses are contingent not only because we have not yet found the true hypothesis; I have suggested that they are inescapably contingent; they can never become absolutely true. In this view there is a real world out there, and science has provided a most valuable method to understand and control that world, but scientific laws are our contingent creation—they do not exist "independently of our study." There is no "true reality"; there is only our more or less useful understanding of it. The very well-established hypotheses constituting the laws of physics have countered their intrinsic contingent natures by centuries of empirical support, but they are not most representative of the science used when studying humans. (To illustrate the everyday contingency of hypotheses, even when they seem well supported empirically, I will bring the diabetes research up to date. Given the inheritable nature of the reduced activity in the glucose transporter in diabetics and their offspring, the results seemed to support the hypothesis that the glucose transporter pathway was the site of the responsible mutation. However, more recent results are showing that the reduced activity is a consequence of other metabolic differences so that recent hypotheses identifying the mutation site are no longer targeting the glucose transporter.) Ian Shapiro's commitment of political science to scientific realism resembles my advocacy of the scientific method as described in the diabetes study. Science has proven to be more useful than other methods in providing us with understanding and control of large sections of the world. But in my view the strength of the scientific method depends upon the uncertainty and flexibility of its findings—upon its recognition that its results are contingent and that consequently their universality must always remain in question. Shapiro's major criticism of method has been aimed at rational-choice theory and similar positions, which, he notes, assumes how the mind works and goes on to explain political and economic behavior by the unrestrained application of that assumption. Shapiro notes that its claim to universality is intrinsic to the failings of rational-choice theory. In its unquestioned assumptions of a simplistic model of human mental activity, and by its forcing of data to confirm its assumptions, this theory shares the logical structure and empirical failings of contemporary theories of cognitive neuroscience like Computer Theory of Mind that I have criticized in Mind/Brain studies. Instead of being asked to choose between method and problems for research guidance, we may find it simpler, and create more congenial bedfellows, to propose that the choice should be between methods whose answers are either absolute or contingent. In that case I would come down strongly in favor of the contingent answers that are found by scientific methods. And it is for that reason, for it's a distrust of truths claimed to be universal, that we are in accord with Shapiro in deploring the claims to universality in the assumptions shared by rational-choice theory and cognitive neuroscience.

In the study of complex human activities like mind, or of similar concepts in the social sciences, the contingent nature of assumptions that guide study should be acknowledged from the start. I suggest that if we stay away from rigid preconceptions about the nature of questions and answers, and instead search for mechanisms that are at the same time useful and contingent, then the methods we need for improved understanding are presently available, for both political science and biophysical studies of humans.

NOTES

1. Marr, *Vision.*
2. Fodor, *Mind.*
3. Brandon, *Concepts.*
4. Shapiro, *Flight from Reality,* p. 8.

BIBLIOGRAPHY

Brandon, Robert N. *Concepts and Methods in Evolutionary Biology.* Cambridge, UK: Cambridge University Press, 1996.

Fodor, Jerry A. *The Mind Doesn't Work That Way.* Cambridge, MA: MIT Press, 2000.

Marr, David. *Vision.* New York: W. H. Freeman, 1982.

Shapiro, Ian. *The Flight from Reality in the Human Sciences.* Princeton, NJ: Princeton University Press, 2005.

Contributors

Sonu Bedi is an Assistant Professor in the Department of Government at Dartmouth College.

Traci Burch is an Assistant Professor of Political Science at Northwestern University and a Faculty Research Fellow at the American Bar Foundation. In addition to race and ethnic politics, her research interests also include American social policy and criminal justice.

Jennifer L. Hochschild is the Henry LaBarre Jayne Professor of Government at Harvard University, and a Professor of African and African-American Studies. She also holds Lectureships in the John F. Kennedy School of Government and the Graduate School of Education. She is the co-author, with Nathan Scovronick, of *The American Dream and the Public Schools* (Oxford University Press, 2003), and the author of *Facing Up to the American Dream: Race, Class, and the Soul of the Nation* (Princeton University Press, 1995) as well as other books and articles.

Gregory A. Huber is an Associate Professor of Political Science at Yale University, where he is also a Fellow of the Institution for Social and Policy Studies and the Center for the Study of American Politics.

Courtney Jung is an Associate Professor in the Politics Department at The New School for Social Research. She is the author of *Then I Was Black: South African Political Identities in Transition* (Yale University Press, 2000). Her forthcoming book, *Democracy and Indigenous Rights: A Preface to Critical Liberalism*, will be published by Cambridge University Press in 2007. She is also the author of a number of journal articles on political identity and liberal democratic theory.

David R. Mayhew is Sterling Professor of Political Science at Yale University. He is the author of *Congress: The Electoral Connection* (Yale University Press, 1974), *Divided We Govern* (Yale University Press, 1991),

America's Congress (Yale University Press, 2000), and *Electoral Realignments* (Yale University Press, 2002).

Philip Pettit teaches Political Theory and Philosophy at Princeton University, where he is L. S. Rockefeller University Professor of Politics and Human Values. His recent books include *Republicanism* (Oxford University Press, 1997), *A Theory of Freedom* (Oxford University Press, 2001), *Rules, Reasons and Norms* (Oxford University Press, 2002), and *Penser en Societe* (PUF, 2004). He is the co-author, with Geoffrey Brennan, of *Economy of Esteem* (Oxford University Press, 2004); and a co-author, with Frank Jackson and Michael Smith, of a selection of papers entitled *Mind, Morality and Explanation* (Oxford University Press, 2004). A new book, *Made with Words: Hobbes on Mind, Society and Politics,* is forthcoming from Princeton University Press.

Andreas Schedler is a Professor of Political Science and the Head of the Department of Political Studies at the Centro de Investigación y Docencia Económicas (CIDE) in Mexico City. He has most recently edited *Electoral Authoritarianism: The Dynamics of Unfree Competition* (Boulder and London: Lynne Rienner Publishers, 2006).

Mark R. Shulman is Assistant Dean for Graduate Programs and International Affiliations and an Adjunct Professor at Pace Law School. He has published widely in the fields of history, law, and international relations.

Robert G. Shulman is the Sterling Professor (emeritus) of Molecular Biophysics and Biochemistry at Yale and is presently a Senior Research Scientist in the Department of Diagnostic Radiology. He formed the Magnetic Resonance Center at Yale and had been the Head of Biophysics Research at Bell Telephone Laboratories before coming to Yale. He is a member of the National Academy of Sciences and of the Institute of Medicine and is presently working on the limits, philosophical and experimental, of brain/mind studies.

Ian Shapiro is Sterling Professor of Political Science at Yale University, where he also serves as Henry R. Luce Director of the Yale Center for International and Area Studies. He has written widely on democracy, justice, and the methods of social inquiry. His most recent books are *The Flight from Reality in the Human Sciences* (Princeton University Press, 2005) and, with Michael Graetz, *Death by a Thousand Cuts: The Fight over Taxing Inherited Wealth* (Princeton University Press, 2005).

Susan Stokes is John S. Saden Professor of Political Science at Yale University. Her most recent book is *Democracy and the Culture of Skepticism: Political Trust in Argentina and Mexico* (Russell Sage Foundation, 2006), co-authored with Matthew Cleary.

Elisabeth Jean Wood is Professor of Political Science at Yale University and Research Professor at the Santa Fe Institute. She is the author of *Forging Democracy from Below: Insurgent Transitions in South Africa and El Salvador* (Cambridge University Press, 2000) and *Insurgent Collective Action and Civil War in El Salvador* (Cambridge University Press, 2003).

David Wootton is Anniversary Professor of History at the University of York, England. He has published widely on early modern intellectual history. His most recent book is *Bad Medicine: Doctors Doing Harm Since Hippocrates* (Oxford: Oxford University Press, 2006). He can be contacted by email: dw504@york.ac.uk.

Index

Italicized page numbers indicate that the information appears in a figure on the page. A page number ending in "t" indicates that the information appears in a table on the page.